JOB SEARCH
HANDBOOK *for*
PEOPLE
with DISABILITIES

Second Edition

Dr. Daniel J. Ryan

jist®
Works
America's Career Publisher

Job Search Handbook for People with Disabilities, Second Edition
© 2004 by Daniel J. Ryan
Published by JIST Works, an imprint of JIST Publishing, Inc.
8902 Otis Avenue
Indianapolis, IN 46216-1033
Phone: 1-800-648-JIST   Fax: 1-800-JIST-FAX   E-mail: info@jist.com

Visit our Web site at **www.jist.com** for information on JIST, free career resources, book chapters, and ordering instructions for our many products! For free information on 14,000 job titles, visit **www.careeroink.com.** Quantity discounts are available for JIST books. Please call our Sales Department at 1-800-648-5478 for a free catalog and more information.

Interior Designer: designLab, Seattle
Page Layout: Debra Kincaid
Cover Designer: Trudy Coler
Proofreader: Linda Quigley
Indexer: Henthorne House

Printed in Canada
08 07 06 05 04   9 8 7 6 5 4 3 2 1

Library of Congress Cataloging-in-Publication Data

Ryan, Daniel J., 1960-
    Job search handbook for people with disabilities / Daniel J. Ryan.—
2nd ed.
          p. cm.
Includes index.
   ISBN 1-56370-989-9 (pbk.)
  1. People with disabilities—Vocational guidance—United
States—Handbooks, manuals, etc. 2. Job hunting—United
States—Handbooks, manuals, etc. 3. People with
disabilities—Employment—United States—Handbooks, manuals, etc. I.
Title.
  HV1568.5.R93 2004
  650.14'087'0973—dc22

                                    2003026447

ISBN 1-56370-989-9

Acknowledgments

I would like to extend my sincere appreciation to these people who helped make this book possible: Lori Cates Hand, and the rest of the JIST gang. Lori was particularly helpful, shepherding this book from its inception.

Again, special thanks also go out to the many helpful sources of information. The folks at the Job Accommodation Network, who work so hard every day to make it easier for people with disabilities as they make their way in the workforce, deserve my thanks and respect. The same is true for the people who comprise the Office of Disability Employment Policy, whose work continues to be inspirational.

The inspiration for this book came from the hundreds of students I had the pleasure of serving whose courage and tenacity made me feel that not only could this task be done by someone like me, but also that it must.

Finally, thanks to Sandy, Aidan, and Talia, whose patience and love made this whole effort possible.

Contents

Introduction viii

Part I: Preparing for Your Job Search

Chapter 1: Assessing Your Skills, Abilities, and Goals 3
Exercises for Self-Assessment 3
Career Assessment Instruments 14
You Are Not Alone 20
Support for Continuing Your Education 20

Chapter 2: Exploring Careers 23
Targeting Specific Occupations to Research 24
Sources of Information 26
Starting Your Own Business 36
Evaluating the Possibilities 37

Chapter 3: More Preparation: Practical Work Experience, Assertiveness Training, and Public Speaking Skills 39
Experiential Education 39
Assertiveness 43
Public Speaking 48

Part II: Marketing Yourself to Potential Employers

Chapter 4: Creating Your Resume 53
Dissecting the Resume 54
What Shouldn't Go on Your Resume? 83
Scannable Resumes 84
Resume Aesthetics 85
Resumes and the Internet 87

Chapter 5: Writing a Great Cover Letter 89
Getting Started with Contact Info 89
Answer Three Important Questions 90
Finishing the Letter 95
Format Tips 95
Sample Cover Letters for Different Situations 95
Online Cover Letter Help 106

Part III: Applying and Interviewing for Jobs

Chapter 6: Networking and Mentors 109
Networking—a Numbers Game 110
Establishing a Network 111
Finding a Mentor 122

Chapter 7: Other Ways to Generate Job Leads 127
Using the Newspaper to Find Leads 127
Employment Agencies 130
U.S. Department of Labor 132
College Career Centers 132
State Vocational Rehabilitation Offices 133
Business Leadership Network 133
Internet Leads 133
Trade Publications 137

Chapter 8: Managing Your Job Search 139
Tracking Contacts 139
Time Management 140

Chapter 9: Applying for Jobs 155
Networking 155
Sending a Resume and Cover Letter 156
Applying Online 157
Filling Out a Written Application Form 157
Improving Your Chances of Getting the Job 159

Chapter 10: Preparing for the Interview **161**
    Doing Your Research 162
    Accessibility Issues 167
    Rehearsing for the Interview 169
    Disclosing Your Disability 171
    Interviewing Styles 185
    The Day of the Interview 188
    Second Interviews 191
    Some Online Interviewing Resources 195

Chapter 11: After the Interview **197**
    Writing Thank-You Letters 197
    Following Up Via the Phone 201
    Sometimes You're the Windshield; Sometimes You're
        the Bug: Handling Rejection 202
    The Uneven Playing Field 205
    Negotiating the Offer 216

Part IV: Succeeding at Work

Chapter 12: Keeping the Job **225**
    Having the Right Attitude 226
    Succeeding at Office Politics 227
    Looking for Projects 230
    Fitting In and Succeeding with a Disability 232
    Normalizing Your Disability for Your Peers
        and Coworkers 232
    Being Ready for the Next Opportunity When It
        Presents Itself 234
    Knowing How to Handle Changes in Insurance 235

Chapter 13: Accommodating Your Disability on the Job **237**
    Real-Life Sample Accommodations 238
    Sample Disability-Specific Accommodations
        from the Job Accommodation Network 242

**Appendix: Job Links from the U.S. Department of Labor
Office of Disability Employment Policy** **253**

Index **267**

Introduction

This book is intended to serve as a resource for people with disabilities as they conduct their job search. Although there are thousands of different books relating to career development and the job search, more than ten years after the passage of the Americans with Disabilities Act, there are few resources that address the universe of specific issues faced by people with disabilities.

There is no implied guarantee that this book will level the playing field for the job seeker with a disability. Sadly, discrimination against people with disabilities is still very present among the gatekeepers to the workforce. The goal of this book is to prepare job seekers to best represent themselves and reassure potential employers that they are capable workers.

What the book will do, hopefully, is help you

- Get a better understanding of the "bigger picture" of who you are.
- Understand what strengths you possess, as well as any areas of weakness.
- Identify possible career fields and potential employers within those fields.
- Position yourself in your job search by establishing contacts within your desired industry or company.
- Find agencies or governmental programs that can assist you.
- Present yourself well on paper and in the job interview.
- Know your rights and protection under the law.
- Give guidance as you negotiate the terms of your job offer and provide suggestions for finding success on the job.

This book is intended to be a starting point for the job seeker with a disability. It gives you an overview of the most important job-search topics and how they relate to the individual with a disability. Once you have mastered the information in this book and are looking for more detail in a particular area, the following JIST books are good supplemental material:

Resumes and Cover Letters

Résumé Magic

Cover Letter Magic

Gallery of Best Cover Letters

Gallery of Best Resumes

Gallery of Best Resumes for People Without a Four-Year Degree

The Quick Resume and Cover Letter Book

Applications

Introduction to Job Applications

Best Jobs for the 21st Century

Networking

Networking for Job Search and Career Success

Job Interviews and Salary Negotiation

Why Should I Hire You? Turn Interview Questions into Job Offers

The Quick Interview and Salary Negotiation Book

Internet Job Search

The Quick Internet Guide to College Majors and Careers

This book is intended to be valuable to career-development professionals as well as job seekers. Through a better understanding of the issues faced by job-seekers with disabilities, career counselors will be better prepared to assist them.

Background

People with disabilities have been relegated to second-class-citizen status throughout history. In ancient times, children with disabilities were viewed unfavorably, varying from being seen as possessed by demons to being viewed as a sign of the impurity of the parents. As a result, they were frequently sacrificed to the gods or abandoned. To this day, the news of a disability in a newborn child, or as a result of an accident or illness, is invariably greeted with feelings of pity and despair. The assumption is that the person with a disability will be unable to lead a "normal life." And a "normal life" is assumed to include gainful employment.

Signs of progress are all around us, however. Persons with disabilities are graduating from high schools and enrolling in colleges and universities in record numbers. Ramps and curb cuts are common, if not mandated, in public places. Assistive listening devices (such as volume controls on telephones), Braille menus in restaurants, voice-recognition software, and even text tags on Web-page rollovers are some of the accommodations that have expanded access to goods and services. Persons with disabilities have not made as much progress into the workforce, however.

One possible reason that persons with disabilities did not take their place in the workforce may have been related to the gatekeeper status of our educational system. Persons with disabilities were routinely either denied access to education or relegated to self-contained special-education classes. It was only in the latter part of the 20th century that laws such as the Education of Handicapped Persons Act, the Rehabilitation Act of 1973, and the Americans with Disabilities Act of 1990 opened up access to education for persons with disabilities from kindergarten through college.

This access to education has helped to narrow the gap between persons with disabilities and the nondisabled, as it relates to both education level and employment. Over time, as more people with disabilities acquire high school diplomas and college degrees, they will be prepared to assume jobs in the new economy.

Employment and Income Statistics

While the unemployment rate has settled in at the lowest rate seen in generations, the majority of people with disabilities remain without work. In fact, a 1998 survey conducted by The National Organization on Disability and Louis Harris & Associates found that the nondisabled were more than twice as likely to be working as were persons with disabilities (see Figure 1).

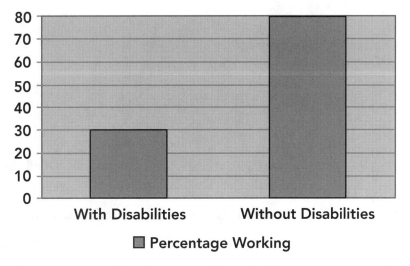

Figure 1 The percentage of working-age adults with full- or part-time employment.

Obviously, the existence of this untapped labor pool adversely affects people with disabilities; it also threatens the continued expansion of the economy. These currently idle workers could prove to be a driving force behind the nation's economic growth, both as producers and consumers.

This fact has recently been recognized by the nation's lawmakers. In the Work Incentives Improvement Act of 1999, Congress removed major disincentives to people with disabilities entering the workforce. The legislation removed some of the most significant employment barriers by providing adequate and affordable health insurance when a person on Social Security Insurance (SSI) or Social Security Disability Insurance (SSDI) goes to work or develops a significant disability while working. It also encouraged SSDI beneficiaries to return to work by providing assurances that cash benefits will remain available if employment proves unsuccessful.

Another disturbing fact, found in a Louis Harris poll, is the gap between the wages of people with disabilities and the wages of the nondisabled. People with disabilities are close to three times as likely to reside in a household with less than $15,000 in total income (see Figure 2).

Cornell University conducted two research initiatives to examine employer practices in response to the employment provisions of Title I of the American with Disabilities Act (ADA) and related civil rights legislation. As part of that

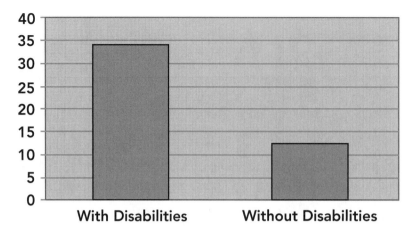

Figure 2 Percentage of adults living in households with less than $15,000 annual income.

research, they asked employers to rate seven possible barriers blocking the employment of people with disabilities.

Barriers	Private Sector Percent	Public Sector Percent
Lack of related experience	49	53
Lack of required skills/training	39	45
Supervisor knowledge of accommodation	31	34
Attitudes/stereotypes	22	43
Cost of accommodations	16	19
Cost of supervision	12	10
Cost of training	9	11

Source: "Disability Employment Policies and Practices in Private and Federal Sector Organizations," Susanne M. Bruyere, March 2000, Cornell University, Program on Employment and Disability, School of Industrial and Labor Relations, Extension Division

How to Use This Book

If you are reading this book, it's likely that you are currently undergoing a major change in your life. Perhaps you are recently unemployed and are looking for a new position. Perhaps you have recently graduated from school and are seeking your first job. Maybe you have been out of work for some time, but some event or combination of events has brought you to the decision to undertake a serious job search. It is even possible that someone who cares about you and is trying to help you with your job search purchased this book for you.

Regardless of the reason, this will not be the most fun book you will ever read (although hopefully it is written in such a way that it is at least enjoyable!). Conducting a job search can be a daunting task. This fact can sometimes be compounded by feelings of depression, serious financial concerns, and general feelings of anxiety. Much of the fear associated with the job search is the fear of the unknown. This book can lessen those. In the course of reading this book, you should begin to realize that you can minimize the role that your disability plays in your overall job search. Although you need to address the issues relating to your disability, they don't need to be the focus of your search.

You can use this book in many ways. Many individuals will find it helpful to read through the book first and then return to the exercises found throughout. Others will want to proceed methodically, going through each exercise as it occurs. One person I know uses it as a mouse pad! Regardless of which way you prefer, it is very important that you at least complete the chapter on self-assessment (Chapter 1) before moving on. The book is written from the perspective of someone who sees the job search much like a full-time sales position. Everything you do in your job search has a counterpart in marketing or sales. Just as a salesperson has a product to sell, so do you: yourself. Your job is to market yourself into the job you want.

The Job Search as a Sales Campaign

Think about unpleasant experiences that you have had purchasing a product. Chances are, your complaint has something to do with the product not living up to expectations, the salesperson's lack of knowledge about the product, or the way in which the person tried to sell the product to you. However, if the salesperson is enthusiastic (without being pushy), friendly, and confident, and can effectively explain how the product's features can benefit you, it is likely you will feel more comfortable making the purchase. Let's say that you raise a concern about a drawback of the product, or mention a competing product that may be more desirable in some way. If the salesperson is able to acknowledge your feelings, address the issue, and re-emphasize the strengths of the product and how they more than compensate for any shortcomings, he or she is likely to overcome your objections and get you to purchase the product. Even if you choose not to make the purchase, it is likely that you will part company thinking positively about the encounter. And if you ever have a need for that type of product again, you may return to that salesperson.

The job search is quite similar to a sales campaign. Perhaps the single most important task for a salesperson is to know the product. A good salesperson will know the product's features and weaknesses and, when possible, how it relates to other products. A good salesperson will be able to talk intelligently about their product and its features. They will also be able to talk about it in a way that relates to the customer's needs.

Another important skill for a salesperson is prospecting. Who is likely to be looking for this type of product? How can you find them? What features are they looking for? How will they use the product? What is important to them? A good understanding of the market will make a big impact on your success. If you are selling toothpicks at the summer picnic, you will be better off spending your time near the corn-on-the-cob tent than at the "make your own dessert" tent.

The third part of this approach is the ability of the salesperson to sell. Having the best product is rarely enough. If it were, most people would have a Betamax video recorder in their home and a Macintosh computer at work. Often, a decent product with a great marketing plan will beat a better product with a poor marketing plan. Simply put, good salespeople know how to sell. They have the discipline to work hard, and they are constantly prospecting for more customers. They are good talkers and even better listeners. They connect with people as individuals, leaving each person they meet better off for the encounter. They share an enthusiasm that bubbles up from the knowledge that they have an excellent product to sell. They know that their product has value, and that some lucky customer will soon make that same realization.

This book will help you be a better salesperson for yourself. It will help you gain the product knowledge you will need to be successful. It will teach you how to do the necessary market research in order to find and qualify potential customers (employers). It will share some of the skills necessary for conducting a sales campaign, including the direct-mail design (a resume and cover letter), generating referrals (networking), handling yourself on the phone, handling yourself on the sales call (interview), presenting the product (dressing and etiquette), closing the deal (negotiating the offer), and how to keep the customer satisfied (first year on the job). And all for $17.95!

PART I

Preparing for Your Job Search

Chapter 1: Assessing Your Skills, Abilities, and Goals

Chapter 2: Exploring Careers

Chapter 3: More Preparation: Practical Work Experience, Assertiveness Training, and Public Speaking Skills

CHAPTER 1

Assessing Your Skills, Abilities, and Goals

Whenever you are lost, the first thing you look for is a map. Once you finally get it unfolded, you look frantically for your destination. This is an important step, but it overlooks an even more important step: looking for your current location (that's why you always see those big YOU ARE HERE marks on public maps). If you don't know where you are, you can wander for a long time without truly knowing whether you are getting closer to your destination or farther away.

This is true if you are looking for a store in an unfamiliar mall, for a street in an unfamiliar neighborhood, or for your "true vocation." In the latter case, it's particularly important that you take the time to determine your current location.

Exercises for Self-Assessment

In order to help you begin this journey of self-exploration, several exercises have been provided here for you. Keep these completed exercises, because you will use them later as you begin your job search.

Write Your Career Autobiography

Get a binder (or a computer disk) and write your career autobiography. This autobiography should include recollections about your education. What courses have you taken? Which courses did you like? Which did you dislike? What do you remember learning in those courses? What have your long-term goals been? What were some of the things you said you wanted to be when you grew up?

Your autobiography should include a section on the projects you have worked on as a part of your jobs, internships, or volunteer experiences. Again, it should include your memories of what was fun or enjoyable about the projects, as well as the parts that you remember less fondly. Take the time to reconstruct in your mind the successes you had. Remember the feelings you had as you tackled the projects. Frustration? Exhilaration? Pride?

Part of this effort should include an inventory of the skills you have developed and any special skills that you have picked up along the way. Also, record those bumps you have felt, and failures or difficulties you have experienced. If you overcame those setbacks, recall how you did it and write it down. If you walked away at the first sign of failure, record that. If you tried repeatedly without improving your result, record that as well. This exercise is extremely valuable, because it forces you to think about valuable experiences you have had in your life, probably jogging some old memories that you might otherwise have forgotten. This kind of introspection, if approached seriously, will give you a keener insight into what you have to offer an employer. It will help you observe your personal character from a more objective distance.

When you have a disability, it is extremely important to take the time to examine your strengths and weaknesses. The fact is that everyone, regardless of whether they have a disability, can score themselves on a variety of different skills and abilities. The most important thing you can do is to identify honestly what your strengths and weaknesses are, and to focus on the strengths. That is not to say that you should ignore all of your weaknesses; in fact, my suggestion is that you do quite the opposite. Take the time to identify your weaknesses, and then look for ways to address them.

It is quite likely that if a weakness is related to your disability, you have already begun to find ways to make accommodations for it. Perhaps you have a reading disability. If so, you may have already developed strategies for addressing that disability. If you haven't, it may be worth discussing with a rehabilitation counselor how you can learn to use some of the available computer technology or text-taping services so that you can access information that is currently in text (printed) form. Another resource available to you to help identify possible accommodations is the Job Accommodation Network, discussed in greater detail in Chapter 13.

Identify Your Skills and Traits

The list in Table 1.1 can help you identify your skills and traits. Consider the following skills and rank yourself on a scale from 1 to 5.

Table 1.1 Skills

Weak 1	Some Skill 2				Average 3	Good 4				Outstanding 5

Abstract thinking	1	2	3	4	5	Customer service	1	2	3	4	5
Accounting/ bookkeeping	1	2	3	4	5	Dancing	1	2	3	4	5
Acting	1	2	3	4	5	Data entry	1	2	3	4	5
Analytical	1	2	3	4	5	Decorating	1	2	3	4	5
Assembly	1	2	3	4	5	Delegating	1	2	3	4	5
Athletic	1	2	3	4	5	Desktop publishing	1	2	3	4	5
Attention to detail	1	2	3	4	5	Drafting	1	2	3	4	5
Carpentry	1	2	3	4	5	Driving	1	2	3	4	5
Cashiering	1	2	3	4	5	Editing	1	2	3	4	5
Choreography	1	2	3	4	5	Electrical	1	2	3	4	5
Coaching sports	1	2	3	4	5	Entertaining	1	2	3	4	5
Collaboration	1	2	3	4	5	Experience with various software	1	2	3	4	5
Complex decision making	1	2	3	4	5	Fashion design	1	2	3	4	5
Computer programming	1	2	3	4	5	Fine motor	1	2	3	4	5
Conceptual	1	2	3	4	5	Flexibility	1	2	3	4	5
Conflict resolution	1	2	3	4	5	Following complex directions	1	2	3	4	5
Cooking	1	2	3	4	5	Foreign language fluency	1	2	3	4	5
Counseling	1	2	3	4	5	Fund raising	1	2	3	4	5
Courage	1	2	3	4	5	Gardening	1	2	3	4	5
Critical thinking	1	2	3	4	5	Grammar	1	2	3	4	5

continues

Table 1.1 Skills (*continued*)

Weak 1	Some Skill 2				Average 3	Good 4		Outstanding 5		
Handling multiple priorities	1	2	3	4	5	Planning	1	2	3	4	5
						Plumbing	1	2	3	4	5
Intelligence	1	2	3	4	5	Problem solving	1	2	3	4	5
Interpersonal communication	1	2	3	4	5	Proofreading	1	2	3	4	5
						Public speaking	1	2	3	4	5
Leadership	1	2	3	4	5	Punctuality	1	2	3	4	5
Listening	1	2	3	4	5	Reasoning	1	2	3	4	5
Managing others	1	2	3	4	5	Reception	1	2	3	4	5
Mathematical skills	1	2	3	4	5	Record keeping	1	2	3	4	5
Mechanical	1	2	3	4	5	Recruiting	1	2	3	4	5
Mediation	1	2	3	4	5	Repairing	1	2	3	4	5
Memorization	1	2	3	4	5	Researching	1	2	3	4	5
Modeling	1	2	3	4	5	Sales	1	2	3	4	5
Musical	1	2	3	4	5	Singing	1	2	3	4	5
Negotiating	1	2	3	4	5	Sorting/coding	1	2	3	4	5
Officiating/ refereeing	1	2	3	4	5	Speaking clearly	1	2	3	4	5
						Teaching	1	2	3	4	5
Operating machinery (list)	1	2	3	4	5	Telephone skills	1	2	3	4	5
						Time management	1	2	3	4	5
Painting	1	2	3	4	5	Typing	1	2	3	4	5
Performing	1	2	3	4	5	Visual design	1	2	3	4	5
Perseverance	1	2	3	4	5	Waiting tables	1	2	3	4	5
Persuasion	1	2	3	4	5	Web design	1	2	3	4	5
Photography	1	2	3	4	5	Writing	1	2	3	4	5
Physical stamina	1	2	3	4	5						

When you have completed this exercise, look back over your list again. When you come to a skill that you enjoy using, circle the number that corresponds with that skill. Then create a page in your binder with a listing of the circled 4s and 5s. These should be the skills you focus on. To add validity to this new abridged list, ask a friend whose opinion you really value to assess the list objectively. A former teacher may fill this role as well. See if there are any discrepancies between your self-perception and the perception of others. Keep in mind that if there is a conflict, it may be because your friend has never had the opportunity to see you using a particular skill.

When you have completed this list, and when you have asked for objective feedback, move on to the next section in this chapter, "Know Your Weaknesses."

Know Your Weaknesses

Coming to a better understanding of your skills is of extreme importance, because it is the foundation upon which you will build your job-search plan. It is also important to take an objective look at your weaknesses. The list in Table 1.1 will give you a look at some of your areas of weakness. Scores of 1 or 2 are indicators of possible areas of weakness. Your weaknesses may or may not relate to your disability. Regardless of the source or cause of the weakness, it's helpful to determine which weaknesses may be a factor in your job search. If a weakness stands in the way of your goal, you may want to address it.

Remediating a weakness may be as simple as practicing a skill you rarely use, or as involved as taking classes at a local university or adult education program. By addressing the weakness before you begin your job search, you show the prospective employer that you have a good self-understanding, and that you are being proactive about self-improvement.

In your binder, draw up a list of your weaknesses and ask someone, perhaps the same person who helped give you feedback on your skills and traits (that is, if you are still speaking!), to look over your list with you. Again, an objective look may be helpful. Sometimes we are our own toughest critics. What you may list as a weakness because you know you can do much better, someone else may see as an average ability. When you have completed this exercise, move on to the next section, which examines disability assessment issues.

Assess the Issues Relating to Your Disability

In addition to your weaknesses, you should also address issues relating to your disability. You need to examine your disability and the way in which it may manifest itself in your job search. You may find that the disability has no impact at all on your choice of career. In fact, many people with disabilities have been employed for years, and their supervisors and coworkers have absolutely no idea at all that they have a disability. In other cases, a disability will require some accommodations. (For a more in-depth discussion about workplace accommodations, see Chapter 13.) For example, a person with diabetes may need to follow a more rigid eating schedule to facilitate the maintenance of their blood sugar levels. In other cases, a disability may require some direct modifications to the workplace (such as the width of doorways or the height of a drafting table) or the way that tasks are accomplished (such as voice-recognition software to aid data entry and word processing).

By considering the ways in which your disability may affect your work, you can anticipate potential questions in a job interview. This will give you the opportunity to fashion your responses in a way that will impress the employer with your preparation and your self-understanding. It may also help to put the employer at ease with the thought of hiring a person with a disability.

The following is a list of disabilities or disability-related circumstances and potential ways they can impact your work or your employer. Keep in mind that whether they actually do affect your work is beside the point. In addition to the challenge of overcoming ways in which your disability does impact your life, you must also deal with the misperceptions of how it might affect your life.

- **AIDS/HIV**

   Regular medication regimen

   Contiguousness/risk to coworkers

   Potential for extended sick leaves

- **Using assistive devices (braces, cane, wheelchair)**

   Stationary—can't get around to do what needs to be done

   Exorbitant workplace modification costs

   Slowness

- **Asperger's Syndrome**

  Impaired nonverbal communication

  Difficulty in adapting to change

- **Asthma**

  Allergies to workplace

  Stamina

- **Attention deficit disorder**

  Difficulty in paying attention to detail

  Need to modify workplace to provide distraction-free environment

- **Cerebral palsy**

  Difficulty in interpreting speech

  Assistive technology costs

  Workplace modifications

- **Chemical sensitivity**

  Workplace modifications

  Change in cleaning contract

  Change in ventilation system

  Guidelines regarding coworkers' use of soaps, lotions, and fragrances

- **Chronic fatigue syndrome**

  Alterations to standard schedule

  Extended use of sick time

- **Chronic illness**

  Extended use of sick time

  Contiguousness

  Regular medication regimen

  Alterations to standard schedule

- **Depth perception**

  Safety issues on plant floor

- **Issues regarding transportation or operating equipment (forklift, automobile, etc.)**

- **Diabetes**

  Regular medication regimen

  Alterations to standard schedule

- **Disfigurement**

  Impact on coworkers, customers

- **Hearing**

  Use of volume-control handset on telephone

  Use of TTY at workspace and elsewhere

  Modification of loudspeaker system

  Installation of visual safety alarms

- **Learning disability**

  Enabling spell-checking software on word processor, modifying other software to include spell-checking

  Installing assistive technology, scanner/reader, speech card in computer

  Submitting directions in written form if the employee has a cognitive processing difficulty

  Leniency on time requirements for duties that require a great deal of reading

- **Missing digit**

  Workplace safety issues

  Modified keyboard or other equipment

- **Missing limb**

  Workplace safety issues

  Equipment modification

  Impact on coworkers, customers

- **Psychological/emotional**

  Regular medication regimen

  Potential for extended leave

- **Speech**

  Use of e-mail for most communication

  Impact on coworkers, customers

- **Tourette's syndrome**

  Impact on coworkers, customers

- **Traumatic brain injury**

  Need for directions to be given in written form

  Impact on coworkers, customers

- **Vision**

  Use of guide dog

  Use of screen-reading program with speech card

  Printing memos and other material in alternative formats, such as large print or Braille

  Audible signals in elevator

  Workplace modifications

In addition to the above possible issues, most disabilities that are visible or have visible effects will require training to educate coworkers. Many disability-related organizations have published materials to help people understand disabilities, including recommended etiquette for interacting with a person who has a disability.

You should also make a list of the issues you may need to address regarding your disability and possible accommodations you may need. It may be helpful to speak with a rehabilitation counselor or one of the people at the Job Accommodation Network, and check your assumptions against their experience. They may even have suggestions for how you might address these issues. (There is more information about the Job Accommodation Network in Chapter 13.)

When you have finished this section, move on to the next section, an assessment of your traits and characteristics.

Determine Your Traits and Characteristics

How would you describe yourself? How would others describe you? Sometimes, our personality traits and characteristics can give us great insight into the types of careers in which we can be happy. While I have met some joke-telling, backslapping accountants, there are a few more people like that in the field of sales. Some career counselors, like John Holland, who developed the "The Self-Directed Search" assessment device, believe that people with certain personality types are more often found in certain career fields. Take a look at the following traits and characteristics, and circle the ones that seem to describe you best.

Abstract	Disloyal	Methodical
Adventurous	Domineering	Orderly
Ambitious	Driven	Practical
Analytical	Easygoing	Quick learner
Artistic	Extroverted	Risk-taking
Assertive	Focused	Self-confident
Businesslike	Goal-directed	Self-starter
Cautious	Honest	Sense of humor
Compassionate	Humble	Sensitive
Complacent	Idealistic	Shy
Concrete	Impulsive	Strong work ethic
Conformist	Insensitive	Supportive
Creative	Introverted	Tactful
Critical	Intuitive	Team player
Curious	Kind	Trusting
Dedicated	Loyal	Upbeat
Discreet		

Once again, the value of this exercise will be far greater if you can ask one or two people to look over your list. You may even want to make photocopies of the sheet and ask them to critique you independently and anonymously. Compare your self-perceptions to the perceptions held by others. Sometimes you will see conflicts, but other times you may find near-universal agreement. When you have finished this exercise, move on to the next section on values.

Identify Your Values

Just as it is important for you to think about who you are and what you have to offer, it is also important that you spend some time thinking about what you are looking for. A big part of this involves deciding what you value. To complete this exercise, write each of the following values down on index cards. Then pick up two cards and decide: "Which of these two things is more important to me?" Take the card that finished in second place and start a pile. Pick up another card and "run it against" the first card. Continue to do this until you have one card that "beats" all of the others. Then continue this for second place, etc. You should end up with a ranking of the values from the following list.

Challenge	Money
Creativity	Opportunity for advancement
Direction from others	Power
Fringe benefits	Recognition
Helping people	Routine
Independence	Security
Leisure (vacation, etc.)	Variety

You now have a better picture of who you are. You have reminded yourself of and recorded your past triumphs and challenges. You have painted a picture of yourself that includes those experiences, as well as the strengths and weaknesses you possess. You have given thought to your values, and to what you really need and want from a job. You have also given some thought as to how your disability may impact your career choice.

Hopefully, these self-evaluation exercises have helped to illustrate a point: Your disability is but one stone in the mosaic of who you are. How many of your weaknesses are direct results of your disability? Probably not many. Most people have myriad strengths and weaknesses. They may excel at certain types of tasks, yet they may struggle with others. This fact is true regardless of whether or not they have a disability. For most people, the key is to know what those strengths and weaknesses are, and then to apply for jobs that require the skills that they have, and to avoid applying for jobs that require skills that they do not possess.

Career Assessment Instruments

Your own assessment of your skills and your personality is quite likely to be accurate; however, your objectivity cannot be assured. Having a friend look over the preceding exercises will help increase the reliability of the information. The problem is that even your friends will have a difficult time being truly objective. It may be worth your while, then, to undergo a more formal career assessment with the assistance of a vocational counselor. The following is a list of career-assessment instruments, along with a brief description of what they measure and how you might find them.

Aptitude and Achievement Assessment

Most of the following assessment tests can be taken with the help of a qualified career counselor. Check with your local vocational rehabilitation office, or look in the Yellow Pages, for a college career center or vocational counseling agency. Some assessments involve a fee, but some are free via your public library or the Internet. It is recommended, however, that you use these instruments only in cooperation with a career counselor. It's easy to misread the results of them, and the results of misreading them can be significant in terms of money and, more importantly, time.

Adult Basic Learning Examination, 2nd Edition (ABLE)

This instrument is used to assess the basic educational achievement of adults, although it is most useful for adults with less than an Associate degree. The instrument tests six different achievement areas: Vocabulary, Reading Comprehension, Spelling, Language (grammar and punctuation), Number Operations, and Problem Solving.

Armed Services Vocational Aptitude Battery

The Armed Services Vocational Aptitude Battery (ASVAB) is a series of assessment instruments that measure Word Knowledge, Paragraph Comprehension, Arithmetic Reasoning, Mathematics Knowledge, General Science, Auto and Shop Information, Mechanical Comprehension, Electronics Information, Numerical Operations, and Coding Speed. In addition, the ASVAB contains the "The Self-Directed Search" assessment device (described below). The results of the test are useful in determining the candidate's suitability for military and nonmilitary careers. The ASVAB is most often used with senior high and postsecondary students. Because it is offered to schools without charge, it is a popular instrument in many school districts. It is worth pointing out that the ASVAB has been criticized because of the timed nature of the instrument and the bias that results for persons with some disabilities.

Differential Aptitude Test (DAT) with Career Interest Inventory (CII)

The DAT is comprised of eight subtests, measuring Verbal Reasoning, Numerical Reasoning, Abstract Reasoning, Perceptual Speed and Accuracy, Mechanical Reasoning, Space Relations, Spelling, and Language Usage. The CII measures interests in the following categories: Social Science, Clerical Services, Health Services, Agriculture, Customer Services, Fine Arts, Mathematics and Science, Building Trades, Educational Services, Legal Services, Transportation, Sales, Management, Benchwork, and Machine Operation. The test is most often used with secondary students through adults.

Tests of Adult Basic Education (TABE)

This instrument is constructed to assess basic skills in reading, mathematics, and language. The TABE is used primarily among individuals age 16 and over.

United States Employment Service General Aptitude Test Battery (GATB) and Interest Inventory (USES II)

This instrument is used broadly among government employment and labor agencies. Designed to assess individuals age 16 and older, the instrument contains both an aptitude assessment and an interest inventory. The GATB measures the following aptitudes: General, Verbal, Numerical, Spatial, Form Perception, Clerical Perception, Motor Coordination, Finger Dexterity, and Manual Dexterity. When combined with the USES II, the GATB is the most extensively researched vocational assessment instrument available. It should be noted that the GATB, like the ASVAB, has been criticized because of the timed nature of the instrument and the bias that results for persons with some disabilities.

World of Work Inventory

This instrument is appropriate for high school through adult populations. In addition to measuring interests according to the broad Dictionary of Occupational Titles classifications, it provides Vocational Training Potentials in the areas of Numerical, Verbal, Abstractions, Spatial-Form, Mechanical/Electrical, and Clerical. The WOWI has several different forms: long and short forms, a Spanish-language form, as well as small font and normal font printing. The WOWI is not timed, but there are suggested time frames for its administration.

Interest Inventories

While the preceding assessment instruments help to measure your aptitude for doing certain tasks, interest inventories help you to identify some of the things you enjoy doing or ways in which your personality may play a role in your career satisfaction.

Career Directions Inventory

This interest inventory is used most often with high school and postsecondary students, although it is often used as a career-planning instrument for the general adult population. It measures an individual's interest within 15 basic interest areas: Administration, Art, Clerical, Food Service, Industrial Arts, Health Service, Outdoors, Personal Service, Sales, Science and Technology, Teaching/Social Service, Writing, Assertive, Persuasive, and Systematic.

Career Occupational Preference System Interest Inventory (COPS)

The COPS is used primarily with secondary students and adults. The instrument provides scores for career clusters in the following areas: Science (Professional and Skilled), Technology (Professional and Skilled), Consumer Electronics, Outdoors, Business (Professional and Skilled), Clerical, Communication, Arts (Professional and Skilled), and Service (Professional and Skilled). The COPS provides separate scoring categories to show you how secondary students scored, as opposed to adults.

Harrington–O'Shea Career Decision-Making System— Revised (CDM-R)

The Harrington–O'Shea is a popular instrument for use with college students and adults; however, it is also used widely with secondary school students. The instrument contains six sections. There are sections dedicated to Job Choices, Favorite Subjects (Academic), Future Training, Values, Best Abilities, and an interest inventory. The interest inventory is based upon the theory of John Holland (see the next section, "The Self-Directed Search"). It reports scores for six basic occupational categories: Crafts, Scientific, The Arts, Social, Business, and Office Operations.

The Self-Directed Search

There are several versions of The Self-Directed Search: for middle and secondary school students and adults with limited reading abilities, college students, and adults. The Self-Directed Search, designed by John Holland, is one of the most popular career interest inventories in use in the world. It is based on Holland's theory that there are six basic personality types: Creative, Realistic, Investigative, Artistic, Social, and Enterprising. The theory also assumes that there are six corresponding work environments, and that individuals will find "person-environment fit" in work environments that most closely match their personality. This instrument is available via the Internet at

```
www.self-directed-search.com
```

Strong Interest Inventory

The Strong Interest Inventory is useful in assessing the career interests of individuals from middle school through adulthood. The instrument reports a score for the six areas of interest described by John Holland in "The Self-Directed Search," as well as 23 basic interest scales and 207 occupational scales.

Instruments for People with Disabilities

There are several programs used in the rehabilitation counseling field to assist in the placement of people with disabilities in vocational education, sheltered workshops, or supervised work settings. You can get information on these instruments by speaking with your state's office of vocational rehabilitation. The following instrument is used in the vocational rehabilitation field but is appropriate for high school and college graduates as well.

McCarron–Dial System (MDS)

The McCarron–Dial System is designed to assist rehabilitation counselors in working with people of all ages with disabilities. It is used to assess verbal-spatial-cognitive, motor, emotional, sensory, and integration-coping skills. It helps to identify specific needs that should be addressed prior to embarking on certain careers.

Computer-Based Guidance Systems

In addition to the instruments listed earlier, there are some computer programs that can help assess some of the same things. Many of these provide almost immediate results and help deliver educational content based on those results.

Discover

Discover is a computer program that assists you in the area of self-assessment, as well as providing information to help you make decisions about possible careers. It also contains a component that assists you in choosing college or graduate programs throughout the United States.

SIGIPlus

Like Discover, SIGIPlus is a computer-based guidance program that assists in self-assessment and career exploration. However, SIGIPlus does not provide information on postsecondary education.

Choices CT

Computer-aided guidance programs, like their paper-and-pencil counterparts, should be used under the guidance of a vocational counselor. It is important to have a professional assist you in interpreting the results. These instruments are not meant to be used like a crystal ball. They cannot tell you "what you should do." Nor, for that matter, can a vocational counselor. What a counselor can do, with the use of these instruments, is help you learn more about your abilities and interests, and how they may relate to different careers.

Assessment Instruments on the Internet

The Internet is another good source of various assessment instruments.

The Career Key

`http://www.careerkey.org/english/`

This site offers a professional career test that measures your skills, abilities, values, interests, and personality. It identifies promising jobs and gives you accurate information about them.

The Career Interests Game

`http://career.missouri.edu/article.php?sid=146`

This is a game designed by the University of Missouri to help you match your interests and skills with similar careers. It can help you begin thinking about how your personality will fit in with specific work environments and careers. Based on the Holland typology, this site is a great place to get an overview of your interests.

The Self-Directed Search

`www.self-directed-search.com`

See the description above.

The Campbell Interest and Skill Survey

`www.usnews.com/usnews/work/articles/ccciss.htm`

This site, provided by *U.S. News and World Report,* gives you an opportunity to take a first step in sorting out particular skills and interests. Readers can download a version of the complete Campbell Interest and Skill Survey and have it scored for a fee.

Personality Inventory

www.keirsey.com

Like the Myers-Briggs Type Indicator, this instrument provides information about your personality type, and will give you added perspective in your self-exploration.

You Are Not Alone

At this point you have completed what is by far the most difficult part of the job search. Introspection is a difficult task, and taking on such a task while facing the uncertainty of a change in your career makes it an even greater undertaking.

Hopefully these exercises and information have helped you to put your disability into a broader perspective. Every person who undergoes a job search has to face their abilities as well as their shortcomings. And people must decide which of their shortcoming they can address, and which ones they will choose to address. This is no different for a person with a disability. You must see which areas of weakness can be addressed—regardless of whether they are related to any disability. Again, my guess is that only a fraction of your weaknesses are related to a disability. I would say that for many people there are ways to address most, if not all, of their weaknesses through the use of various reasonable accommodations.

The process of self-assessment as it relates to one's disability is an even greater challenge for individuals who have an acquired disability. If your disability occurred later than adolescence, it is possible that it is not yet completely integrated into your sense of self. If you are still having some difficulty coming to a complete integration of your disability into your self-concept, you are not alone. This happens frequently in cases of late-onset or acquired disability. In this case, you may wish to contact a counselor, because it can be helpful to discuss these issues with someone, particularly with a professional who has worked with people experiencing the same challenges. Although it is not impossible to work on these issues at the same time that you are conducting your job search, there is some advantage to addressing them beforehand.

Support for Continuing Your Education

When people complete an assessment of their abilities and compare them to the requirements for their career goals, they sometimes find that there is a gap that may require continuing their education. If so, resources are available to make education more affordable. The best resource for financial aid is the Heath Resource center.

HEATH Resource Center's Financial Aid for Students with Disabilities

`http://www.heath.gwu.edu/`

The HEATH Resource Center of the American Council on Education operates a national clearinghouse on postsecondary education for individuals with disabilities. The site's Financial Aid for Students with Disabilities publication is updated annually and provides information on U.S. federal student aid programs and other financial aid programs for students with disabilities. The publication also includes a list of 29 sponsors of scholarships specifically designated for students with disabilities. Disabled students may also wish to request a copy of *Strategies for Advising Students with Disabilities — A Postsecondary Student Consumer's Guide.* Contact the organization at

HEATH Resource Center
2121 K Street NW, Suite 220
Washington, DC 20036-1193
Phone: 1-800-544-3284 or 1-202-939-9320 (both numbers voice/TTY)
Fax: 1-202-833-4760

CHAPTER 2

Exploring Careers

When you have a good idea of who you are and what you have to offer, the next step is to determine the possible careers that match up favorably with your interests, values, strengths, and weaknesses. Many of the interest inventories mentioned in Chapter 1 will give you a list of occupations that match your individual profile. This list is an excellent starting point.

I have conducted workshops for high school students, incoming college freshmen, and adults. I often start job-search workshops with a simple question: "How many people here think that they have a pretty good idea of what the job of a police officer is like? A judge? A forensic scientist?" Usually, many if not most of the people in the audience will raise their hands for the first two, and several will raise their hands for the last. I then follow up with those who raised their hands the first time: "How is it that you know what a police officer does?" Unfortunately, from time to time someone will share his or her experience with being fingerprinted, etc. Some people will have a police officer in the family or as a close friend. For most people, however, their understanding of the job of police officer comes from watching *NYPD Blue, COPS, Law and Order,* or *Homicide.* Along the same lines, people base their opinions on what the job of a judge is like from watching *Judge Judy,* or from watching the Scott Peterson trial. (As for forensic scientist, depending on how old they are, they cite Quincy, ME or Grissom from *CSI.*)

Having a misunderstanding about a career is even worse than having no understanding at all. If you decide to pursue a career as a forensic scientist because of scenes in your head of the glamour of Las Vegas or South Florida, or if you shy away from law enforcement because of the constant car chases, you are making a poor decision. My father was a police officer for over 35 years, and I remember him telling me that the only realistic police show that he had ever seen was *Barney Miller*.

Unfortunately, many people make career decisions based on the Hollywood version of careers. There are hundreds, if not thousands, of disenchanted lawyers out there who have been practicing for years and have yet to get an opportunity to stand in front of a jury box waxing eloquent about the Constitution or the rights of the oppressed. For the most part, they are cooped up in a library researching past cases, or sitting in a deposition asking questions of unethical home remodelers or accident victims. Unfortunately for them, they found out too late that they made the wrong choice. By this time, many feel that they may have too much time invested in their career to change now. Some decide to change anyway.

Accountants and career counselors don't have the same problem. You don't see too many accounting sitcoms. (When Joe Pesci or Charles Grodin played roles as accountants, you never really saw them balancing a ledger.) Career counselors whine a lot about how psychiatrists get all of the good roles! Regardless of whether you are interested in careers in law, accounting, or vocational counseling, there are legitimate sources of information on those careers.

Targeting Specific Occupations to Research

At this point, you should gather up the results of any of the assessment instruments that you have used. Most of the instruments discussed in Chapter 1 will have generated a list of occupations that match closely with the profile derived from your responses. Take these lists and write each occupation on an index card. You may find that some of the occupations have been mentioned in several different instruments. Take note of that by writing on the index card for that occupation the number of times it has been mentioned.

Now, look through the index cards. Which of these job titles sound attractive to you? Put those in a pile with a Post-It Note labeled "Interesting." Of the remaining cards, which job titles sound unappealing? Put them in a second pile with a Post-It Note labeled "Not Interested." It's likely that you will have several cards left, because they represent jobs in which you are neither interested nor disinterested. For these jobs, you will need more information before you can make an intelligent decision. Put these cards in the first pile. Now go back to the "Not Interested" pile. Separate these cards further into two piles. One will consist of those jobs for which you have significant firsthand information, and you know for sure that you are not interested in them. The second group should include those jobs about which you have little quality information. Put the second group into that first pile so that you can investigate them more fully.

The first pile is probably much larger than the remaining pile of cards. This is because it would be inadvisable to rule out any possible options before you have enough solid information to make an informed decision.

I know this firsthand. When I took an interest inventory in my senior year in high school, it came back with a listing of occupations. Near the top of the list was a job that caused me to distrust the entire survey. The job title was…Funeral Director. Funeral Director! I couldn't sit through an entire episode of *Scooby-Doo* without being freaked out! I certainly couldn't spend the rest of my life working with dead bodies all the time—injecting embalming fluid and dressing corpses. "Where do they get these survey results, anyway?" I asked myself. I shared the results with a few friends, no doubt providing them with doubts about their own results, along with a lot of laughs.

Now I look at those results with a different perspective. Although I still can't sit through an entire episode of *Scooby-Doo,* now it's for different reasons. Having friends who are funeral directors, I now know that they may spend little or no time actually doing any work with corpses. Many funeral homes have people on their staffs who are very good with that aspect of the business. I now also realize that much of the work of a funeral director is not too unlike the work that I do every day. Funeral directors work with people who are having a difficult time. These clients have suffered a significant loss and are looking for a person who can be an empathic listener and who can help them get through this trying time. There are many comparisons made between the stages of grief that one goes through when a loved one dies and the stages of grief that an individual goes through when they lose a job. In each case, a trained counselor can make that experience less difficult.

Now, while I have no regrets about the road my career has taken, it was foolish and immature of me to have completely disregarded the results of my interest inventory based on my misperception of what a funeral director's job was like. So spend the time now and explore all of the possible options that are available to you and which, at some level, appear to match your interests, skills, or aptitudes. Perhaps you will determine that your preconceived notion was correct, and that you would not be interested in or suited for a particular career. At the same time, it is possible that after an initial investigation, you may find that you wish to further explore a position that you thought would hold no interest.

So take that pile of cards and put the job titles into your binder (or word processing document), with one job per page. Then go and gather information from sources that will help you better understand that occupation.

Sources of Information

There are numerous sources of quality information about occupations and the world of work. Some of these come from government sources like the United States Department of Labor. Other sources include commercial publishers that collect information from a variety of corporate and governmental sources. Finally, you can find useful information from corporations through their public and investor relations departments.

Reference Publications

The first place to look will provide you with the most basic information. This resource is the O*NET, the Occupational Information Network, an easy-to-use database available on the Web browser. It contains comprehensive information on job requirements and worker competencies. O*NET replaced the Dictionary of Occupational Titles as the most comprehensive source of information on occupations in existence. This information is based on data collected from employers across the country, and each "occupation" refers to the "collective description of a number of individual jobs performed, with minor variations, in many establishments." The information was compiled by the United States Department of Labor's Employment and Training Administration and is published in book form by the USDOL, JIST Works, and other publishers. It is also available on the World Wide Web at:

```
http://www.doleta.gov/programs/onet/
```

Vocational counselors and job seekers use the O*NET to gather information on occupations. Each entry contains an eight-digit Standard Occupational Classification code and information outlining Tasks of the Occupation, Knowledge, Skills, Abilities, Work Activities, Work Context, a Job Zone Component, Interests, Work Values, Related Occupations, and a Link to Wage and Employment Data.

Example

19-4092.00 - Forensic Science Technicians
Collect, identify, classify, and analyze physical evidence related to criminal investigations. Perform tests on weapons or substances, such as fiber, hair, and tissue to determine significance to investigation. May testify as expert witnesses on evidence or crime laboratory techniques. May serve as specialists in area of expertise, such as ballistics, fingerprinting, handwriting, or biochemistry.

Tasks

Examines, tests, and analyzes tissue samples, chemical substances, physical materials, and ballistics evidence, using recording, measuring, and testing equipment.

Interprets laboratory findings and test results to identify and classify substances, materials, and other evidence collected at crime scene.

Collects and preserves criminal evidence used to solve cases.

Confers with ballistics, fingerprinting, handwriting, documents, electronics, medical, chemical, or metallurgical experts concerning evidence and its interpretation.

Reconstructs crime scene to determine relationships among pieces of evidence.

Prepares reports or presentations of findings, investigative methods, or laboratory techniques.

Testifies as expert witness on evidence or laboratory techniques in trials or hearings.

Knowledge

Chemistry	Knowledge of the chemical composition, structure, and properties of substances and of the chemical processes and transformations that they undergo. This includes uses of chemicals and their interactions, danger signs, production techniques, and disposal methods.
Public Safety and Security	Knowledge of relevant equipment, policies, procedures, and strategies to promote effective local, state, or national security operations for the protection of people, data, property, and institutions.

English Language	Knowledge of the structure and content of the English language, including the meaning and spelling of words, rules of composition, and grammar.
Law and Government	Knowledge of laws, legal codes, court procedures, precedents, government regulations, executive orders, agency rules, and the democratic political process.
Computers and Electronics	Knowledge of circuit boards, processors, chips, electronic equipment, and computer hardware and software, including applications and programming.
Mathematics	Knowledge of arithmetic, algebra, geometry, calculus, statistics, and their applications.

Skills

Reading Comprehension	Understanding written sentences and paragraphs in work related documents.
Science	Using scientific rules and methods to solve problems.
Critical Thinking	Using logic and reasoning to identify the strengths and weaknesses of alternative solutions, conclusions or approaches to problems.
Active Listening	Giving full attention to what other people are saying, taking time to understand the points being made, asking questions as appropriate, and not interrupting at inappropriate times.
Coordination	Adjusting actions in relation to others' actions.
Equipment Selection	Determining the kind of tools and equipment needed to do a job.
Writing	Communicating effectively in writing as appropriate for the needs of the audience.

Judgment and Decision Making	Considering the relative costs and benefits of potential actions to choose the most appropriate one.
Mathematics	Using mathematics to solve problems.
Complex Problem Solving	Identifying complex problems and reviewing related information to develop and evaluate options and implement solutions.

Abilities

Inductive reasoning	Combining pieces of information to form general rules or conclusions (includes finding a relationship among seemingly unrelated events).
Oral Expression	Communicating information and ideas in speaking so others will understand.
Information Ordering	Arranging things or actions in a certain order or pattern according to a specific rule or set of rules (e.g., patterns of numbers, letters, words, pictures, mathematical operations).
Oral Comprehension	Listening to and understanding information and ideas presented through spoken words and sentences.
Flexibility of Closure	Identifying or detecting a known pattern (a figure, object, word, or sound) that is hidden in other distracting material.
Near Vision	Seeing details at close range (within a few feet of the observer).
Written Expression	Communicating information and ideas in writing so others will understand.
Written Comprehension	Reading and understanding information and ideas presented in writing.
Category Flexibility	Generating or using different sets of rules for combining or grouping things in different ways.
Fluency of Ideas	The ability to come up with a number of ideas about a topic (the number of ideas is important, not their quality, correctness, or creativity).

Work Activities

Getting Information	Observing, receiving, and otherwise obtaining information from all relevant sources.
	Translating or explaining what information means and how it can be used.
Identifying Objects, Actions, and Events	Identifying information by categorizing, estimating, recognizing differences or similarities, and detecting changes in circumstances or events.
Documenting/Recording Information	Entering, transcribing, recording, storing, or maintaining information in written or electronic/magnetic form.
Analyzing Data or Information	Identifying the underlying principles, reasons, or facts of information by breaking down information or data into separate parts.
Judging the Qualities of Things, Services or People	Assessing the value, importance, or quality of things or people.
Communicating with Supervisors, Peers, or Subordinates	Providing information to supervisors, coworkers, and subordinates by telephone, in written form, e-mail, or in person.
Making Decisions and Solving Problems	Analyzing information and evaluating results to choose the best solution and solve problems.
Handling and Moving Objects	Using hands and arms in handling, installing, positioning, and moving materials, and manipulating things.
Communicating with Persons Outside	Communicating with people outside the organization, representing the organization to customers, the public, government, and other external sources. This information can be exchanged in person, in writing, or by telephone or e-mail.
Interpreting the Meaning of Information for Others	

Hands-on Work with the O*NET

After going through the O*NET for each of your chosen occupations and recording a brief synopsis in your binder or word processing file, go back and read the descriptions all over again. Which of the descriptions reinforced your understanding of that occupation? Which of them surprised you? Write a couple of pages about what you learned from that experience. Write about how you feel about any progress you have made, or about frustrations you may be feeling.

When you have completed that exercise, and while you are still in an objective state, go back over the list and put a check mark next to those positions that you would like to gather more information about. At this point, you should still err on the side of collecting information on any jobs for which you have any interest in learning more about.

For those positions for which you want to pursue additional information, the next logical step is to refer to the Occupational Outlook Handbook.

The Occupational Outlook Handbook (OOH)

The *OOH* is published by the United States Department of Labor Bureau of Labor Statistics, and it includes a great deal of updated and detailed information not found in the O*NET. The information included in the *OOH* centers on broader employment categories (several hundred, as opposed to the greater number of occupational titles in the O*NET) and encompasses the following:

The DOT Code

The Nature of the Work

- Tasks performed, equipment used, supervisory relationships
- Variations within the broad category
- Variations in duties based on seniority or supervisory relationship
- Impact of technology

Working Conditions

- Hours
- Environment

- Physical demands, stress, injury

- Protective clothing or equipment required

- Travel

Training, Qualifications, and Advancement

- Types and duration of appropriate training involved

- Source of training (apprenticeships, education, on-the-job training, etc.)

- Educational requirements

- Desirable skills and characteristics

- Certification or licensure required for entry-level or advanced positions

- Opportunities for advancement

Job Outlook

- External and internal forces that may impact demand for a particular occupation within that category

- Number of job openings currently and anticipated

- Vulnerability to economic cycles, foreign competition, technological advances

Earnings

- Typical earnings of workers at various stages in the occupational category

- Type of compensation package (benefits, salary, stock options)

- Earnings within sectors (private, government, not-for-profit, self-employed)

Related Occupations

- Those categories that are similar in terms of skills, abilities, aptitudes, etc.

Sources of Additional Information

- Trade and professional associations and contact information, unions, and government agencies where job seekers can find more information about an employment category

You can explore the *Occupational Outlook Handbook* by visiting the Department of Labor's Web site at:

www.bls.gov/oco/

The *OOH* can be a very valuable tool, in that each occupation category is covered in some depth, and the information it contains is relatively timely, because the handbook is published every two years. Look through the *OOH* description for each of the occupations listed in your binder that you are still interested in researching. Take notes, including references to those aspects that may be most important to you (salaries, opportunities for advancement, required training, etc.).

After you have done this for each of those occupations, take another couple of pages to reflect on this part of the process. What have you discovered? What themes run through the occupations you have chosen to research? What have you found out that has surprised you? What has excited you? What has turned you off?

Now read over your entries once again. After having read these descriptions, and in covering your notes, which occupations have you decided that you have learned enough about to rule out as a possibility? Some of these may have been occupations that were in your original "no interest" pile. That is probably likely, but hopefully you will find that the last couple of exercises were still worth your effort. Certainly you can never be worse off for having gained knowledge on a certain topic. But more importantly, by having gone through this effort, you will be less likely to second-guess yourself later. You will always be able to go back to your workbook and read your notes, and hopefully discern why you ruled out a certain occupation.

It is also very possible that your narrowed list of interest will include some occupations that were in your "no interest" pile. It is also possible, if not likely, that your new list will include some occupations that were mentioned in the results of more than one of your assessment instruments.

Review your new list. What do the occupations that remain have in common? For each occupation on your "intermediate list," jot down the questions you would like to explore further. You are at the point now where you will need to dig deeper to find your information. You must go to sources that will provide in-depth information on that particular occupation. One good place to start is with professional associations and trade groups, covered in the following section.

Professional Associations and Trade Groups

Many organizations have formed to serve the collective interests of individuals in certain career paths. Sometimes these organizations are national or international; however, they may have regional, state, or local chapters as well. Attending meetings of these organizations (when it is allowed under their rules, of course) is a great opportunity to stay up-to-date on developments in the field, and to make some excellent contacts.

The last section of the *OOH* includes information about these organizations; however, if you cannot find sufficient information there, you can turn to the Encyclopedia of Associations. This reference text is available at most libraries, and it is a great source for you if you are looking for information on organizations such as The American Mathematical Society, the Society of American Florists, or even the Dilbert fan club.

Many of these organizations will gladly provide you with information if you request it. That information can give you added insight into a field. Going to one of their meetings in person is even more valuable. These meetings can be a nonthreatening way to get to know people who are in the field. These people are a great source of information—far better than anything you can read about in a book. These meetings also serve as an important networking resource for the members. The meetings often include announcements about opportunities that are available in the field. These positions are also often listed in the organization's newsletter.

Informational Interviewing

When you are seeking information about what a career is really like, your best source of information is someone who is actually in that job. These individuals can provide you with timely information and can add dimension to the information you have already gathered about a position. They are in a position to tell you how the job has changed in recent years, what skills they use every day, how they perform their day-to-day tasks, what the opportunities are for advancement, and what they have heard about possible job openings within their organization or with other companies in the field.

Some people are a little nervous about asking people to share this kind of information with them. This topic will be addressed in greater detail in Chapter 6.

At this point, let's just address the issue with this thought: What person would not feel flattered by someone's sincere interest in what they do and how they got to where they are today? Who doesn't feel a little bit more important when someone turns to them for advice on a very important topic?

How Do You Set Up an Informational Interview?

Informational interviews are usually arranged through one of your networking contacts. You will either be contacting a personal friend or relative, or you will be contacting the friend, relative, or business associate of a mutual acquaintance. The request you will be making is a simple one. "I would like to meet you for coffee, lunch, at your office, or at your leisure, as I am considering a career in your field, and I would like to learn more about it."

It is important that you make it clear up front that you are only hoping to come away with information. If you imply that you have any expectation at all that this individual may be in a position to offer you a job, or that you may ask him or her to hire you, it may cause the individual to deny your request for the meeting.

What Topics to Cover in an Informational Interview

Most informational interviews last in the neighborhood of 30 minutes to an hour. That does not give you a great deal of time to gather the important information you are seeking. Depending on the individual you are interviewing and the information you have already gathered from other sources, you might want to use some of the following questions as a guide during your interview.

- What are the duties that you feel are most essential to your position? (This will be a very important question as you determine which, if any, duties will be impacted by your disability.)

- How different are those duties from someone performing this type of job at another organization?

- How did you reach this position—what was your career path?

- Was that the typical career path for this type of position?

- What skills/traits/background are employers looking for when they hire for these types of positions?

- Has there been a lot of hiring activity in this area?

- Is the field growing, stagnant, or in decline?

- This conversation has solidified my decision to pursue a career in this area. What suggestions would you have for me as I attempt to break into this field?

- Are you aware of any opportunities currently available in this field, or positions that could be seen as a possible stepping-stone to this field?

- Would you be willing to keep your eyes and ears open for me in the event that you hear about any positions for which I might be able to compete?

- Would you mind if I stayed in touch with you, contacting you every month or so to see if you have heard about anything, and to update you on my progress?

- Is there anything else you would suggest that I do?

- Is there anyone else that you would suggest I speak to about this field?

There is one question you should never ask in an informational interview: "Will you hire me?" This question violates the agreement established at the request for the meeting, and will make the person you are speaking with feel awkward, uncomfortable, and perhaps even angry. It will definitely make them less likely to help you in the future. It will also make it less likely that the individual will agree to this type of interview with anyone in the future. Nobody likes a pushy salesperson, and this is doubly true when the "customer" is not in a position to buy.

Starting Your Own Business

Your study of potential opportunities may result in your deciding that you would like to start your own business. If so, you will want to repeat some of the steps mentioned earlier from two perspectives. You will want to speak to people who are in that field, but you will also want to speak with other entrepreneurs who have recently set out on their own. One thing you may hear is that before you begin a new business it is helpful to "try it with training wheels"—work for someone else in that field so that you are confident that you have enough of an understanding of the business to make a go of it.

There are many resources to help you start your business ranging from government (Small Business Administration or local Industrial Development Agency), to banks and not-for-profits organizations such as SCORE (Service Corps of Retired Executives). Touch base with them to get information that will put you in a better position to decide if this is the option you want to pursue.

Evaluating the Possibilities

At this point you have gathered enough information about all of your potential choices so that you can make an educated choice about your future. You know what your skills are, and you know which jobs require people with your skills. In addition to the information you have found in books or on the Web like O*NET and the *Occupational Outlook Handbook*, you have had the chance to hear it "straight from the horse's mouth." With this information, you should have a pretty good idea of which occupations would hold your interest.

Now is the time to go through with what Benjamin Franklin referred to as a T-square. In your binder, create a page for each option. In the left column, write all of the positives about pursuing that occupational goal. Some categories might include salary, opportunities for advancement, type of work, growth prospects for that field, work setting, etc. Now do the same thing for the negatives.

After you have completed a T-square for each position, spend some time evaluating them. Which occupations, on the whole, still seem the most appealing? Which ones have some appeal, but have equally weighty drawbacks (you would need to go back for additional training, etc.)?

T-square for Pharmaceutical Sales Position

Pros	Cons
Opportunities for nearly unlimited income	No stable source of income
Chance to "be my own boss"	Limited direction from supervisors
Opportunities to travel	Travel a strain on family
Working with people all the time	Stress of needing to be "on"

(continued)

T-square for Pharmaceutical Sales Position (*continued*)

Pros	Cons
Company car	Advancement means relocating
Good benefits	Excessive hours
Having a part in making people's lives better	Little security
No need for further formal education, just sales training	

Keep in mind that making a decision about one option does not necessarily rule out any of the other options for good. You might decide later in your career to make a change, and enter one of the other fields. Or, after an extended period with no success in reaching your current goal, you might decide to go back and pursue a different goal.

Not all goals are mutually exclusive. In fact, you may find that some goals allow for you to pursue different goals simultaneously. For example, you may choose to pursue two goals—retail management and human resources. In order to compete for jobs in human resources, you may need to return to school to pick up some courses in benefits, labor law, or even counseling. You could begin enrolling in the course work, and at the same time you could be applying and interviewing for positions in retail management. If you are offered a position in retail management, you may become enamored with the field, and the human resources goal may fade. The course work will not be wasted, however, because it will help you to be a better manager.

When possible, look for ways in which you can pursue several goals at once. This will allow you the flexibility to look at more opportunities. Obviously, the more opportunities that you are open to accepting, the more likely it is that you will be offered one.

CHAPTER 3

More Preparation: Practical Work Experience, Assertiveness Training, and Public Speaking Skills

Some of the challenges that a job seeker with a disability shares with all job seekers are more pronounced. Although the challenges often vary by the individual as well as by the nature of the disability, too many people with disabilities fail to take advantage of opportunities to foster their own career development. Others, because of experiences they had while growing up, may not have had the chance to develop, through a variety of experiences, in self-confidence or other areas such as public speaking. If you lack skills in these areas, there are steps you can take to address these concerns.

Experiential Education

Lack of experience is the number one thing holding back the employment of people with disabilities. This is an important issue for all job seekers, but it is particularly crucial for people with disabilities. Showing that you have practical experience is the one thing that can go the furthest in proving that you will be able to perform the essential functions of the job.

What is experiential education? It can come in many forms. In its most common form, it is an experience that is related somehow to more formal "in-class" education. It is an important part of many high school and college experiences. The value is that you can gain practical experience that, when accompanied by the kind of theoretical knowledge you have gained in the classroom, gives you a more three-dimensional understanding of the work.

Obviously, it's to your advantage to become involved in some form of experiential education while you are still enrolled in school. Schools often have well-established contacts and can help you break into a company in which you are interested. The fact is, however, that it is never too late to get this kind of experience. Many people who are considering making a career move will volunteer with a not-for-profit agency in the evenings or on weekends. This gives the volunteer the feeling of fulfillment that comes with helping out a good cause, as well as some practical experience in a field of interest.

What forms can experiential education take? These experiences come under various labels, some of which are used almost interchangeably. These programs can include apprenticeships, internships, cooperative education, service learning, practicum, student teaching, and volunteer work. The following sections discuss these forms of experience in more detail.

Apprenticeships

Usually associated with the skilled trades, an apprenticeship is a form of on-the-job training. The apprentice works with a skilled veteran craftsman for a period of time, after which the apprentice becomes a fully functional tradesman.

To learn more about apprenticeships, visit the following sites on the Web:

The Office of Apprenticeship Training, Employer and Labor Services

`www.doleta.gov/atels_bat`

This U.S. Department of Labor site offers information on apprenticeship programs from across the country.

Job Corps

`jobcorps.doleta.gov`

This federally funded job training program is for at-risk youth, ages 16 through 24.

Internships

An internship is usually a one-time work experience done by a student who is at least at the high school level. Many interns are in college and have taken some coursework that is related to the field. The intern works in a professional setting under the supervision of at least one practicing professional for a period of around three to four months (or one college semester). The student may or may not get academic credit for the internship. Some companies pay interns, whereas others do not.

For more information about internships, see the following Web sites:

InternWeb.com

www.internweb.com

This site has the benefit of some well-written information about internships, as well as an easily searchable database of internship opportunities.

Workforce Recruitment Program

http://www.dol.gov/odep/programs/workforc.htm

A program available to college students specializing in assisting students with disabilities to acquire internship opportunities is the Workforce Recruitment Program run by the Office of Disability Employment Policy of the U.S. Department of Labor. More information on this program can be found on the ODEP Web site.

Entry Point

www.entrypoint.org

This is another great resource for internship opportunities for students with disabilities in Science, Engineering, Mathematics, and Computer Science. Entry Point, a program of the American Association for the Advancement of the Sciences (AAAS) is a summer internship program that partners with NASA, IBM, The National Science Foundation, Lucent Technologies, Seagate Technologies, Procter & Gamble, and Texas Instruments. Check out the Web site for more information on the program.

Cooperative Education (Co-op)

Cooperative education is usually a work experience done by a student who is at least at the high school level. Cooperative education usually spans more than one semester. These students are enrolled in high school or college and have accumulated a significant number of credit hours in their major academic study area. The co-op involves work assignments that are related to the student's academic and career interests. Co-op students are almost always paid, and they earn academic credit. The typical program plan is for students to be involved in the work setting at the same time that they are taking classes in this area, thereby maximizing both experiences. Examples of career fields that regularly suggest co-op education are engineering, physical therapy, and pharmacy.

For more information about co-op opportunities, check out the National Association of Colleges and Employers' JobWeb:

www.jobweb.com

Service Learning

Service learning is a term used to describe what is usually a component of an individual academic class. The idea is to augment the academic content of a class with practical experience. Service learning does not involve pay and is usually arranged at a not-for-profit organization. Supervision is not often a major component of service learning.

Practicum

A practicum is similar to service learning in that it usually does not offer pay and usually is completed as part of an academic class. Most practicum experiences are centered on human-service occupations such as social work and counseling.

Student Teaching

In order to complete a degree in education, a student must first demonstrate competency in the area of teaching. To that end, students are placed in a classroom setting where an experienced teacher supervises them. The supervising teacher observes the student teacher in the preparation and delivery of classroom presentations and lesson plans. These are rarely if ever paid experiences; however, the student teacher does receive academic credit.

Volunteer Experiences

For the most part, the experiences described above are all associated with a structured academic setting. Many individuals arrange practical work experiences on their own as well. The volunteer experience can be very flexible. Depending on the employer's need and the volunteer's availability, this may involve a full-time commitment for several weeks, or it may involve the volunteer coming to help out when they can.

For more information about volunteer opportunities, check out the following:

Idealist

www.idealist.org

A clearinghouse of volunteer opportunities, which you can search based on your interests, skills, and dates of ability.

SERVEnet

www.servenet.org

A free matching service for volunteers and organizations.

Assertiveness

Throughout the job-search process, it will pay to have developed your assertiveness skills. These skills will help you as you communicate your decision about which career you want to pursue. They will help you as you approach your networking contacts. You will need them as you interview for positions. You will need them as you negotiate an offer, and you will need them as you negotiate accommodations in the workplace.

It is possible that you have already developed significant skills in this area. Many people with disabilities have had to learn to be very assertive as they have negotiated the educational system. From advocating for access or an appropriate Individualized Education Plan (IEP) in the K–12 setting, or advocating for academic accommodations in higher education, you may have had to be extremely assertive to have gotten where you are today.

Sometimes, however, this is not the case. Sometimes the struggle in the K–12 setting is so great, or the resistance from health-care providers is so strong, that it is the parents of the person with a disability who have become more assertive and staunch advocates for their son or daughter.

Not only is this unfortunate from the standpoint that the parents have had to fight so hard for what should have come more easily, it is unfortunate because it keeps the person with a disability from doing more of the fighting for herself or himself.

When this is the case, it actually slows the personal development of the person with a disability. Regardless of the reason for a lack of assertiveness, it is important that you overcome this weakness.

Perhaps you are unsure of whether or not you are assertive. Some people believe they are assertive, when in fact they are perceived as meek. Others feel that they are assertive, but are perceived by others as being just plain aggressive. Generally speaking, assertive people are considerate of others but make decisions based on their own needs. Aggressive people tend to act based on their needs but without consideration for how those actions might affect others. Nonassertive (passive) people make decisions with the feelings of other people in mind, intent on avoiding conflict at any cost. These questions may help you determine whether or not you are assertive:

1. If someone asks you to do something or go somewhere, and you don't want to, are you fairly likely to say no rather than go along so as not to hurt their feelings?

2. Are you comfortable asking for favors, or do you constantly find yourself apologizing when you ask for help?

3. If someone older (parents, teacher, relative) expresses a strong opinion with which you disagree, are you comfortable presenting your opinion in a reasoned way?

4. Do you find yourself able to resist peer pressure?

5. Are you proud of your accomplishments? Are you comfortable being complimented for those accomplishments?

6. If someone does something that bothers you (such as cutting in front of you in a line), do you bring that to their attention?

7. Do you feel comfortable maintaining eye contact throughout a conversation?

8. Are you more likely to demand something than to ask for it?

9. If someone disagrees with you, do you view that person as "wrong"?

10. If you compromise with someone, do you feel like you have lost?

If you answered yes to questions 1 through 7, you are likely to be consistently assertive. If you answered yes to questions 8 through 10, you are probably consistently aggressive. If you answer most of questions 1 through 7 with a yes, you may be assertive, but could improve. If you answered four or fewer of the first seven questions with a yes, you can definitely use some help in becoming more assertive.

Possible Sources of Nonassertiveness

There are a lot of sources for nonassertiveness. Many of the causes affect everyone. Some of the causes of nonassertiveness can be made much worse by the presence of a disability. Use the table that follows to identify problem areas for you. By identifying the sources of nonassertive behavior, you will be in a better position to address them.

Sources	Description	Yes	No
Insecurity	Sometimes nonassertive behavior stems from a person feeling insecure about their abilities or their right to voice their opinion. In some cases, this insecurity manifests itself as aggressive behavior.	❏	❏
Fear of Rejection	An overriding concern for the approval of others drives some people to do things that they believe will please others rather than please themselves.	❏	❏
Fear of Conflict	Some people are afraid to act assertively because they are afraid that it will lead to conflict. These people have usually had bad experiences with conflicts in the past. These experiences may have fed the person's insecurities and low self-esteem.	❏	❏

(continued)

(continued)

Sources	Description	Yes	No
Questionable Abilities	Many people who are not assertive act that way out of deference because they perceive that others know better. This comes less from an inflated perception of the abilities of others, and more from low self-esteem.	❏	❏
Poor Communication Skills	If you have trouble communicating effectively, you will have trouble presenting yourself in an assertive way. This can be true when another person is condescending or nasty, as well as when a person extends a compliment.	❏	❏

Tips for Becoming More Assertive

Becoming more assertive is not something that will happen overnight. It will take time, and it will take a great deal of practice. Some of the activities will seem a little monotonous, but as you repeat them, you will find that you are more able to respond in a confident, assertive way.

Be Willing to Take Risks

It is only by taking chances that you can fail, but it is also only by taking chances that you can truly succeed. If you are willing to forgive yourself if you stumble, it will be easier to take a chance.

Be Happy About Your Successes

Don't dwell on negative experiences. Learn from them and move on. Take a minute to enjoy the successes that you have as well. It's OK to be proud of your accomplishments. If someone says "Nice job!," don't say "It was nothing." Say "Thanks. It was a lot of hard work, but I am really happy with the way it turned out." And mean it!

Keep Learning and Improving

If you need improvement in an area, keep working on it. Ask for suggestions. Ask questions to better understand something. It is far better to ask a question and admit that you don't understand something than to pretend that you do and be stuck.

Forgive Yourself

It's okay if you never quite get it down perfectly. Ted Williams was the best hitter in the history of baseball. He has held this distinction even though he failed to get a hit more than 6 times out of 10. Forgive yourself for being human. Although you are bound to make mistakes, so have your parents, your friends, and your teachers. I know that I've made some dandies!

Practice Speaking Assertively

Be direct. Speak about how you feel, what you see, what conclusions you draw. Do it in a clear and specific way:

> "Jenny, when you smoke in my car, the windows get all foggy at night and it makes it hard for me to see."

> "Jim, when you don't call and tell me you are going to be late, I waste my time waiting for you when I could be doing something else."

Listen to Your Voice

Listen to yourself talk, use a tape recorder, or have someone else help you with this. Listen for uncertainty. Listen for tremors or signs of no confidence.

Be Aware of Your Body Language

If you look meek, you will be perceived as meek. Practice making eye contact. Sit alertly in your chair. Don't cross your arms. Don't fidget.

Listen

Listening is crucial to acting assertively. If you aren't sure what the other person is saying, you will be less sure about your response. Listen carefully, check to be sure that you understood correctly if necessary, and then respond.

Be True to Yourself

Remember that it's okay to say no. It's okay if others are disappointed.

Don't feel obligated to do everything that is asked of you. If someone has been in a car accident and needs your help, by all means, go and help them. If someone wants you to help him or her move a sofa during your daughter's piano recital, tell them that you are unable to help. Don't feel the need to apologize and explain why you can't help.

Acting assertively is as much about feeling confident about your worth as a human being as it is about anything else. If you have spent a lot of your life hearing people focus on the things that you can't do rather than on the things you can do, it's natural that you will not feel as confident about yourself. Bruce Willis, George Clooney, and Doug Flutie are not the best singers that you will ever hear, although they have all tried, and they would all like to succeed in this arena. Michael Jordan was a pretty poor professional baseball player. Wouldn't it seem ridiculous if they listened to their critics and felt less about themselves because of one area where they didn't excel? That's no more ridiculous than you buying into the opinions of others and dwelling on the few things you can't excel at, rather than on the many things you can do very well.

Public Speaking

Surveys of people's biggest fears show that the number one fear of the typical person is speaking in public. It rates ahead of dying, air travel, buying a car, and going to the dentist. Public speaking! This means that more people would prefer to be eulogized than to deliver a eulogy!

That fear can be reduced, but it takes practice. You need to recognize that public speaking is a skill worth having, and you have to set your mind to accomplish it.

It is unlikely that to win your job you will have to stand up and deliver a speech to a standing-room-only arena. It is almost certain, however, that you will need to give a credible performance in an interview, and there is a good chance that you will need to speak with a group of people at some point in the interview process. These groups are often called search committees, because they assist in the search for candidates for a particular position. Sometimes they are called focus groups. Regardless of what they are called, it is quite possible that sometime in the job search process you will speak with a group of people who represent various constituencies within the organization. These people may be potential coworkers, peers, customers, or supervisors.

Because of this possibility, it is worth your while to practice your public speaking. Practicing these skills will help build your self-confidence and your assertiveness as well. As you practice, keep a few basic guidelines in mind.

Know Your Material

If you are giving a speech to a professional association, you are going to make every effort to be sure that you know what it is that you will be speaking about. You need to take the same care as you go into a job interview, or make a presentation to a search committee. In the case of a job interview or a presentation to a search committee, this means that you go in with a thorough knowledge of yourself—an understanding of your strengths and weaknesses, as well as your potential. It means that you have also done your research on the company, and that you have a good idea of how you would be able to contribute.

Rehearse

This is not the same as memorizing. Your answers will be different each time you interview, because the questions will be different. The key here is to anticipate what kinds of things might be asked, and simulate how you would answer them. Have a friend practice with you, or tape yourself so that you can get a more objective sense of how you are doing.

Speak to the Listener(s)

As you prepare to make a presentation or go into an interview, you need to constantly remind yourself to think from the listener's perspective. The odds of someone remembering what you say have a great deal to do with the extent to which what you say resonates with each person as an individual. Using words like "you" while you are speaking will help force you to put things in that listener's terms.

Keep It Brief

People have limited attention spans, so you need to communicate your message clearly and concisely. Otherwise, you risk losing their attention, and they will remember little of what you have said. Do not feel the need to explain in detail why you respond the way you do. Just give the answer or make the point. If the audience is confused about why you made the point you did, they will ask you. Dale Carnegie was world renowned, partly because of his skill as a public speaker. If you were to take a Dale Carnegie course, you would practice making speeches that are two minutes long. Make your point, make it with confidence, and sit down.

Create an Image in the Listener's Mind

You could tell an audience about how you took a trip to the Butterfly Conservatory in Niagara Falls, Ontario and saw 1,000 species of butterflies, and they might remember it. If you tell them that you walked through the conservatory wearing a red shirt, knowing that it is an attractive color to the butterflies, and that within five minutes of standing as still as you could, nearly a hundred butterflies landed on your shirt, and, when your husband took a picture and you had it developed, all you could see was your face in a sea of oranges, yellows, and browns, they will remember. That is the power of imagery. If you tell a search committee that you are a "people person," it may mean next to nothing, because the phrase is so overused. If you tell that committee about how you spend your weekends taking inner-city children on hiking expeditions with your church, they will have a much clearer idea of what you mean.

Mean What You Say

Too many people make the fatal mistake of trying to put on airs, speaking about things that they don't completely understand, or that they don't feel much passion about. Others try to "snow" people by saying what they think the listeners want to hear. These are huge mistakes. Nothing comes through more clearly than a phony person giving a speech. If you truly mean what you say and are passionate about it, those attitudes will come through, too.

Join a Speaker's Club

Many areas have clubs where you can practice your public speaking in front of friendly faces. This is also a great way to expand your network. One large organization of such clubs is Toastmasters International. You can probably find a club near you. There are currently more than 8,500 clubs meeting in more than 60 countries. For more information, check out

`www.toastmasters.org`

PART II

Marketing Yourself to Potential Employers

Chapter 4:   Creating Your Resume

Chapter 5:   Writing a Great Cover Letter

CHAPTER 4

Creating Your Resume

The first question you need to ask yourself is: "Do I need a resume?" That leads to the next question: What is a resume?

What is a resume? First of all, let's talk about what it isn't. It isn't your life story. This isn't the time to tell about every experience that you have had. Think of it in terms of music. A life story is similar to an anthology—a collection of all the songs by a band or an artist. The Elvis Presley anthology is made up of hundreds of songs sung by Elvis. Few people other than die-hard Elvis fans would buy the anthology, however.

A resume is more like a "greatest hits" album. The record companies have released collection albums of Elvis' love songs, Elvis' gospel hits, Elvis' movie music, as well as many others. These albums appeal to certain specific groups of people. They may buy the album because they like Elvis, or they may buy it because they like gospel music.

So, a resume is a vehicle by which you can communicate those things about your background that you feel the employer will be most interested in. It is your opportunity to put into words, as concisely as possible, why you are right for a particular position.

You will not be starting from scratch. Go back to the autobiography that you wrote in Chapter 1. You should be able to use it to cut and paste information to put into your resume. This will give you the raw material that you can later fashion into your resume.

The next question is relatively easy to answer: "Do I need a resume?" The answer is probably yes. Many job openings will only require you to fill out a job application. It will ask for specific information that the employer will use to evaluate your candidacy. Supplementing that application with a resume will provide you with

53

an opportunity to address some of the things that you can offer the employer that may or may not have been asked for on the application.

It is a good idea to have a resume available in the event that it is asked for, or in the event that you believe it will add value to your application. With that in mind, it is advisable to provide a brief summary of your background, strengths, and accomplishments.

What goes on a resume? There are many different possible components to a resume. Depending upon your background, and upon the requirements of the position, these different components may or may not be included in your resume. Also, depending upon the importance of each component as it relates to your background, and the requirements of the position, these sections may be found at different places on the resume. For example, if you have just recently completed your education and have little work experience, you may decide to list your education near the top of your resume, ahead of your experience.

Keep in mind that an employer is likely to spend twenty seconds or less reading your resume. With that in mind, you need to be sure that the resume is clear, concise, and well laid out, and that the most important things (in terms of what the employer is looking for) are present and easily found.

As you are writing the resume, keep pausing to ask yourself "How will this be read? What will the employer be looking for?" The focus should be on the reader, and the resume should be structured to hold their attention for at least the full twenty seconds, or longer if possible. If you can keep their attention longer, it will be more likely that your resume will stand out and that you will be asked to come for in an interview.

That brings up perhaps the most important point: A resume is not designed to get you a job. It is unlikely that anyone will hire you based solely on information that they find on a sheet of paper. A resume is really best used with one goal in mind— to pique the interest of the reader sufficiently to invite you to come in to interview for a position.

Dissecting the Resume

There are two widely used formats for a resume, as well as several hybrids that combine some features from each. The following sections describe both types of resumes and detail the information that you should include on them.

Chronological Resumes

A chronological resume lists all your work experience in the order in which it happened, starting with your most recent job. If your work history has been steady—no huge gaps or job-hopping—this is the best format to use.

Vital Statistics

The most important information on the resume should be located right at the top. That is the place to list your name, address, and telephone number. This should be obvious; unfortunately, however, I see plenty of resumes of college graduates (including individuals with a Master's degree) from which the telephone number is inadvertently left off. Sometimes people move or change phone numbers, and they forget to change their resume to reflect the changes.

There are a few other suggestions worth passing along at this point. If you do not have an answering machine, it will be worth investing in one. Employers are likely to be too busy to attempt reaching you too many times. Of course, if you have an answering machine, think twice about your message. The fact that you do a great Homer Simpson impersonation may absolutely crack your friends up, but it's less likely to impress a prospective employer.

You may also want to include other information at the top. Perhaps you would consider including your e-mail address. E-mail can be a very valuable tool, and it's becoming a primary means of business communication for more and more people every day. The convenience of using e-mail is the speed with which the message can be delivered and the detail that can be included. That value can be negated if you don't use your e-mail regularly. Responding a week after an employer has contacted you will not impress anyone.

Some people also include the URL for their Web page, where they may also have a more detailed resume, and perhaps even a portfolio of sorts. This may include images, video, and/or audio clips, as well as links to other printed material. This can add significant value to your application, but it also carries some risk. You need to be sure to give the Web page(s) the same kind of scrutiny that you would give your resume. You certainly don't want to have typos, grammatical errors, or other mistakes seen by a prospective employer.

Also, be sure that you feel comfortable with an employer visiting your Web site. It's the computer equivalent of the medicine cabinet in your home—few can resist taking a peek to see what else they find. If the employer has any curiosity at all, they may poke around a bit and look at your other pages, and perhaps even the links. Do you really want an employer to know that you are a big Yanni fan? Or a member of Alcoholics Anonymous? Or a collector of South Park memorabilia? If not, think again about including your URL on your resume.

Objective

For many people, the objective is the hardest part of the resume to write. It may also be the most important. This is your best opportunity to clearly communicate what it is that you are interested in. Written to appeal to the employer, the objective can quickly sum up the answer to the question "What does this person want?"

Some people believe that an objective is unnecessary, because a good cover letter will address this topic, and address it more completely in a few sentences than an objective can in one. I believe that these people are half-right. Certainly a cover letter provides an opportunity to elaborate more fully on your career objective. The problem with cover letters is that they are often separated from the resume at some point during the screening process. The other problem is that "elaborate" is a double-edged sword. There is definitely a value in being able to sum up what you want in a clear and concise way, like you do in a statement of your career objective.

If you choose to include an objective, it should be written to interest the employer in reading further. It should give a clear indication that you know what you want. As recently as ten years ago, it was more acceptable to have an objective that stated "Seeking an entry-level position with opportunities for advancement." The theory behind this type of objective was that you did not want your resume to rule you out of any jobs that you would consider taking. The idea was to boil the objective down to its least common denominator so as to appeal at some level to just about everybody.

That philosophy made at least some sense in an age when the costs of having your resume typeset precluded you from tinkering with it too often. Today, however, in the age of the desktop PC, laser printer, and fancy word-processing programs, you can make a resume at home that looks as good as or better than the ones that were produced professionally ten years ago. So, if you can personalize each resume, why not? If you went grocery shopping, how appealing would it be to pick up a can with no picture on the label, with just the word "Vegetables" or "Fruit"? Now, if you hate lima beans, you may definitely pass up a can that says "Lima Beans," but you would probably be more likely to pick up a can that says "Corn," or a can of some other vegetable that *appeals* to you.

So, while it is important to try not to include information that will turn an employer off to your candidacy, it is even more important that you do everything you can to make them interested in learning more about you. Because the objective is usually found near the top of the resume, it is particularly important that you make sure that it captures the employer's interest.

So, in one or two sentences, you want to state some combination of what it is that you are seeking, and what it is that you can offer.

Self-Serving or Uninteresting Objectives

- *Seeking an outside sales opportunity with a progressive-thinking company that will provide me with an opportunity for advancement.*

What company doesn't like to think of itself as "progressive"? Also, why are you worried about advancement already? You haven't even been hired for *this* job yet.

- *Seeking to advance my career in the exciting world of pharmaceutical sales.*

Every wasted word that you put on your resume decreases the impact of all the other words. If the employer spends even a half second reading the adjective "exciting," it does two things. It increases the chance that a more important word—an action verb or an accomplishment—will be missed. Secondly, it gives the reader the impression that you are trying to snow them.

- *Seeking management position.*

This is a common mistake, particularly among first-time job seekers. It does not tell the employer anything, except perhaps that you have not given a great deal of thought to what it is that you want to do.

- *Seeking a challenging position in social services.*

Again, this adjective adds very little to the objective.

The Same Objectives, Revisited

- *Seeking outside sales position requiring proven closing skills.*

This clearly states what you seek, and emphasizes that you have the requisite skills.

- *Seeking pharmaceutical sales position utilizing my background and experience in organic chemistry as well as my excellent interpersonal communication skills. Willing to travel and/or relocate.*

Again, this shows that you are focused, and that you can make a contribution. It also states that you are willing to do what it takes to move up the ladder.

- *Seeking retail-management training position, utilizing my six years of experience in retail sales.*

Clearly states the goal and summarizes your qualifications.

- *Seeking a position as a crisis counselor.*

Short and to the point.

Education

This section will vary depending on your level of education, the time that has elapsed since you completed it, and how vital the education is relative to the position you are seeking. If you have recently graduated from high school or college, you may wish to put the Education section right after the objective. You should list this information in order of importance, which usually means that the most recent information goes first. For example:

Bachelor of Science in Accounting	
Gettysburg College, Gettysburg, PA	May 1999
Associate degree in Business	
Mississippi Valley Community College, Biloxi, MS	May 1997

In most cases, you should drop your high school diploma from your resume after you have completed a college degree. There are two exceptions to this rule. One exception would be if you know that the person reviewing the resumes or the interviewer is a graduate of the same institution. I would suggest shying away from this unless there is a particularly strong bond among the alumni from that school. The second exception would be if your high school training was technical in nature, and if those skills will be especially relevant to the position for which you are applying.

Example:

> Associate degree in Medical Technology
> Aims Community College, Sioux City, IA   May 1999
>
> Burgard Vocational High School, Sioux City, IA
> Regent's Diploma, Certificate in Dental Hygienist Training   June 1997

When listing your education, you may wish to list the date that you received your degree. Do not list the dates that you attended. Listing the date doesn't help you out at all. Even if you are some kind of prodigy and finished a Bachelor's and a law degree in five years, it raises more concern than excitement (how mature will a 22-year-old lawyer be?). If it took you longer to finish your education than it took the person reviewing your resume, what will their reaction be? Will that person make assumptions about you? The accomplishment is what counts, not how long it took you to achieve it.

The fact is, for many students with disabilities, the high school or college experience may take a bit longer to complete. Depending on when the disability was acquired or diagnosed, there may have been a period in which the student had to "stop out" for a time to complete rehabilitation. For students with some types of disabilities, one of the most common types of academic accommodations involves a reduction in course load, resulting in a longer period of enrollment and a delayed graduation. By citing the dates of your *enrollment*, you run the risk of raising questions about your disability before you have a chance to sell your skills and abilities in an interview.

More and more often, it takes students longer than two years to finish an Associate degree, and longer than four years to finish a Bachelor's. In fact, nationally, fewer than 60 percent of those students who begin college as freshmen finish within six years. So, regardless of how long it takes you, completing a degree is what is most significant, and thus it is what is most important to put on the resume.

Not all relevant education comes in the form of a college degree or a high school diploma. It is appropriate to include in the education section any formal training that you have received from professional training organizations. Sometimes this training results in some sort of certificate. In this case, you should list the certificate in much the same way as you would list your other degrees. In other cases the training will result in increased knowledge in a certain area, but will not lead to any particular degree. In those cases, you may choose to include it in the education area, put it in a "Related Course Work" section, or a combination of the two.

EDUCATION
Associate degree in Metallurgy
Ponte Verde Community College, Ponte Verde, FL   May 1997

Certificate in Dental Technology
DTT Technical Institute, Jacksonville, FL   January 1998

Experience

In the experience section, you will recap any experiences you have had that are relevant to the position for which you are applying. This is a place for you to illustrate how the skills that you have can be transferred and applied to the position for which you are applying. Refer to the skills section of Chapter 1 and to the autobiography section of your binder or file. You may be able to more or less cut and paste sections from the autobiography directly into the experience section of the resume, and then just edit it from there.

Think broadly in terms of your experience. Do not feel restricted to include just full-time paid work experience. If you have had an internship or volunteer experience that is related to the type of job for which you are applying, it is worth including. If you decide to include those types of unpaid experiences, you may wish to change the heading to "Related Experience."

Generally, people list their experiences in reverse chronological order—the most recent experience comes first. Include all of the experiences that you believe will be relevant to the position for which you are applying. If you are applying for a job in retail management, those four years you spent as a cashier or bagging groceries in a supermarket become very relevant. If you are applying for a job as an elementary-school teacher, those three summers you spent as a nanny for the same family during college will be very relevant as well.

EXPERIENCE
Produce Manager, Wegmans Supermarket, Slidell, LA
1997–Present

Supervise and train all produce staff.

Responsible for monitoring inventory.

Increased volume by 12% over the past five years by using innovative displays, cooking classes, and product demonstrations.

Reduced spoilage by 17% by utilizing just-in-time ordering process in conjunction with the central warehouse.

Intern, Wegmans Supermarket, Slidell, LA
Summer and Fall semesters, 1996

Assisted accounting and finance office in design and implementation of streamlined inventory process.

Assistant Manager, Foot Locker—Shops at Canal Place—New Orleans, LA
May 1985–May 1990

Responsible for opening and closing store, balancing cash drawer with receipts, and scheduling sales staff.

Established in-store promotional campaigns, resulting in the store winning the "Store of the State" award in three of the last four years of my employment.

Sometimes, however, you will have experiences that are significant, but not as obviously relevant to the position for which you are applying. Using the above examples, the four years bagging groceries will not be as relevant to the school superintendent who is hiring an elementary school teacher, nor will the three years as a nanny seem all that relevant to the general manager of a retail store. The fact that you spent four years at *any* job, or that a family (or employer) would want you back for three consecutive summers, *is* relevant. Having another section titled "Other Experience" will give you an opportunity to point out that fact, without spending a lot of space describing it.

OTHER EXPERIENCE
Stock Clerk, Tops Friendly Markets, North Tonawanda, OH
1993–1995

Camp Counselor, Camp Mohawk, Lake Conesus, OH
1990–1993 (summers)

VOLUNTEER EXPERIENCE
Network Administrator, Cystic Fibrosis Foundation
Summer, 1998

Established networked database using Windows NT, allowing several staff members to have access to shared files, including the donor database.

The experience section(s) should be direct and to the point. It should outline two important areas—those things that you accomplished, and those things that you did as part of your normal responsibilities. These things do not have to be described in complete sentences; however, they should be grammatically correct in every other way (verb agreement, etc.). This section should make use of high-powered action words. Although sometimes adjectives are helpful in more completely communicating an idea, the most important words in this section of your resume will be the nouns and the verbs.

The following is a list of high-powered action words you can use to describe accomplishments:

Achieved	Designed	Illustrated
Administered	Detailed	Implemented
Advised	Developed	Improved
Arbitrated	Dissected	Increased
Assembled	Distilled	Installed
Attained	Distributed	Instituted
Audited	Diverted	Instructed
Budgeted	Edited	Interpreted
Built	Enforced	Interviewed
Collaborated	Established	Inventoried
Communicated	Estimated	Investigated
Constructed	Evaluated	Judged
Counseled	Extracted	Lectured
Created	Facilitated	Lifted
Decided	Filed	Listened
Decreased	Financed	Maintained
Delegated	Formulated	Managed
Delivered	Generated	Mediated
Demonstrated	Guided	Navigated

Negotiated	Raised	Scheduled
Networked	Razed	Selected
Observed	Received	Sketched
Operated	Recommended	Sold
Organized	Reconciled	Solved
Oversaw	Recorded	Sorted
Painted	Recruited	Spoke
Performed	Reduced	Studied
Persuaded	Referred	Summarized
Photographed	Rehabilitated	Supervised
Planned	Rendered	Supplied
Predicted	Renewed	Surveyed
Prepared	Repaired	Synthesized
Presented	Reported	Systematized
Printed	Represented	Taught
Processed	Researched	Trained
Produced	Resolved	Transcribed
Programmed	Responded	Translated
Proofed	Restored	Traveled
Publicized	Retrieved	Tutored
Purchased	Reviewed	Upgraded
Quelled		

These action words can help add a little punch to your experience section by bringing your accomplishments to life. As I mentioned before, prospective employers do not read resumes word for word; rather, they scan them. In order to catch the reader's eye, you want to use appropriate buzzwords that will stand out.

Buzzwords

Peppering your resume with the appropriate buzzwords can also help your resume stand out, particularly if it is scanned into an electronic file for searching at some later date. Examples of buzzwords that might be searched could include:

C++	Mediation
Engineer	Peer-review
Grant	Bilingual
ISO 9000	COBOL
LAN	Branding
Quality-control	Value-added
Team-based	Compliance

Military Experience

If you have spent any time in the military, either on active duty or in the reserves, you should include that information on your resume. Depending on the job for which you are applying, the tasks you performed in service to your country may or may not be relevant to the potential employer. If your experience might be relevant, you should describe it in the same amount of detail that you used in the experience section. And even if the responsibilities are not directly relevant to the employer, pointing out your service record has value on its own.

In this section you should include your service dates, rank, assignments, and discharge date (and type). Also include the skills you developed. Most veterans acquire certain skills as part of their military experience, regardless of what their responsibilities were. These include leadership, teamwork, and, of course, discipline. These are skills that are in very high demand in the workforce, and they are difficult to acquire. If you have learned these skills, you should communicate that fact as often as you can, on your resume and in your interviews.

MILITARY EXPERIENCE
Second Lieutenant, 2nd Armored Division, United States Army,
Fort Knox, KY 1992–1996

Commissioned as an officer in ROTC; served as trainer/instructor on small arms range.

Skills/Abilities

It is sometimes worthwhile to include a special section of your resume dedicated to enumerating any special skills that you may have. These are things that may be found between the lines in other areas of your resume; however, in some circumstances you should consider spelling them out. When an employer has a certain skill set in mind, it helps if that skill can be found right on your resume. This is particularly true if the skills are not usually held by all applicants.

Things that you could include in the skills section of your resume include any languages you speak; any special tools/machinery that you can operate; any computer programming languages or programs with which you are proficient; as well as any other skills or abilities that are directly related to the position for which you are applying.

> **Skills/Abilities**   Proficient in C++, Cobol, and Visual Basic.
>
> Experienced in establishing LAN and telecommunications networks.

or

> **Skills/Abilities**   Licensed to operate 4-axle, 18-wheeled tractor-trailer rigs.
>
> Experienced with pneumatic pallet-jack.
>
> Fluent in Spanish.

Athletics

In the same manner as military experience, athletics can help you develop important skills and attributes. If you played intercollegiate sports, you can put this on your resume under a heading such as "Athletics." You could also put this information in any of a number of other sections. For example, if your athletic experience is related to a community organization, you may want to include it under a heading such as "Community Activities" (see below).

If you gained your athletic experience as part of a disability-related organization, you will need to make an important choice. By including something like "Special Olympics Gold Medal for 5K run," you will do two things. First of all, you show that you have been involved in athletics, and that the reader can make assumptions about the attributes you possess (discipline, teamwork, etc.). The second thing you do, however, is alert the reader to the fact that you have a disability. This may raise questions in the mind of the reader about your ability to do the job.

In cases like this, the decision is, of course, up to you. Unless you know the person reading the resume, or unless you have a strong secondary connection to the individual, or unless you know that the company that is hiring has a strong history of nondiscrimination toward people with disabilities, I would suggest that you omit this information from your resume. You can mention this accomplishment later, in an interview.

The risk of including the information is that it gives the employer the chance to screen you out of consideration based on prejudice or misinformation. If the person suspects that you have a disability, you are no longer in control of what they think of you. They will begin to fill in the spaces between the lines, based on their own perhaps limited encounters with people with disabilities. They may make assumptions about what you can or cannot do, without giving you the opportunity to elaborate on your skills and how you could use them to accomplish the responsibilities of the position.

The fact is that your disability may have little or nothing to do with your ability to perform the job in all of its dimensions. In fact, if you have done your homework and have followed my suggestions regarding self-assessment, you will know exactly what the job requires and how, with or without accommodations, you can meet those requirements. But when the person sees that information on your resume, they could assume anything. They might assume that you are deaf or blind, or that you are a quadriplegic. You will have no control over what they think.

You can clear up some of the misconceptions by including in your cover letter information about the exact nature of your disability and how it affects you. Chapter 5, "Writing a Great Cover Letter," discusses this strategy further.

Omitting indirect references to your disability from your resume does not mean that you need to somehow hide from those accomplishments. It is my belief, however, based on a decade of working with people with disabilities, that employers are much more likely to discriminate against someone who has a disability than they are to discriminate in favor of someone because they have a disability. At the risk of sounding repetitious, a resume is intended only to pique the interest of the employer enough that you are granted a job interview. If the employer is more likely to use disability-related information against you, why not wait until you are face-to-face with him or her to approach the topic? This will give you the opportunity to directly address any questions that the employer may have.

In its new context, the information may serve to humanize your candidacy even more. Having been a "Silver Wheels" football player will appear even more impressive when you can explain the commitment, dedication, and stamina that it requires, as well as the fund-raising experience that comes with it. Using the interview as the vehicle for describing this activity also provides you with the opportunity to give evidence of how you have been successful despite your disability. This may help the interviewer understand how you will be able to be successful in the workplace as well.

Community Activities

Listing community activities, particularly leadership positions related to those activities, gives you an opportunity to show another dimension to your activities and employment. It can show that you are willing to go the extra mile to help people, on top of your regular employment. Or, in the absence of relevant employment, your volunteer activities can still demonstrate that you have skills, experience, and character.

Sometimes community involvement comes in the form of experience with tasks that can be valuable to an employer. In these cases, rather than just including a bulleted list that may give the impression that you are just a "joiner," you can provide a sentence or two that describes your involvement in the activity.

COMMUNITY ACTIVITIES

Marketing Manager, Names Project AIDS Awareness Activities: May 1993–June 1994

Directed a public relations effort related to the public display of the AIDS Quilt at the Koessler Center in June, 1994.

Member, Kiwanis Club of Des Moines: 1985–Present

Led the Holiday Jellybean sale, netting profit of over $15,000 in 1997 alone.

Before I leave the topic of community activities, I offer one word of caution. Sometimes people will make judgments about you based on the type of activities in which you are involved. If an activity is related to a religious organization, or to a political cause or party, think twice before you include that information on your resume. You do not want to provide any reason for a person to discriminate against you.

At the risk of sounding repetitive, remember that the resume is a tool that you use to get face-to-face with an employer (or at least on the telephone). After an employer has met you and sees what a wonderful person you are, they may overlook the fact that you were in charge of the lawn signs for the Ventura for Governor campaign, even though the employer voted for his opponent. Without knowing your personality, the employer can use only the resume to make decisions about you, and they may rely on preconceived notions about people from groups that can be considered by anyone to be "controversial."

As for your involvement in any disability-related groups, be selective. Raising money for Cystic Fibrosis or planning a benefit auction for the Attention Deficit Disorder organization shows only that you are involved in worthy causes. Being the treasurer of the local Tourette syndrome chapter or the founder of the Atlanta Amputees Association can raise questions in the mind of the employer.

It is worth noting that there is nothing "wrong" with being a member of a disability-related chapter or founding an association for amputees. The trouble is, people who read resumes are human, and they will use assumptions (right or wrong) to fill in the blanks about people. If they see that you got your degree from Harvard, they will assume that you are likely to be bright and rich. If they see on your resume that you were the captain and linebacker for the Oklahoma football team, they may assume that you are big, and that you have lived on a farm. It is only in an interview that you can begin to straighten out those assumptions and allow the employer to understand that you went to Harvard on a full-ride academic scholarship (the employer was only half-right!).

Honors and Awards

If you have been recognized in any way for achievements, you should consider listing these accomplishments on your resume. Certainly you would want to include any professional awards (Salesman of the Month, Realtor of the Year, Outstanding New Professional, etc.). Sometimes community involvement is recognized with awards or certificates. You may want to include an award like the United Way Volunteer of the Year award on your resume as well.

Other honors and awards may be academic, athletic, or civic, or they may be related to athletic achievements.

HONORS AND AWARDS
- Dean's List seven consecutive semesters at Regis. (*Note—you could include this information in the education section instead*)

- Rookie of the Year Award—Metlife Seacaucus office—Highest sales volume for a first-year agent, 1996.

- Business First "Forty under 40" Award—Recognizes community involvement for local citizens under the age of 40.

Professional Associations

Your membership in any professional associations should also be included on your resume, particularly if you held any leadership positions within the organization. If you were only a dues-paying member, and if the association has no relevance to the position you are pursuing, you may want to omit this section. If not, you will want to list the name of the organization, the dates of membership, and any positions held.

PROFESSIONAL ASSOCIATIONS
National Society of Black Engineers, 1997–2000.
Membership Chair, Texas A&M Chapter, 1999.

References

There are a variety of opinions on the topic of whether or not you should include references on your resume. Because employers often request references before reaching a hiring decision, there appear to be three viable options:

- Ignore the issue completely on your resume, but keep a single page of references available in the event that an employer asks for them.

- Include a line at the bottom of the resume stating "References Available Upon Request," and then keep a single page of references available in case they are requested.

- Include the references directly on your resume.

Let's begin with an analysis of including the references on your resume.

Pros

1. Shows that you have confidence in what the referents might say about you.

2. If the employer knows one of your references personally, they might pick up the phone and call, thereby giving your candidacy more consideration.

3. If the employer doesn't know the reference personally, but recognizes the name as an individual who is respected, some of that respect rubs off on you.

4. If your candidacy is "on the bubble," an employer may call one or more of your references to help him or her make the decision.

Cons

1. Adding a references section may mean that your resume goes to an extra page, or that something valuable is cut.

2. The employer may know the reference and dislike or distrust that individual.

3. The employer may contact the reference and find out that the reference doesn't have too many good things to say about you.

Let's address the cons first. If you must make a choice between listing your references or listing the fact that you are fluent in three languages, decide which one is likely to be more important to the employer. If the languages are English, Latin, and Greek, perhaps listing a contact who is a leader in the field would be more valuable to your candidacy. If those languages are English, Spanish, and Mandarin, it is likely that this information is more important to the employer than your references. If this is the case, simply preparing a separate sheet that lists your references and keeping it available will be more appropriate for you.

The second two cons are fairly easy to address. You should ask someone to serve as a reference for you only if:

- The person knows you well enough to speak intelligently about your abilities.

- The person has seen you perform successfully in some endeavor.

- You are confident that this person will be able to speak knowledgeably, positively, and enthusiastically about your candidacy.

- The person is generally or universally liked. You may never know if there is a personal history between the two people, but by staying away from controversial individuals, you help your chances.

Regardless of whether you include references on your resume or simply list references on a separate sheet of paper, there are certain pieces of information that you should include:

References

James Nadbrzuch	Talia Princessa	Aidan Matthews
Business Manager	Proprietor	HR Manager
PCI Electronics	Talia's Collectibles	Hunter Foods
3700 PCI Blvd.	1556 Hertel Avenue	3212 Workerman Rd.
Ponte Verde, FL 95012	Del Boca Vista, FL 95212	Jackson, FL 95023
803-345-7898	803-456-5646	803-455-4100
jimn@pci.com		aidan@huntfoods.com

If you ask someone to serve as a reference for you, you should provide the person with a copy of the resume that you will be using in your job search. If you want the person to talk about particular skills, you should provide the person with that information as well. If you have not been in regular contact with the reference (perhaps he or she is a former employer), you should try to bring the person up-to-date on your accomplishments and career goals.

Also, if you include your references on your resume, in your cover letter you should give the employer permission to contact those references. Some employers will shy away from contacting your references without your written consent because of their interpretation of some regulations, including the Fair Credit Reporting Act. By giving permission outright in your letter, which you sign, you should clear up any confusion.

Hobbies, Interests, and Personal Information

Some resumes contain a section title that says something like "Hobbies," "Interests," or "Personal Information." In these sections you often see things like:

Enjoy skating, biking, and bird watching.

or

Avid reader, singer/songwriter, and accomplished mime.

The rationale behind including this type of information has some merit. Proponents argue that including this information on your resume shows that you are not just one-dimensional, and that you are in fact quite interesting. My opinion is, however, that if you can fit only a few hundred words on your resume, you had better pick the most important words you can. It seems highly unlikely that the words "mime" or "skating" would make that cut.

Other people choose to share personal information, also as a way of showing their multidimensional background. Often you see things like:

> 6'2", 215 lbs.
>
> Single, willing to travel and/or relocate.

or

> Married for 12 years, two children (3, 9)
>
> Health—Excellent

In all of my years of helping people with their resumes, I have seen hundreds with the line "Health—Excellent," and not one that said "Health—3–6 months to live," or "Health—My gout is killing me!"

Including personal information is, in my opinion, just asking for trouble. If the information is not directly relevant to the job, why include it? Providing this information simply gives the employer an easy way to discriminate against you. Marital status, religion, health, sexual preference, disability status, ethnicity, and plans for raising a family are all topics that would be excluded from any legal line of interview questioning. You have absolutely nothing to gain by bringing up these topics yourself.

By the same token, do not include a picture on your resume. This was in vogue a number of years ago and then thankfully faded away. Now with the low cost of scanners and digital cameras, some individuals are including digitized images on their resume as a way of distinguishing themselves from other applicants. Unfortunately for these candidates, they are distinguishing themselves, but not in a positive way (unless, of course, they are Brad Pitt or Cameron Diaz!).

There are, however, a few jobs for which a photo is helpful, even necessary. Positions like model, spokesperson, or actor often require that a customary "head shot" photo be sent along with the resume and portfolio.

Samples of Chronological Resumes

The following are different versions of chronological resumes. The first Martin Rowan resume does not fit on one page. By changing the layout and style, and by deleting some text, the most important information can all fit on one page.

| Applebee's | July 2004–August 2004 | **Host, Server's** |
| Mamaroneck, NY | | **Assistant** |

Gained valuable communication and public relations skills by providing quality customer service. Handled disputes with customers and performed troubleshooting tasks to improve customer relations.

| Rite-Aid Pharmacy | May 2003–August 2003 | **Sales Associate** |
| New York City, NY | | |

Responsible for directly assisting the customer on the sales floor and handled customer cashier accounts. Managed inventory levels to maintain constant availability of products.

| Atlantic and Pacific Corporation | August 2000–May 2003 | **Sales Associate** |
| New York City, NY | | |

REFERENCES WILL BE FURNISHED UPON REQUEST

Martin P. Rowan
38 Heath Street
Brighton, MA 02135
(617) 831-0302
rowan@scranton.edu

EDUCATION:

Graduate of Clarkstown South

Bachelor of Science May 2005, University of Scranton, Scranton, PA

Major: Finance
Overall GPA: 3.1/4.0
Management GPA: 3.3/4.0
Related Coursework: Corporate Finance, Managerial Accounting, Investments, Managerial Economics, Managerial Science, Financial Statement Analysis, Marketing.

COMPUTER EXPERIENCE:

Proficient in the use of spreadsheets, word processors, graphic presentation software, database software, the Internet, and a variety of research tools, including Bloomberg and Lexus.

AFFILIATIONS, VOLUNTEER WORK:

Phi Delta Quo Fraternity, Secretary 2003–2004.

Vice-President of Rush, 2002–2003.

Financial Management Association (FMA): Member.

KIDSDAY—Helped to raise money for underprivileged children.

ACTIVITIES/HOBBIES:

Phi Delta Quo Intramural Coordinator; Varsity High School Tennis Captain; Working Out, Baseball, Skiing.

WORK EXPERIENCE:

| PaineWebber | June 2005–August 2005 | **Financial Analyst** |
| Weehawken, NJ | | **Intern** |

Responsible for reconciliation of daily intercompany analysis. Organized and implemented routine performance criteria and reports distributed to senior management.

Analyzed, valued, and monitored performance of corporate debt and derivative security instruments held in firm portfolio. Responsible for a component of weekly intercompany financial reporting.

Martin P. Rowan

38 Heath Street
Brighton, MA 02135
(617) 831-0302
rowan@scranton.edu

Objective: Seeking a position in financial services.

Education: Bachelor of Science in Finance, May 2005.

University of Scranton, Scranton, PA. GPA 3.1.

Computer   Proficient in the use of spreadsheets, word processors, graphic
Experience: presentation software, database software, the Internet, and a variety
of research tools, including Bloomberg and Lexus.

WORK EXPERIENCE:

PaineWebber   **Financial Analyst Intern,** Summer 2005
Weehawken, NJ

- Responsible for reconciliation of daily intercompany analysis.
- Organized and implemented routine performance criteria and reports distributed to senior management.
- Analyzed, valued, and monitored performance of corporate debt and derivative security instruments held in firm portfolio.
- Responsible for a component of weekly intercompany financial reporting.

Applebee's, Mamaroneck, NY   **Host, Server's Assistant,** Summer 2004

Rite-Aid Pharmacy, New York City, NY   **Sales Associate,** Summer 2003

- Stock and cashiering duties.

Atlantic and Pacific Corporation   **Sales Associate,** August 2000–May 2003
New York City, NY

- Handled customer cashier accounts.

AFFILIATIONS, VOLUNTEER WORK:

Phi Delta Quo Fraternity, Secretary 2003–2004, Vice-President of Rush, 2002–2003

Financial Management Association (FMA), Member

KIDSDAY—Helped to raise money for underprivileged children

Darlene L. Brady
34 Brentwood Manor
Cupertino, New York 14120
716-836-5411

OBJECTIVE   To contribute extensive clerical experience to a challenging position.

WORK EXPERIENCE

STATE College, Amherst, NY
Records and Registration
Secretary: 2/2000 to present

- Utilized *computerized* scheduling system.
- Operated multi-line phone system.
- Coordinated all aspects of registration fairs.
- Investigated and responded to all student and alumni questions and problems.
- Performed secretarial responsibilities for several counselors.

NORTH TONAWANDA HIGH SCHOOL, North Tonawanda, NY
Guidance Office
Secretary: 1990 to 2000

- Provided secretarial support to Guidance Counselors.
- Handled phones, mail, typing and filing.
- Performed data entry of scheduling, grade reporting, and transcript information.
- Generated and printed reports, lists, and schedules.
- Served as liaison to BOCES on maintenance of networked computer system.

DENNIS G. IMWACKI, D.P.M., North Tonawanda, NY
Medical Billing Secretary: 1988 to 1990

- Performed data entry of daily charges and accounts receivables on computer and ledger cards.
- Coordinated printing and mailing of all billing and insurance pickups.
- Handled incoming phone calls and appointments.
- Prepared transcription and balanced daily log sheets.
- Undertook front desk receptionist/secretary responsibilities as needed.

EDUCATION   TONAWANDA HIGH SCHOOL, Tonawanda, NY
Regents Diploma——Business and Cosmetology

COMPUTER SKILLS   PC, Windows XP, Microsoft Word and Access, Internet, E-mail.

REFERENCES   Available upon request.

Functional Resumes

Some job seekers may have an atypical background compared to most people applying for a given position. Sometimes a person may have been out of the workforce for a number of years because of an illness they or a family member may have had. Some people take a "time-out" from their career in order to raise a family or to attend to another priority or opportunity that presented itself. Other individuals, at some point in their career, may have been laid off or let go from a previous position and have been unemployed for a year or more. For these individuals, there is value in writing your resume in a way that takes the emphasis away from those gaps in time.

Other job seekers are simply pursuing a career change. They may have been laid off or let go recently, or they may have left a career on their own because of a change in life goals. For these individuals, a functional resume can shift the emphasis away from the jobs they have held and focus it on the skills and accomplishments they achieved or acquired during their career.

Writing a functional resume is not all that different from writing a chronological resume, because many of the basics will remain the same. Regardless of what form of resume you write, the most important information will still be listed at the top, with less-vital information found below. With this in mind, you will still begin your resume with your contact information:

Richard Gruber
1745 Claudia Drive
Detroit, MI 45687
513-245-6784
tat@hotmail.com

Objective

After you list your contact information, you will want to communicate your objective. Including an objective on a functional resume is arguably even more important than including it on a chronological resume. This is because of the nature of the resume—your background may not be typical of those who are applying for the position, and you will need to show in a clear way that you are interested in that particular position.

Another way to approach the objective, however, is to include a brief statement of background that explains why you are seeking this position.

> **Background:** Seven years experience in customer service and constituent relations. Seeking an opportunity to put these skills to use in college admissions.

Education

You may want to include your education information near the top; however, in most scenarios in which a functional resume is used, there is more-relevant information that should be found closer to the top of the resume. That information may include skills that were developed in the workplace or as part of your formal education. It may also include any other significant awards or achievements you have. Wherever you include the information, the format is really no different than for the chronological resume:

> **Education:** Bachelor of Arts in Political Science: May, 1990.
> Xavier University, Cincinnati, OH. GPA 3.75.
> Dean's List 7 semesters.
> Varsity Division I Baseball.

Experience

The section in which you highlight your skills/abilities, accomplishments, and experience is what truly separates the functional resume from the chronological resume. On the functional resume the focus is on the functions you performed, the experience you gained, or the skills you developed. On a chronological resume, that information may be found, but the focus is on the position you held and the dates that you held it.

There are many different ways to shape this section of a functional resume. How you decide to include the information is up to you. You will see some samples here and in the sample resumes at the end of this chapter. Look them over, and if you find one that seems to make sense, use it. If not, it's possible that there may be a better way for you to convey that information. Regardless of what some people may tell you, there is no science to resume writing, just art.

The following are some sample headings for use in your experience section.

SELECTED ACHIEVEMENTS AND RESULTS
Training

- Developed weekend leadership training program for 20 sales associates.

- Wrote and designed 60-page training manual for scout troop leaders.

- Designed orientation program for den mothers that was adopted by state council.

Sales

- Consistently maintained highest or second-highest percentage close rate in region.

- Achieved several awards and bonuses based on special promotions.

- Met or surpassed sales goals for each quarter.

CAREER HIGHLIGHTS

- Outstanding Young Women in America, 1994.

- Harriet Tubman Leadership Award, Bethel Council.

- Successfully developed merchandising plan for *Amtiva* product line.

- Opened three new store locations with revenues of over $30 million.

SUMMARY OF QUALIFICATIONS

- Self-starter who successfully launched and sold two businesses with revenues of over $500,000 each.

- Accomplished public speaker, giving two dozen or more presentations annually with audiences of between 30 and 2,300.

- Extensive leadership skills acquired through holding elected positions for over a dozen community, civic, and professional associations in the past 10 years.

Although the functional resume will serve to take the focus off of specific positions you have had, you still need to recount your professional employment. You can do this in a simple section in a variety of ways.

Work Experience

Manager, Wilson Farms   1994–1998
Clerk, Quality Markets   1990–1994

You may also need to cover gaps of time during which you were not employed. It is easy to cover up several months by listing the years rather than the exact dates (as in the example above). If the period is significantly longer, this will not be as helpful. Although some individuals suggest that you leave the dates out altogether, I believe that this may not be the best approach. You may want to include a statement that explains your absence from work for that time period, but leave it in the work experience section so that it is not a main focus. For example, consider the following examples:

| **Work Experience** | Manager, Wilson Farms | |
| | Clerk, Quality Markets | |

| **Work Experience** | Manager, Wilson Farms | 1994–1998 |
| | Clerk, Quality Markets | 1980–1988 |

(From 1988–1994, I raised my child, who has now entered school.)

| **Work Experience** | Manager, Wilson Farms | 1994–1998 |
| | Clerk, Quality Markets | 1980–1992 |

(From 1992–1994, I was recovering from a back injury resulting from a car accident.)

You need to determine, based on the specifics of your own personal situation, which approach is best for you. Your approach may also change depending on how many gaps you have had in your employment history. You may choose to ignore the cause of the gaps. Or, as in the example shown above, you may chose to provide a context that helps explain the gaps.

The other sections of the functional resume will be similar to the ones found in a chronological resume. Obviously, if you have a section that highlights your skills elsewhere, there will be no added value in repeating the same information with a skills/abilities section. By the same token, if you have included your military experience, your community activities, or any other information toward the top of your resume, there is no need to repeat it elsewhere.

Sample Functional Resumes

Sean J. Walther

128 Wellington Road
Omaha, NE 10216
(816) 832-1148
ryan@creighton.edu

Career Summary:

Six years of increasing responsibility within customer service and sales. Proven troubleshooter. Excellent rapport with customers, sales staff, and prospects. Experienced public speaker.

Education:

Master of Business Administration
Creighton University, Omaha, Nebraska: May 1998
Bachelor of Arts in Political Science
Creighton University, Omaha, Nebraska: May 1988

Program Development:

Planned and implemented Customer Appreciation Week.

Designed several in-service programs for sales staff members on selling via the telephone.

Developed product pages for publishing on the World Wide Web.

Designed and implemented several PC and mainframe systems, including prospect-tracking system.

Conceived, designed, and produced *Horizons*, an eight-page advertising supplement; funded 90 percent with co-op ad revenues.

Supervision:

Manage budget of more than $640,000.

Train and supervise staff of 22 as well as coordinate 12 summer hourly workers.

Chair of the United Way Executive Committee, 1999–2001.

Customer Service:

Hear individual grievance cases involving sales misrepresentation.

Counsel customers individually and in groups relative to objections and financing.

Administer and interpret qualifying assessment instruments.

Professional Affiliations and Leadership Positions:

National Association of Sales Administrators

Chair, Region II 2003 Conference Committee

Consultant, 2001 Teleconference

Member, 2001 National Conference Program Committee

Member, Region II Advisory Committee

Western Nebraska Consortium of Auto Care Professionals

Awards and Achievements:

NASA Region II Outstanding New Professional, 1998

Who's Who in American Sales, 2000–2002

Related Experience:

Sonic Lube, <u>Coordinator</u>, Customer Service, 1998–Present.

Reciprocity, Telesales Representative, 1997.

Sunshine Markets, <u>Intern</u>, Spring 1997.

Other Experience:

Metropolitan Life, <u>Account Representative,</u> 1995–1996.

City of Buffalo Division of Planning, <u>Economic Market Analyst,</u> 1993–1995.

Omaha County Department of Criminal Justice, <u>Confidential Investigator</u>, 1991–1993.

First Omaha Corporation, <u>Financial Consultant</u>, 1988–1991

Community Involvement:

Treasurer, North Buffalo Community Development Corporation, 1995.

Member, Board of Directors, North Buffalo Community Development Corporation, 1992–1995.

First Vice President, North Buffalo Kiwanis Club, 1994.

References

Peter Thunt
President, Hunt Real Estate
5570 Main St.
Williams, NE 14221
(816) 633-9400

Seymour H. Knowles, IV
Assistant Director, Buffalo Sports
Memorial Auditorium
Buffalo, NE 14202
(816) 856-7300

Ando Topolski

113 McKinley Parkway
Purchase, WA 13443
(297) 756-2467
scull@aol.com

Career Summary:

Twelve years as a human resource specialist, with extensive knowledge of payroll and benefits.

Benefits Administration

401(k) and 403(b) administration

Evaluation of HMO options

Flexible spending accounts

Training and Staff Development

Developed programs in substance abuse prevention.

Presented orientation, stress-management, time-management, and conflict-resolution programs.

Compensation

Designed payroll system using Foxbase.

Administered deferred compensation program.

Developed severance packages.

Recruiting

Coordinated all college on-campus recruitment.

Participated in numerous job fairs.

Conducted first-level screening interviews.

Work History

CSAT Products, Williams, WA   1995–2005

Elgin Industries, Walla Walla, WA   1990–1995

Professional Affiliations

Society for Human Resource Management

Industrial Relations Society

References Furnished upon Request

What Shouldn't Go on Your Resume?

There are certain things that have no place on your resume. Some of these things were mentioned earlier, but are worth mentioning again. One common mistake found on resumes is the word "resume." Including that word as a heading on your resume does not add anything to the resume, because virtually anyone in the business or professional world can recognize a resume on sight. The same is true for the headings Vita, C.V., or Curriculum Vita.

Perhaps the most common problem with resumes, or the most common reason why a resume will screen you *out* of a possible job, is the presence of errors, such as typos, misspellings, or grammatical mistakes. A resume may contain only a few hundred words. Given that fact, you cannot afford to have any of those words convey to an employer that you are anything but fully competent.

Most word processors can help you with words that you might misspell. The problem with relying on computers alone to "proofread" your resume is that the computer doesn't know what you meant to type. This is a problem when you use the wrong word or verb tense, or when you type a word incorrectly, but where the mistyped word is a different word spelled correctly. With this in mind, and for all of the reasons mentioned in this section, you should have a friend or friends read your resume from the viewpoint of the prospective employer.

Another thing that should be absent from your resume is anything that is false or misleading. "Padding" your resume with exaggerations, half-truths, or outright falsehoods may give you a short-term advantage; however, if the truth is uncovered in the job interview, you will forfeit that advantage, and more. If the truth is uncovered after you have started with the employer, you may lose your job, and then you'll have a potentially dangerous reference out there.

Another mistake made on resumes is to include information of a personal nature. As was mentioned earlier, including information on health, marital status, height, weight, etc. is not advisable. Including such information is as likely to rule you out of a job as it is to give you an advantage. And this information is even more likely to take up valuable room that you could have used for other, more pertinent information.

It is also advisable to exclude salary history or requirements. This topic is best discussed face-to-face after an actual job offer. See Chapter 11 for more information on salary negotiations.

Scannable Resumes

One of the recent changes to the art of resume writing has been the advent of the computer scanner. Like a copier, a scanner duplicates the image found on a piece of paper. Rather than reproducing the image on paper, however, the scanner makes a digital reproduction, which is then examined by an Optical Character Recognition (OCR) program that translates the image into the words that it recognizes from the page. This technology has been of great value to major employers like IBM, which receives up to two million unsolicited resumes a year. By using this scanning and conversion technology, an employer can convert the paper resume to a text file, which it can then search electronically to identify every resume on file that contains the word "forklift" or "C++" or "landscaping."

To that end, entire books have been written to explain how to best take advantage of this new technology and avoid the pitfalls it introduces. For example, you should avoid special formatting such as underlined words, italics, script fonts, etc., because the formatting may confuse the computer and your word may be lost. As the OCR technology continues to improve, however, these problems will likely disappear.

Another strategy for writing a scannable resume is to focus more on the nouns in your resume than on the verbs. Words like "PowerPoint" or "forklift" or "cyclotron" are more useful to someone who is doing a text search than are words like "operated," "designed," or "organized."

As we will discuss in Chapter 7, almost every job-search method has a place in your job-search master plan. To ignore the recommendations for writing a scannable resume, and then to submit it to an HR department where it is likely to be scanned, is to risk making that resume less likely to help you. On the other hand, you should not rely too heavily on any job-search method in which you or your resume will be treated as impersonally as being digitized and relegated to some huge database somewhere.

The key to most successful job searches is to have the opportunity to discuss your candidacy with an individual who has the responsibility of deciding who will be hired. The best way to make that happen is to get that individual to actually read your resume at some point, preferably after speaking to a mutual acquaintance.

Resume Aesthetics

This section comes last on purpose. Many clients approach career counselors with one of several burning questions: What color paper should I use on my resume? Should my resume be one page or two? What font should I use?

While there is value in how you answer these questions, they are less vital to your success than *what your resume says*. So here is my response to those questions.

What Color Paper Should I Use?

This question cannot be answered easily without first asking "For whom is the resume written?" If you are submitting a resume for 95 percent of the jobs out there, the answer is that white, cream, ivory, and gray are all acceptable. Whichever color you choose, buy enough of it to print both your resume and your cover letter. You may want to purchase matching envelopes as well.

If you are applying for jobs in the more creative fields—advertising, the arts, etc.—people are more likely to be receptive to resumes that are more out of the ordinary. One client decided on a resume that was printed on manila file folders with the candidate's name on the tab. The idea was that the collateral materials that the candidate sent (such as samples of other creative work) could be stored in the folder. Another client pursuing a career in the music industry decided to print a resume that looked like an album's liner notes (if you don't remember what an album is, ask your grandparents!). In each case the candidate was successful in finding a job. I highly doubt that the resume got them the job; however, the resume obviously did not rule them out of the job, either.

How Many Pages Should My Resume Be?

Again, the answer here depends on a combination of the job for which you are applying and your own background. Only the most extraordinary recent high school or college graduate will need more than one page to convey a good summary of their background. The best way to prepare your resume is to start with the career autobiography that you wrote, and translate it into resume style. Then go through the resume and delete all the information that would be irrelevant to the employer to whom you are submitting this resume. Then go back through and delete all those things that are probably not going to be too valuable to that employer. As you go through this process over and over, you will likely come to a point where you will need to decide to either a) cut out one of two valuable pieces of information so that you can reduce the resume to one page, or b) include one of several marginally important pieces of information so that you can make the resume an even two pages. That is a judgement call that you can make with input from a career counselor, friends, and family.

What Font Should I Use?

Another decision that you make can affect the length of the resume too. The question of what font to use can be answered by the eye. Try printing your resume using different fonts, and ask the people you trust which one they prefer. I would suggest that you use a 12-point font or, at the smallest, a 10-point font. A smaller font enables you to put more text on the page; however, it makes it more difficult for the employer to read. You may also want to experiment with the margins that you use. Reducing the margins from the default of 1.25" to 1" all around can increase the amount of text you can include on the resume. But you'll need to check how your margins look by viewing a draft printout. You might not like the result.

What Text Formatting Should I Use?

Formatting is also a personal style choice. Scannable resume guidelines not-withstanding, some people choose to underline all their past job titles while boldfacing all the employer names. Others may choose to italicize their e-mail address. These choices are really a matter of personal preference; however, I would strongly urge you to not overdo the formatting, and to be consistent throughout. Do not italicize one employer and then boldface the next. Although some formatting can make the resume more eye-appealing and can help the reader subconsciously organize and process the information, too many styles can muddle the information and confuse the reader. By the way, even if you do prepare a scannable resume without any formatting, that does not preclude you from using those styles in the version of your resume that you send to companies that do not scan resumes.

Should I Post My Resume on My Web Site?

Millions of Americans have their own Web spaces and URLs. Posting a resume on your Web site seems like a logical choice. I would caution you, however, to consider the information listed in your resume and ask yourself whether you want to make it available to the world. I am surprised by the number of people who have unpublished telephone numbers but who have their resumes on the Web for the world to see. You will want to also ask yourself who it is that you expect to see your resume on your Web site. Companies spend millions of dollars in advertising and marketing efforts to drive the right people to the companies' Web sites. What is your strategy going to be?

Finally, consider what other information you have on your Web site. When potential employers look at your resume on your Web site, they may be tempted to learn more about you. Do you want them reading your blog where you complain about your current job and salary? Do you really want them to see your shrine to your favorite reality show contestant?

If your site is fairly professional, a different option would be to include a brief synopsis of your accomplishments and skill sets. Also include a contact form so that they can reach you for a more complete resume.

Resumes and the Internet

As technology evolves, you may find the Internet playing a bigger role in your job search. You can use the Internet to find more information about preparing resumes. Or, you may end up e-mailing your resume to a potential employer. The following two sections give more details on each of these possibilities.

Online Resume Resources

There are a number of great resources for resume writing on the Internet.

For information on a number of resume books, check out the JIST Works Web site:

```
www.jist.com
```

Purdue University, through its Online Writing Lab, has produced the following site:

```
http://owl.english.purdue.edu/handouts/pw/index.html
```

The University at Buffalo has several resume-related publications at the following address:

```
www.ub-careers.buffalo.edu/career/student.shtml#job
```

And the New York State Department of Labor has prepared a publication to help you with writing an electronic or scannable resume:

```
www.labor.state.ny.us/working_ny/finding_a_job/career/dinores.htm
```

E-Mailable Resumes

Some organizations will accept your resume via e-mail. If you want to submit your resume in this manner, contact the company and find out if they are able to receive the resume as a file attachment, and if so, what kinds of attachments are acceptable. This way you can send an e-mail message indicating that your resume is attached as a Microsoft Word document, for example, or as a PDF file. If they are able to accept such files, you can be more sure that the resume will be formatted the way that you intended.

CHAPTER 5

Writing a Great Cover Letter

If there's one thing about the job search that people dread more than writing a resume, it's writing a cover letter. The reason the cover letter is so daunting is that it is both more personalized and more formal than a resume. Unlike a resume, where bullets and sentence fragments are acceptable, a cover letter should read like any other professional letter. It should be grammatically perfect, and it should contain no errors of fact.

To have any chance of standing out, the cover letter must be written for a particular position, or for one of several positions within one organization. That means that each cover letter you write needs to be specific to that reader. And it also needs to flow in a reasonable and comfortable manner.

Anxiety levels around writing a cover letter are only made worse by the writing habits that we have developed. If you have not been in the workforce for long, or if you have been employed in a setting where you did not need to communicate in writing with other individuals, your letter-writing experience may be limited to holiday and greeting cards, or the thank-you notes that your mother made you send your aunt in response to that scarf she sent you.

Even if you have been in the workforce for a while, it's quite likely that you write far more messages through e-mail than via letter. The nature of e-mail is so different from the formal business letter, and sometimes people forget that. The result is cryptic letters with no real flow.

Getting Started with Contact Info

The first step, and the easiest, is to put your contact information and the recipient's address at the top of the cover letter. If you have preprinted personal letterhead stationery, you do not need to include any other contact information on your letter. Assuming that you do not, the information to include at the top of your letter is the following:

> Street address
> City, state, ZIP code
> Telephone number
> E-mail address

Some people include this information in a heading that is identical to the heading on their resume (also including their name). Others just put the information flush at the left margin or indented near the right margin.

Following that information, skip a line and put in the date. Then put in the recipient's name and complete address, as it would appear on the envelope. Then skip a line and begin your salutation. This could range from

> To whom it may concern:

to

> Dear Mr. Orrange:

Or, if you are personally familiar with the addressee:

> Dear Bob:

And then you move on to write the body of the letter!

Answer Three Important Questions

The anxiety of writing a cover letter does not have to be overwhelming. The key is to answer a few questions before you ever put your pen to paper (or your fingers to the keyboard):

- Why you are writing?

- What do you want to say?

- What do you want the person reading the letter to do in response to having read it?

Why Are You Writing?

A cover letter, by definition, is a letter that accompanies and explains something else. In this case, it will accompany a resume. The "why" question, and how you answer it, will determine the content of the letter. For example, some people will write a cover letter and submit a resume in response to an advertisement in the help-wanted section of the newspaper. In that case, a cover letter might begin:

To whom it may concern:

or

Dear P.O. Box 6501:

Now, I won't tell you to "Stop right there!" but I will warn you that any letter will be more effective if it is addressed to an actual individual than if it is addressed as above. You may decide that it's much easier to send a generic cover letter than to ferret out contact names and personalize each letter. That's a fine decision, but you should understand that the response rate for this type of letter is likely to be lower than if it were addressed to Joan Doe, Director of Marketing.

So hopefully, the ad that you're responding to included a contact person to whom you can address your letter. (Incidentally, some companies will list the name of a fictitious individual in their classified advertising. It allows them to funnel all the mail and telephone calls to the appropriate person without that individual being inundated with calls after the search has been completed. I once worked for a company that used this method, and was amazed at how many times the receptionist would have people trying to get past them, claiming to be close personal friends of Ishmael O'Malley from the HR department.)

Dear Mr. O'Malley:

I am writing this letter in response to the ad that was placed in Sunday's *San Jose Mercury News.* In the ad you stated that you are looking for an energetic self-starter with experience in the area of sales. I believe that you will find from my enclosed resume that my background matches your requirements quite nicely.

or

Dear Ms. Kern:

Thank you for taking the time to discuss the opening for a manufacturer's representative that appeared in the *National Business Employment Weekly* on March 24th. After our conversation, I was even more convinced that my background will provide an excellent match for this position.

Now, often you will be writing a cover letter for a reason other than simply responding to a help-wanted advertisement. In fact, as you will see later, although you should not overlook *any* reputable job lead, there are far more productive uses for your time than reading want ads. Hopefully you will have plenty of opportunities to access what is referred to as "the hidden job market"—a name given to the vast number of job openings (reportedly up to 85 percent of all openings) that never make their way into the want ads or the employment agencies. If you are writing a letter to a networking contact, the letter will carry much more weight than if you were addressing it to a stranger.

> Dear Mr. Farber:
>
> Recently I was speaking with Mr. Joe Donaruma from your accounting division regarding the exciting things that are taking place at Regional Information Systems. The more we spoke, the more his enthusiasm excited me. Knowing my interest in keeping my programming skills on the cutting edge, he suggested that I contact you about the possibility of coming on board with RIS to work on the new integrated database project. He got me so excited that I came right home to write this.

or

> Dear Mrs. Cleary:
>
> As a member of the United Way development committee, I have had the chance to work with your CEO, Tom Miller. Yesterday he and I had a conversation about the upcoming relocation of my current employer to Sri Lanka, and he suggested that I contact you directly to see if we can explore my background, and the extent to which it may be appropriate for the need that you have in servicing the XYZ account.

In either of these cases, you have an advantage over the "cold" letter—the letter that is written without the benefit of having some third party known to both you and the employer. The fact is, when a letter comes in that makes reference to someone that the employer knows, in some small way, that letter comes from that third individual too. Certainly, in the case of Mrs. Cleary, she cannot afford to simply disregard the letter, because it is possible that the CEO will follow up and check on it. Even in the case of the letter written to Mr. Farber, he will want to accord you at least the same respect that he would give to Mr. Donaruma, as the letter writer is sure to tell Mr. Donaruma what the results of his inquiry were. How the letter writer was treated will certainly reflect on Mr. Farber.

What Do You Want to Say?

With the first paragraph of the cover letter, you will hopefully have captured the reader's attention sufficiently to keep him or her reading. Cover letters, like resumes, are more likely to be scanned than read word for word. The opening of the letter will dictate the extent to which your letter will actually be read. Assuming that your opening was strong, including a reference to a third party known to you and the reader, there's a good chance that he or she will read on.

The second part of the cover letter gives you an opportunity to succinctly sum up the reasons why you believe that your background warrants bringing you in for an interview. You can usually do this in one or sometimes two paragraphs. Those paragraphs should be crafted carefully, so as to keep the employer interested enough to keep reading rather than scanning. With that in mind, brevity, clarity, and organization will be very important.

Some Sample Second Sections

In these samples, you will see how you make the transition from the introduction to laying out your qualifications for the position.

> As you will see from my enclosed resume, I have recently completed my Associate degree in Medical Technology. As part of that degree, I completed an eighteen-month co-op experience with CMD Medical Group, where I started as a records clerk and eventually completed rotations in phlebology and serology. This experience gave me training on the Cyclotron 4000, which I understand is used at your office as well.

> Outside of my formal curriculum, but equally valuable, has been my volunteer experience with Hospice Greensboro. I was exposed to Hospice as they cared for my ailing aunt while I was in high school. I was so impressed with the service and dedication of their staff that I began volunteering eight to twenty hours a week, and I have done this for three years. In that time I have developed a clearer understanding of the human side of medical technology, and have learned to always treat each individual as a person first, and as a patient second.

In the illustration above, two paragraphs were used to make two different aspects of the writer's background stand out. Although there may be times when this approach seems appropriate, more often you will find that it is to your advantage to keep this section down to one paragraph. Once again, it's worth pointing out that the stronger the introductory section, the more likely that the reader will actually read your letter, regardless of whether you use one or two paragraphs for the second section. Otherwise, you run the risk that the reader will read the first paragraph and either stop reading or skip to the ending.

A one-paragraph version of the same letter might be arranged like this:

> I believe that an interview would show you that my combination of education and experience makes me uniquely qualified for this position. I have received an Associate degree in Medical Technology from Central Carolina Community College, maintaining a 3.8 average while concurrently working twenty or more hours a week in paid and volunteer positions. In my co-op and through my volunteer work, I have gained the practical experience to go along with my academic preparation, and more importantly, I have come to appreciate the human element in the work we do and the people we serve.

Neither version provides all the information that we would like to convey. You should not expect your cover letter to do that. The key is to provide enough information to interest the reader in finding out more without providing so much information that the reader stops reading and moves on.

What Do You Want the Person Reading the Letter to Do in Response to Having Read It?

The third section of the cover letter should be a call for action. It should let the reader know what you want. You can take a passive or an assertive approach to this section, depending on a combination of the position for which you are applying and your comfort in following up with the employer.

An assertive approach:

> I will call you within ten days to confirm that you have received this letter and to see if you are interested in exploring in greater detail the possibility of my joining your firm. If you have any questions in the meantime, please contact me at 555-456-7234.

A passive approach:

> I sincerely believe that I would be an excellent fit for this position. I am confident that if you grant me an interview for this position, you will feel the same. I look forward to hearing from you, and to discussing my candidacy in greater detail.

There is rarely any reason to mention your disability when writing your cover letter. The one exception might be when the employer is specifically seeking people with disabilities for the position. In most other cases, the cover letter, like the resume, is not the preferred means of disclosing your disability. The cover letter is simply a means to address why you are sending a resume to the employer. Any discussion of your disability is best left for later on in the process.

Finishing the Letter

To finish the letter, I would stick with a closing that is comfortable for you and appropriate for business correspondence. Endings such as "Sincerely," "Respectfully," or even "Thank You" are all appropriate closings. Following the closing, you should skip a line or two (making room for your signature) and type your name. Then you should skip another line and type

> Enclosure

This indicates that your resume is enclosed.

Format Tips

There are several different formats for business correspondence, all of which have their supporters. Many word processing programs will provide assistance with this process, giving you samples from which to choose. If you are using a typewriter, however, you will have to go it alone. Here are examples of the most common cover letter formats:

- **Full block.** This style aligns the text of your letter to the left as well as to the right. This is an option on most word processors, but it's close to impossible with a typewriter. It also looks a bit awkward, as you may have one line that is crowded with text, followed by a line with huge gaps.

- **Block left.** This style aligns all of the text to the left side of the page. Text at the right side of the page will appear more jagged.

- **Indented.** The indented style is the style most people are accustomed to. With this style, each paragraph is indented three to five spaces on the first line. Also, the date, closing, and signature move nearer to the right margin in this format.

Sample Cover Letters for Different Situations

Each cover letter should be written specifically for one opportunity. Sometimes you will be writing in response to an advertisement. In these situations, you should read the ad carefully, in terms of what is said as well as what isn't.

In Response to an Ad with Contact Information

This ad is looking for possible career changers, with a two-year training program that will prepare you for that change. The fact that it's a paid training program should take away some of the risk of entering a commission sales field. Although the ad does not refer to it as a commission sales position, the words "You expect your compensation to be based upon your achievements" is likely to mean just that. This is obviously a topic you will want to cover in the interview. A cover letter for this type of position might look like this:

128 Elm St.
Wobegon, MN 55437
December 12, 2005

Mr. Ralph Bartolotta
Financial Metrics
1350 Checkingham, Suite 300
North Tampa, FL 33600

Dear Mr. Bartolotta,

Please accept this letter and the enclosed resume in response to your ad in the *National Business Employment Weekly.* As a salesman for fifteen years in the electronics and software industries, I am excited by the prospect of entering the field of financial services.

As you will see from my resume, I have achieved a high level of success in both of my two previous positions. I am a proven closer, with a history of meeting and exceeding my goals, sometimes by more than 50%. Those goals have not been modest ones, either. In each of the last five years I have set my goal to include membership in "The Million Dollar Summit." Not only did I achieve that goal in each of those years, but for the past three years I have been "Top of the Class."

I realize that you are likely to have plenty of questions about my background that you just can't answer by looking at my resume. By the same token, I have questions about this position that are not addressed in your advertisement. To this end, I will contact you sometime in the next week to set up a time when we can get together and discuss those questions. If you have any questions in the interim, please feel free to contact me at 212-355-6765.

I look forward to speaking with you.

Sincerely,

Darrel Ventura

Notice the assertive tone in the last paragraph. If you are applying for a position in sales, you are likely to be comfortable with a job-search approach that is similar to the approach you will need to take as a sales professional. If you are not comfortable with this type of close, you may not be comfortable in sales.

An assertive close is usually advisable for anyone, regardless of the field for which you are applying. You may never be able to reach the hiring manager (strategies for this will be discussed in Chapter 6), but it is a way of exhibiting confidence. And if you're successful at getting through, it gives you a better opportunity to influence your chances of being hired. This type of close is not recommended unless you are sure that you will be able and willing to follow through. If you say that you are going to call and then don't, the employer may wonder whether this failure is indicative of your character or work ethic.

In Response to a Blind Ad

An assertive close is out of the question when you are responding to a "blind ad"—an advertisement with no company name or contact listed, usually only a post office box.

A letter written in response to a blind ad might look like this:

128 Wellington Road
Plano, Texas 75247
May 31, 2005

The Wall Street Journal
2020 Melrose Center
Beverly Hills, CA 90210

To whom it may concern:

Fifteen years in automobile sales and five years as the highest-volume salesperson in the region make me an outstanding candidate for your Real Estate Sales Regional Management position. The fact that for the past three years I have concurrently served as a district manager, with responsibility for the training and success of 40 salespeople, makes interviewing me a very productive way to spend your time.

I believe that the key to my success as a district manager has been the success I have had as a sales professional. The people I supervised knew that I not only "talked the talk," I also "walked the walk." I also had firsthand knowledge of the tools that they would need to be successful, and I made it my first priority to see to it that they always had those tools available to them.

I certainly understand the differences between the sale of automobiles and the sale of real estate. I believe, however, that there are many more similarities than differences. Both are tangible goods with emotional, sensory, and intellectual factors influencing the buying decision. They are also both big-ticket and long-term buying decisions. Most importantly, the fundamentals for both positions are identical. The keys are to listen to the customer, understand their needs, have a full understanding of your product, and have a solid understanding of the competition's attributes.

I hope that this letter and the attached resume will sufficiently arouse your interest, and that you will invite me for an interview. I look forward to hearing from you.

Respectfully,

Alex P. Keaton

Enclosure

To a Personal Contact

When sending a letter to a personal contact, or to an individual to whom you were referred by a personal contact, the approach is different.

---

222 Marbury Court
Ruff, OR 87654

Hugh Merkel
Director of Operations
New Era Cap
Derby, NY 14256

May 27, 2005

Dear Mr. Merkel:

I am writing this letter at the recommendation of David Suffoletto, who suggested that given my background, I should contact you about a position in your embroidery department. He told me about the new contract you have received with the Arena Football League. I am sure you are all very excited!

As you will see from my enclosed resume, I have extensive experience in the area of hand stitching, and for the past five years I have worked as a machine stitcher with a local promotional products manufacturer. For the last two years I have been trained and certified on the Singer 6000 computer-aided embroiderer, which I understand you use at New Era.

I am very excited about the possibility of working with your successful and progressive company. I will be in town visiting my family next week, and I would really like to meet with you and discuss this position. Please call me at your convenience and let me know if there is a time next week when you will be available. I will be available at the number on my resume until Sunday, and beginning Monday, I can be reached via my sister at 716-572-2345.

Thank you for your consideration.

Sincerely,

Ben Ross

Combination Cover Letter/Resume

Some people will choose to send a letter that is a combination cover letter and resume. While this is not my preferred method, it is worth including a sample of this type of letter. Here is one written for this purpose.

---

128 Wellington Road
Alexandria, VA 14788

June 12, 2005

Mr. Aidan Matthews
General Manager
Talia Machine Tools
1200 Preservation Avenue
Arlington, VA 14722

Dear Mr. Matthews:

This past weekend I was speaking with Mike Farber, and he informed me that you are looking for a tool and die maker for your Arlington shop. He mentioned that you have recently upgraded your operation to have the latest in technology.

I am writing to you because I believe that I have the skills that you are seeking. In particular, I have:

- An Associate's degree in Applied Technology from AT&T Technical Institute, where I received straight A's
- Experience on the EM50
- Four years of experience operating the Deere Carbide Grinder
- An outstanding work ethic
- An honorable discharge from the U.S. Marine Corps
- A keen sense of technology and machining
- A willingness to prove myself

If you are still in need of a tool and die maker, I believe that I am your man. Please call me at 708-232-1125 at your earliest convenience. In addition to Mike, you can also check with my current supervisor, Mr. Frank Vastola at Vastola Machines (708-881-4205), to help you better gauge my abilities.

I look forward to hearing from you.

Sincerely,

Robert Ray

For a Job for Which Your Disability Is an Asset

The cover letter is another medium where you may decide to disclose your disability. Although it is seldom advisable to disclose your disability in a resume, there may be times when disclosing within a cover letter may be advisable. While these cases may be infrequent, they deserve mentions.

There may be instances in which your disability may be an asset to you when you are applying for jobs. If you are a recovering alcoholic, you will be able to offer an added dimension if you apply for work as a social worker at an agency that offers counseling or other services to alcoholics. This scenario also holds true if you have a seizure disorder and are applying for a job where you would be working with a similar population.

In these cases, you can mention the disability in the cover letter with the knowledge that a) your disability will give you a certain level of credibility with your clientele that, if not necessary, is at least advisable; and b) that the person reading the letter will be less likely to discriminate against a person with a disability if people with disabilities are a significant portion of the organization's clientele.

Here's a sample cover letter for just such a situation.

234 Wyndham Lane
Danvers, MA 02456

May 21, 2005

Cheryl Incorvia
Meadowbrook Services
2100 Main Street
Salem, MA 02460

Dear Ms. Incorvia:

I am writing this letter in response to the ad placed in Sunday's *Boston Globe.* I am particularly interested in applying for the position of Counselor in Training for your summer camp for people with cerebral palsy.

I attended Camp Mohawk for several years myself when I was in grammar school. I have very fond memories of the activities, the setting, and, more importantly, the many friends I met there. The staff was always great, and they always had a cure for homesickness. They obviously had genuine concern for the campers, and it showed in everything they did.

Since my camping days, I have completed high school, and I have just completed my Associate's degree in Human Services at North Shore Community College. I intend to enroll at Emmanuel College in the fall, where I hope to receive a Bachelor's in Psychology. I have also been very active in the "Lobster Bytes," the technology club at North Shore. My experience in conducting workshops on web page design, as well as general computing topics, would be of great value to you as you roll out your "Computer Camp" program this summer.

I feel confident that I will not only be able to provide you with the skills and abilities you seek in a CIT, but that I will also be able to serve as a positive role model for the campers.

I look forward to hearing from you, and to the possibility of returning to Camp Mohawk (and this time with a semi-private bath!).

Sincerely,

Kimberly Roberts

Enc.

In Regard to a Lead from a Friend

Hopefully, a lot of the cover letters that you write will be following up on a conversation with a friend or networking contact. As was discussed earlier, this type of letter has a far greater impact on the reader. Part of the reason for this increase in impact is because of the possibility that the reader will contact the third party directly and inquire about your candidacy. This is great for you in many ways, but it may also provide some challenges.

Depending on how you have prepared this networking contact, there may be the risk that they will disclose your disability. What may seem like an innocent comment by the reference can have a huge impact on the potential employer. I remember speaking with someone who was serving on a search committee for an entry-level position at a college. This person knew the person one of the semifinalists referred to in her letter. It was decided that this person should be contacted along with the other references in order to decide whether to bring the candidate to campus.

The person mentioned in the letter was a faculty member on that campus who knew the candidate very well. As the faculty member was describing the candidate, she said, "She was a student in a summer seminar I taught at another school. She was one of the most well-prepared students I ever had the pleasure of teaching. She could speak French better than most of the students I have had who could hear perfectly."

Now this was obviously meant to be a compliment, and should be taken as one. The fact is, however, that the compliment also inadvertently communicated that the person had a hearing impairment. This may be a positive thing, because if the person who was making the call was on good terms with the faculty member, they might have followed up on the comment and found out that the candidate was, in fact, just what the employer was seeking. If the employer had any negative stereotypes about people with disabilities, however, it could be a very negative thing.

If you suspect that your networking contact or one of your references may disclose your disability, you may find it helpful to disclose your disability in your cover letter. This strategy gives you the opportunity to place your disability in a more appropriate context. The following is a sample of this type of disclosure:

113 McKinley Parkway
Bemidjii, MN 09543

December 27, 2005

Mr. Juan Epstein
Assistant Principal
Christopher Columbus High School
1 Middle-High Circle
St. Paul, MN 09550

Dear Mr. Epstein:

Yesterday I was speaking with Ralph Bartolotta, and he informed me that he had spoken with you about my availability to serve as a long-term substitute teacher. I would be very interested in speaking with you about this possibility.

As you will see from my enclosed resume, I received my Bachelor's degree in Elementary Education from Hamline University this month, and I have received Provisional Certification to teach. I finished one semester behind schedule because of an auto accident I was involved in during the summer of my junior year. As a result of that accident, I now use a motorized wheelchair. I know that this will not prevent me from being an asset to Christopher Columbus, as I had no trouble getting around the school last semester when I visited several classrooms as part of your school's S.A.D.D. programming.

I completed my student teaching in Social Studies at Hubert H. Humphrey High School, under the supervision of Ms. Patty George. I stayed connected with HHH High for an additional semester as advisor to the yearbook committee, filling in for the regular advisor while she was on maternity leave.

My references are on file with the Hamline Career Center, and I would be happy to have them sent if you are interested. I will call you before the semester begins to verify that you have received this and to inquire about the possibility of setting up an interview. If you have any questions in the interim, please do not hesitate to contact me.

Sincerely,

Daniel Rainmano

Online Cover Letter Help

There are many sites on the Internet where you can find additional resources on writing a cover letter. Some that you may want to check out include:

The University at Buffalo has some sample cover letters at

> `www.ub-careers.buffalo.edu/student.shtml#job`

TrueCareers, a job-related site that caters to technology professionals, is located at

> `www.truecareers.com`

The New York State Department of Labor has a collection of cover letter information at

> `www.labor.state.ny.us/working_ny/finding_a_job/winedge/`
> `coverle.htm`

JobStar, an organization that serves people in California, offers help at

> `http://jobsmart.org/tools/resume/cletters.htm`

Monster.com, a private job-search site, has sample cover letters at

> `http://content.monster.com/resume/`

To ease your concerns about grammar and style, Jack Lynch, a student at Rutgers, has prepared

> `http://newark.rutgers.edu/~jlynch/Writing/`

You can find information about several books on cover letters at

> `www.jist.com`

PART III

Applying and Interviewing for Jobs

Chapter 6:   Networking and Mentors

Chapter 7:   Other Ways to Generate Job Leads

Chapter 8:   Managing Your Job Search

Chapter 9:   Applying for Jobs

Chapter 10:   Preparing for the Interview

Chapter 11:   After the Interview

CHAPTER 6

Networking and Mentors

Several times in the preceding chapters I have talked about the need to go beyond the more traditional methods to find job opportunities. One of the very best ways to do that is through networking.

Perhaps the richest source of job leads you will have is the network of contacts that you have already developed. These individuals should be equipped with a good understanding of what kind of work you are looking for, as well as a copy of your resume. As they become aware of job openings, they will likely share that information with you. This is one of the reasons why you should remain in regular contact with these individuals, so that you can assess the information they have received since your last meeting with them.

The majority of jobs are filled through networking. Again, it is not necessarily a question of someone you know giving you a job. More likely, it will be a question of someone you know hearing about an opening, and with their support and words of recommendation, you may be given an opportunity to interview for the job and speak for yourself.

The concept behind networking is simple: People make hiring decisions based on a variety of factors that include the skills that the applicant possesses, the tasks that are essential to the position, and the credentials (degrees, certifications, and so on) of the job seeker. Another major factor in this mix is less tangible, but equally important. The manager must answer the questions "How will this person fit in? Will I like him or her? Is this the type of person I want on my team?"

Most hiring managers will admit that these are sometimes the hardest questions to answer. It costs an employer a lot of money to go through the process of recruiting and training a worker. If that worker does not stay for at least a couple of years, that hire will be looked upon as a failure, and the money spent will be seen as a bad investment. Because the amount of time that an interviewer can spend getting to know each candidate is limited, they often look for other ways to supplement their knowledge of candidates when possible. That's one of the reasons employers pay more attention to resumes and cover letters that come from *referrals,* people they know and trust.

Unless the referred candidate is a relative, or unless the position is with a privately held company (or perhaps a government [political] patronage position), it is unlikely that the person will be hired without meeting certain formal criteria. If those criteria are met, however, the person who knows someone, or knows someone who knows someone at the company, will have the edge.

This chapter also discusses mentors. Having a mentor will serve you in many ways. First of all, it will provide you with sound, seasoned advice. You will have the opportunity to gain a broader perspective on the issues that will affect your search. You will also benefit from the established network that your mentor has. This chapter will provide you with information on how to establish these kinds of relationships, as well as how to use them to assist you in your job search.

Networking—a Numbers Game

A generation ago, people spoke of "six degrees of separation." The idea was that we, as humans, are all interrelated, and that you can find a connection to any individual with a maximum of six intermediaries. More currently, there is a parlor game (perhaps even an actual board game by now) called the *Kevin Bacon Game.* The idea here is to choose an actor or actress, or another person from popular culture, and then find who can name the people who connect that individual with Kevin Bacon in six steps or less (by the way, we have no idea why Kevin Bacon was chosen over anyone else out there). [For example, Matt Damon has a Kevin Bacon Factor of 2: Matt was in *The Legend of Bagger Vance* with Charlize Theron, and Charlize Theron was in *Trapped* with Kevin Bacon. To try this out for yourself, visit the "Oracle of Bacon" Web site at www.cs.virginia.edu/oracle/.]

Chances are, you will have a "Bacon Factor" of your own that is less than 7. And if you can have a "Bacon Factor" of less than 7, certainly you must have a factor that is even less for the hiring manager for your perfect job. The key is to begin putting your contacts on paper and trying to establish your quickest route to that dream job.

Establishing a Network

Think of your network as sort of a spider web, with you positioned at the middle. The strongest strands of this web will be the strands that connect directly from you. It is likely that there are dozens, if not hundreds, of people who will make up this inner ring of contacts. Think about it for a second: How many people do you know pretty well? There are your parents and the rest of your immediate family. Then there is your extended family—aunts, uncles, cousins, etc. These may be the strongest links of all, because they carry with them the bond of blood.

Also in that first strand are your close friends and next-door neighbors, as well as your friends' parents and siblings. You also have a direct link to former teachers, baby-sitters, coaches, clergy, counselors, and employers. You may know coworkers, classmates, teammates, or people from a club or scouting organization.

Perhaps you have a postal worker who has delivered your mail for a while, a person at the bank whom you have come to know over the years, a dry cleaner, or a person who cuts your hair. You may include some of the people you met while conducting your informational interviews. All of these people (and there are plenty I may have left out) could fit into the inner ring of your personal web. Look at the following list for some ideas of people you might consider as networking contacts.

Networking Candidates

Accountant	Guidance counselor	Police officer
Aunts/uncles	Hair stylist	Postal worker
Barber	Lawyer	Priest/minister/rabbi
Cousins	Librarian	Rehab counselor
Dentist	Next-door neighbor	Social worker
Doctor	Parents	Teachers
Dry cleaner	Physical therapist	Veterinarian
Electrician	Plumber	Waiters/waitresses
Florist		

One of the first challenges many people face in networking is getting over this noble, romantic notion of "going it alone." Some people feel ashamed if they have to ask their parents or friends for help. This pitfall is particularly a risk for people with disabilities because of the added desire for independence. You need to get over this feeling, and quickly. Your parents, friends, former teachers, and anyone else you are close to are very interested in seeing you succeed. As I mentioned before, none of them are likely to just give you a job, but they are probably in a position to help you make the contacts you need to get the job you want. This is the number one way most people find a job. You cannot afford to overlook it.

Focusing on the First Ring

You will want to focus your early energies on the first ring of networking contacts. Throughout the process, as you begin your self-assessment, as you explore the world of work, and as you prepare your resume, you should seek out those closest to you for their advice, counsel, and job leads. Start with those who are closest to you. These people will be easier to approach and will help you perfect your "pitch." These are the people who know you best, and they will be in the best position to provide you with meaningful feedback.

Keep in mind, though, that these people may also be the ones who have a vested interest in seeing you pursue a certain course of business. Your mother, for example, may believe that you have perfect pitch and that you should be a professional singer. Your father may be hoping that you will choose to follow him in the family appliance-repair business. A math teacher may have always thought that you should be an accountant, and your neighbor may actually believe that you should take any job that will get you to move and take your annoying stereo system with you!

As long as you realize that their input is just one perspective, you will be better off. As I mentioned before, they are likely to all have different suggestions on things you should add to or subtract from your resume. They may all recognize different strengths and weaknesses in you. Those different perspectives will become even more valuable when you start to hear some of the same things over and over again. If lots of people perceive the same strengths in you, these strengths are likely to be true.

In addition to helping you know your strengths and hone your approach, this first ring of contacts will also be a great source of job leads. If everyone in your inner circle knows that you are interested in a position in pharmaceutical sales, and if they all have copies of your resume, it is quite likely that one of them will come across an opening. They might hear about it while at their doctor's office, while getting their hair done, or in an out-of-town newspaper they were reading while on vacation. This is like having a posse of deputized job seekers. If you arm them well, they may help you find what you want a lot more quickly.

You may have an inner ring of fifty or a hundred people, and that can keep you quite busy. Obviously you will seek to involve them all at different levels, counting on your sister more than your barber or dentist. You should count on all of them, or at least most of them, as you begin to qualify your job leads. To find out more information about that pharmaceutical job, make an appointment for an annual check-up with your physician. Between deep breaths and saying aaahhh, let the doctor know that you are looking for work, and ask her what she thinks about jobs in the field of pharmaceutical sales. Chances are, she can share the names of a dozen or more people who are in the field whom you could call for an informational interview.

Not all of the people in your inner circle will be equally valuable. But if everyone in your inner circle was able, on average, to share the names of three people who might be able to help you, you have just created a second ring that is almost three times the size of your inner ring. As you explore this second ring, you will begin to see an interesting dynamic emerge. Many of the people in the second ring will be on the list of more than one of your inner-ring people. This will be one of the first moments where that interconnectedness that was discussed earlier will be evident. (Keep in mind that Matt Damon's buddy, Ben Affleck, was also in the movie *Reindeer Games* with Charlize Theron, who again, was in *Trapped* with…Kevin Bacon!)

The Second Ring

Contacting the people in the second ring will be a bit more challenging than it was to contact the people in your first ring. Again, to make this a bit easier, start either with the contacts of the people who are closest to you, or with those people who were mentioned by more than one of your inner-circle members. As you approach these people, and as you gain more confidence doing so, shift to contacting the people who you think might be in the best position to help you *directly*.

Making Contact by Telephone

One of the greatest tools at your disposal as you conduct your job search will be the telephone. Some people would rather do just about anything else but use the telephone a great deal, but in this case it is the most efficient way to generate the leads that you need. One thing that can take the edge off of those negative feelings is to have a plan so that your conversations are short and productive.

Although there is an advantage to conducting your first networking meeting with an individual face-to-face, that's not always possible. Also, repeated face-to-face meetings with a busy networking contact could burn the person out more quickly. Using the phone has many other advantages as well:

- **Saves time.** You can make many more phone calls in a day than you can make personal visits. Time spent traveling to and from appointments is time that could be better spent speaking with someone who can help you.

- **Saves money.** Gas, parking, and eating meals away from home all add up in terms of cost. By staying home and using the phone, you can avoid all of these costly items.

- **Saves face.** Chances are that your contacts are busy people. Even though they have a real interest in helping you succeed, they may prefer to help you *when their schedule permits it*. By pinning them down to a specific time, you may end up waiting as they wrap up a meeting. Or worse, they may need to cancel the meeting, causing them to feel guilty and you to feel aggravated. Those feelings of guilt don't help you in the long term either, because the person will be more reluctant to initiate contact with you if they feel guilty about missing the last meeting.

- **Reduces error.** The more effort you expend to keep your records accurate and up-to-date, the better off you will be. At home you will have access to your computer and/or your job-search binder. Scribbling a few notes in your car or on the bus makes it more likely that your records will be less than perfect.

- **Increases results.** The phone is even more helpful when you are trying to arrange the first conversation with someone. Some people try to do it all in person, and end up hitting the roadblock of a receptionist, secretary, or other gatekeeper. Rarely do people appreciate uninvited visitors to their workplace, even if that person was referred by a friend. Showing up in person is much more of an imposition than calling on the phone.

There are ways you can increase your efficiency on the phone. One of the best ways to do this is to arrange your telephone calls so that you can actually catch the person there, rather than leaving a message on voice mail or with an assistant. Every line of work has its own schedule, and as such there are some times that are better than others to actually reach someone. You should always ask your contact how they prefer to be contacted, and the best time to do so. If this is an initial contact, you should ask the person who referred you to tell you the best time to reach their referral.

Regardless of what line of work your contact is in, there are a few guidelines that are generally helpful. Usually you will increase your chances of reaching your contact if you call early in the morning, or after the "official" workday has ended. It is quite likely that the type of people you will be contacting will not be "clock-watchers," and that they will be putting in extra hours to accomplish the added work they have taken on. By calling outside of the regular work hours, you may find them less distracted by other people and appointments.

Although not as effective as calling outside of office hours, you may find some advantage to calling between 12:00 and 2:00. While you run the risk of your contact being at lunch, you increase your chances of getting around the secretaries and assistants, who see it as their job to protect your contact from people like you who might interrupt their work. Over time you may win these gatekeepers over; until then, you need to avoid any obstacle that will keep you from your goal—speaking to the person who can help you.

Another good way to increase your success is to know ahead of time what you want to accomplish. Perhaps this is an initial contact in which your goal is either a personal or phone appointment. Or maybe you are just touching base to update the person on your progress and to ask about any possible leads. Regardless of what motivates you to make the call, it is important that you know ahead of time what you want to say and what you want to accomplish.

Once you know what your goal is for making the call, you should try and write out what you want to say. By scripting your call ahead of time, you can accomplish a great deal. You can reduce the chances that after you hang up you think of all the things you *should* have said. Scripting also gives you the chance to practice your calls ahead of time, making sure that you are comfortable with each word you are using so that you won't get hung up on any of them.

As you script your call, try to anticipate what the contact may ask you. You should be prepared to give a two-minute or less summation of why you should be hired for any given situation. This answer should seem natural, yet cover the most important points. By having some answers ready for potential questions, you will reduce the chance of being caught off guard by a question.

Sample Scripts for a First-Time Phone Contact

Candidate: Hello, Mrs. Lipinski, this is Dan Ryan. I'm a friend of Shannon Miller's, and she suggested I give you a call.

Contact: Oh, yes, she mentioned that you might call. How can I help you?

Candidate: Well, I finished my degree in exercise science at Missouri, Columbia, and I am looking to learn more about the job outlook for this area. I was wondering if there was a time in the next few weeks when you might have a half hour to spend with me to fill me in on your perspective.

Contact: Things are little crazy around here right now. I have been eating lunch at my desk this whole week.

Candidate: Shannon told me that there is a lot going on over there. If I could join you at your desk sometime, I'd even be happy to supply lunch. (Light chuckle) Or, if it would be better for you, I could meet you for a cup of coffee before or after work someday.

Contact: I'll tell you what. Why don't you come in on Wednesday of next week at noon. We can get a couple of sandwiches down at the lunch counter and bring them up here, if you can stand the mess.

Candidate: That would be great! I really appreciate your taking the time to meet with me. I will see you Wednesday at noon!

This script shows a sample of initial resistance that was not too severe. You may encounter people who are a little tougher to pin down. You should stick with it, but don't push too hard. You don't want to alienate someone who could have helped you.

Candidate: Hello, Mr. George? My name is Dan Ryan. I'm a friend of Joe O'Brien's, and he suggested that I give you a call. I have recently moved back to town, and I am looking for a job as an admissions counselor.

Contact: How can I help you?

Candidate: Joe said that you were pretty well plugged in to the higher education field in this area, and that you might be able to help me find some potential opportunities.

Contact: Well, I do have some contacts in the field, but I have to tell you that I am really backed up at work right now.

Candidate: I really would only need around fifteen minutes of your time. If you could just steer me toward those schools that may have an opening, I would really appreciate it. I would be happy to meet you some morning before work, if that's more convenient for you.

Contact: Unfortunately, I have barely had time to breathe lately. My secretary broke her ankle and she has been out for the past two weeks. I hate to say no, but I really don't think I'm going to be able to help you.

Candidate: Wow, it sounds like you really are swamped. I won't take up any more of your time right now, but would it be all right if I called you in a couple of weeks to see if things have calmed down any?

Contact: Well…sure. She's out for at least the next week or so, so maybe you should make it three weeks.

Candidate: No problem. I really appreciate your help. I'll give you a call at the end of the month. Good luck catching up!

Contact: Thanks!

This script shows a candidate sensing the fine line between assertiveness and aggressiveness. Instead of ruining future chances by pressing the point, a future call was arranged. There is no guarantee that these two will ever actually meet, but let's play out another scenario:

Candidate: Hi, Mr. George? This is Dan Ryan. I spoke with you last month. You were a little swamped back then. Have things gotten any better?

Contact: (gruffly) No, not much. How can I help you?

Candidate: I'm not sure if you remember me, but I am a friend of Joe O'Brien's, and he suggested I call you to see what I can learn about the admissions field locally.

Contact: Oh yeah. I saw Joe last week and he asked if you had called. I'm sorry to say that things are still pretty backed up here. I'm still not in much of a position to help.

Candidate: To be honest, I really only have a couple of quick questions right now. I met with Frank Vastola and he filled me in a little about Tipton Community College and Jackson State. Perhaps you can give me an idea of who I might contact over at Delhi. Frank said that he heard that they might add a transfer counselor this year.

Contact: Sure, I know Sid Jackson over at Delhi. He is their Dean of Enrollment Management. I'll tell you what. I'm going to see him Wednesday at a retirement luncheon for a colleague from an educational software company. I will ask him what's going on in the transfer area, and see if he already has someone in mind for the opening. Why don't you give me a call late Wednesday afternoon?

Candidate: Thank you very much. I really appreciate your help. I will give you a call Wednesday afternoon.

Effective Listening

One of the keys to effective use of the telephone is listening. Listening over the phone is much more difficult than in person, because you are relying on only one ear, and you do not have the benefit of facial expressions. If there is any question about what your contact has said, restate it so that they can clarify or affirm what you heard. This is far better to do than to assume that they said or meant one thing, while they really said another.

Most people make the simple mistake of talking more than listening. While you may have important information to convey in each call that you make, you will surely gain more from the time you spend listening. One key to effective listening is to refrain from interrupting. This kind of behavior is sure to turn your contact off. So, too, will taking the liberty of finishing your contact's sentences for him or her. Some people pause mid-sentence, and out of either impatience or a desire to show that they are on the same wavelength, the other person will speak the words that they think the other person is looking for.

To listen effectively, try to eliminate extraneous distractions. Turn off the radio, television, and any other appliances. Focus all of your attention and energy on the person who is speaking. Listen for cues that contradict what the person is saying. If you hear hesitation, uncertainty, or enthusiasm, it can change the meaning of the words that are being spoken. Listening for inflection and pauses can give you a more complete picture of what is being said.

Getting Past the Gatekeepers

One other important suggestion is to try and find the most direct way to reach your contact by phone. If you can find out the employee's direct-dial number, you will reach that person a lot faster than if you have to call the organization's switchboard. Try to get that number from the individual if you can, or from the person who referred you. If you cannot get it from them, there are other ways to find this information. Sometimes the organization will have a voice-mail tree that provides a departmental or organizational directory. These directory trees are sometimes available only after-hours to direct people to the appropriate voice mailbox. Sometimes you can get the direct number from a company's Web site. Other times you might be able to find the direct-dial number of the secretary or assistant (switchboards are a bit less protective of these people). The telephone number of an executive and the secretary are often only a digit or two apart. If you get stuck in a voice mail web, you can usually press 0 or 0# and make your way back to a switchboard to start over. After a few tries you may strike gold!

Brush Up on Your Speaking Skills

Finally, another important thing to consider if you will be using the phone is your speaking ability. Something as simple as smiling while you speak, even though the person on the other end of the phone can't see you, will impact how you are heard. Positioning your mouth in a smile changes the way your voice sounds and helps you communicate interest, enthusiasm, and attention.

Practice speaking with a friend, or with a mirror and a tape recorder if necessary. Do you sound friendly as you answer questions? Confident? Enthusiastic? Do you speak clearly? Are you able to enunciate well? If not, continue to practice. If this does not help, it may be to your advantage to contact a speech therapist.

If your disability is related to your speech, it may be to your advantage to rely on written and/or electronic communication where possible. This will allow you to establish a relationship before you introduce the fact that you have a disability.

Using E-Mail

Some contacts will prefer to use e-mail for their communication. This can work to your advantage, too, because you can use this medium 24 hours a day and it allows your contact to respond at his or her convenience. One suggestion, however: Although e-mail is a less-formal method of communication, don't get sloppy. Make sure that you don't have typos or other errors in your messages. Also, keep them short and to the point. This will take up less of the contact's time, and that will be appreciated.

E-mail has advantages over other forms of communication. It is much faster, allowing for more timely exchange of information. Also, as written correspondence, it gives you the same advantage that scripting your phone conversations provides—the chance to say exactly what you want.

E-mail also has its drawbacks. As a form of written communication, it lacks the chance for nonverbal exchanges that face-to-face conversations provide. It also lacks the inflection and volume control that you get when you speak on the telephone.

The speed and ease with which e-mail can be used can also encourage it to be overused. Do not bombard your contact with e-mail. It is likely that they are already overloaded with the amount that they receive as part of their own work. Use it with the same frequency that you would use the phone.

If you do use e-mail, print your messages—both the ones you write and the ones you receive—or store them in a folder for future reference. This will be a better record than the notes you take after a face-to-face meeting or telephone conversation.

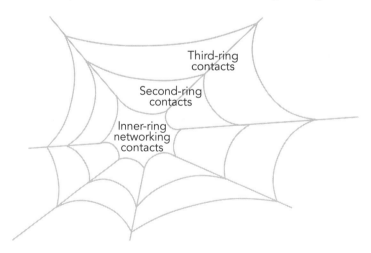

Third-ring contacts

Second-ring contacts

Inner-ring networking contacts

Organizing, Prioritizing, and Following Up

At this point your network is beginning to take that web shape. You can also begin to see what exponential growth can do.

It's a good idea to maintain a note-card file or use a contact-management software program to track your activity with your leads. The card should contain each person's contact information and notes about each interaction you have had with him. The card might look something like this:

Networking Card

Johnson, Navin R.

Work Address	Home Address
Chevron Oil	21 Elm St.
1250 Sheridan Drive	Pensacola, FL
67656	
Pensacola, FL 67664	813-456-6543
813-455-7654	

E-mail address: njohnson@chevron.com

Preferred contact: Phone

Best time to contact: Mornings before 10:00

Meeting notes:

12/12/04	Dropped off 5 copies of resume.
	Suggested I call Mrs. C. Nussbaum from Cooks Know How and Mr. Reiner from Opti-Grab.
1/4/05	Updated him on meeting with Mrs. Nussbaum and phone call with Mr. Reiner.
5/3/05	Stopped by to tell him that I took the job with ProShare. Delivered a box of Gump Chocolates with a thank-you note.

Keeping track of this kind of information is vital to your success. It is also a good skill to develop (if you haven't already) to help you on the job once you get it.

You should also schedule follow-up calls with contacts you have spoken with. This will help you keep them apprised of what you are doing, and it will jog their memories for any leads they may have to pass your way. If you use a contact-management program (such as Outlook, Sidekick, Lotus Agenda, Day-Timer, or any of the others on the market), you can use the calendar function to remind you. If you are using a note-card file, purchase a good calendar folio and mark the dates for follow-up calls.

The time interval between follow-up calls is something that you will need to determine on a case-by-case basis. If this is a lukewarm contact, or if there is little likelihood that there will be any developments since your last call, you may choose to wait six weeks between calls. If the contact is more receptive and more likely to be in a position to help, you may schedule a follow-up call for a week later. In each case, however, be sure that the interval is mutually agreed upon.

As you make contact with the people in your second ring, you will need to constantly reprioritize your prospects. Each time you get a new name, you need to decide whether this is a lead you should follow up on immediately, or if you should put it off while you contact the remaining people in your second ring. You should make these decisions carefully. You don't want a great lead to grow stale while you pursue every single name that you received before it. You also don't want to put off contacting someone so long that the first-ring person who gave you their name takes your lack of follow-through as a lack of interest and decides against helping you further.

Often, networking will pay off with a number of job interviews before you have visited everyone in your third ring. If you have 50 people in your inner ring and they each give you three people to contact on average, and if those people on average give you two people, you will have gone through at least five packs of those 100-count index cards, and you will have begun to understand why early in this book I told you that looking for work was at least a full-time job in itself.

Here's another tip: Don't toss the card file the minute you get that dream job. Keep the file, and keep adding to it as you meet new people. As I mentioned before, it's unlikely that this next job will be the one that you stay in until you retire. This group of people may be able to help you again in the future. And keep those people in mind as you go along. Refer people to that Realtor friend as they look for a new home, or keep your ears open for job leads for your friends who are looking. As you maintain these contacts and make more, your personal web will extend further and further. Who knows—you may even meet Kevin Bacon!

Finding a Mentor

One of the truly great benefits of networking is the possibility of finding a mentor. If you find a person who has an interest in your career, as well as a wealth of practical experience, your career can benefit greatly. Several types of mentors can be of particular value to you. The following sections discuss each mentor type.

People Without Disabilities in a Similar Field

This individual will be able to give you an inside look at the day-to-day work in your chosen field. This person can give you a historical perspective on the field and on where he or she sees the field going in the next five years. A good mentor will give you good advice about which professional associations you should join, and which will only serve to take up your time. You will get advice on magazines, books, or trade journals that can provide you with information on issues that are at the forefront of your field.

People with Similar Disabilities in a Similar Field

If you can find someone who is successful in your chosen career, you will have found a gold mine. If any questions arise in an interview about your ability to perform the essential functions of the job because of your disability, you will easily be able to answer emphatically, using your mentor as an example.

This type of mentor will be in an excellent position to help you on many fronts. Most importantly, this person will be able to share with you a wealth of information about the ways in which his or her disability has affected them on the job. He or she may be in a position to give you a feel for what accommodations might be necessary and appropriate for you in the workplace. You can learn ways in which the disability has had no impact whatsoever. This information will be invaluable to you as you interview for positions in this field. Just having access to this kind of information will surely boost your confidence when you are in an interview.

Obviously, this individual will be able to provide you with information about your chosen field, as well.

People with Similar Disabilities in a Different Field

Sometimes the most important information you need to know will be related somehow to your disability. While you may not find a person with a similar disability in the field you want to enter, it's likely that you will be able to find a person with a similar disability who is working in a different setting. Although career or vocational counselors can be helpful, there is an added value in hearing from a person who has a better perspective on how your disability may interact with your work.

This person will be able to share opinions on issues like how and when to disclose your disability during the job-search process. I have shared my opinions on this issue throughout this book; however, you are sure to find something more authentic when it comes from a person who has faced what you are facing. The best thing to do is to take all of the information you can gather and then decide what makes the most sense for you and your particular situation.

This individual may also be aware of valuable resources for a person with your type of disability. Many support groups, public and private agencies, and technology companies exist to help people with disabilities, particularly in the area of employment and placement. Like all of the other resources in this book, they should not be overlooked.

A Long-Term Relationship

Although a mentor can be a great asset as you explore entering the field and while you think about ways your disability may affect you on the job, don't let the relationship end there. Many mentoring relationships have lasted for the better part of one's career. By cultivating this type of long-term relationship, you can benefit from your mentor's expertise at critical times in your career. Decisions about special projects, opportunities for advancement, and whether to stay or go can all be made with a higher level of confidence if you have the counsel of someone you trust.

By the way, don't feel you have to stop at one mentor. If your mentor is someone from another organization, you should also seek out a mentor from within your current organization when possible. In addition to possessing knowledge and experience in the work world, this person will also possess a better understanding of the culture of the organization in which you work. Keep in mind that this person, like any mentor, will possess only one perspective, but that perspective is likely to be a valuable one to consider.

Don't feel that this relationship will be all one-way, and that you will just be "using" your mentor. It is likely that your mentor will benefit a great deal from their relationship with you as well. Many mentors find that the mentoring experience can be an exhilarating one. It has invigorated many careers, because it refocuses the individual's attention in a new way and energizes that person as they see the organization and the world through your eyes.

You have something else to offer other than letting some "old-timer" live vicariously through your career. You may also have an opportunity to help your mentor gain new skills. Many people entering the workforce for the first time, for example, are far more likely to feel comfortable with newer technology. While your mentor may have a microwave and VCR that both blink 12:00 all day, you may have a good deal of experience using the Internet or some of the newer software packages. The fact is that in the early days of the Internet (shortly after Al Gore invented it), the net was populated mostly by three groups—members of the government-education community, techies, and people with disabilities. Much of the computer technology that was intended to meet the needs of people with disabilities (Optical Character Recognition, scanners, and voice-recognition software) has made its way into the mainstream. If you have experience with technology or a newer programming language, share it with your mentor. Your mentor will likely benefit from this relationship because of the fresh perspective you will bring to the problems you discuss.

Some companies have formal mentoring programs, and some of them work very well. Sometimes, however, people find that it is difficult to make that kind of forced relationship work. If that is the case, try to seek out someone for a less-formal relationship.

Chances are the mentor you choose has benefited from a relationship with a mentor of their own in the past. And sometime in the future, you will probably mentor someone else as well.

CHAPTER 7

Other Ways to Generate Job Leads

Although the most effective way to search for a job is through networking, you do not want to ignore some of the more traditional means, either. There are certainly plenty of people who have had luck in their job search by utilizing the want ads, the Internet, and other tools.

Using the Newspaper to Find Leads

Whenever I lead job-search seminars, I ask "Where do you find out about job openings?" Each time I do, a bunch of hands will go up, and the first person will always say "the newspaper." After that answer, 90 percent of the hands will go down. When I probe a little further, I find that the person is always referring to the want ads in the classified advertising section of the newspaper.

The newspaper is in fact a decent source for leads. On a typical Sunday morning, in a major metropolitan newspaper, you may find 1,000 or more job listings. In addition to daily newspapers, many communities have a special newspaper full of job listings. Still, you should keep in mind that research has shown that fewer than 25 percent of all jobs ever make it to the want ads.

Want Ads

But it's worth discussing a few drawbacks to applying for jobs that you find through the want ads. First of all, the circulation of your local newspaper may be in the tens of thousands (or much more in many cases). That means that there will be a lot of people looking at the same ads that you are reading. The higher the number of people who know about a job, the higher the number who will apply for it. The higher the number that apply, the more difficult it is to make your resume stand out. Although that fact should not scare you off, it should help you understand that it is not advisable for this to be your primary source of job leads. Obviously, networking is a far more productive method.

Many want ads use P.O. boxes as their address. Employers do this to avoid being overwhelmed with phone calls inquiring about the position. The danger in responding to a P.O. box is that the box may belong to your current employer. More than once an employee has been "outed" as a job-seeker because of just this scenario. Before you apply to this type of ad, check to see whether your HR department uses this method. Also, ask around and see whether there is an opening of this type within your organization. Obviously, you will be in a better position to compete for this job if you hold the inside track. Just keep your fingers crossed that it isn't *your* job they are advertising to fill!

Another drawback to answering want ads is that many do not include a contact person. This denies you the opportunity to follow up with an actual human being.

You should keep in mind that some companies post their openings in the newspaper for reasons other than finding the right candidate. Some organizations, particularly ones that follow Affirmative-Action guidelines, are required to post their openings in the newspaper to show that they are making an effort to recruit candidates from protected classes. Other organizations have a policy that they advertise each opening that will be filled. Many jobs are filled internally or have been promised to someone (probably somebody who's a good networker) long before the ad is taken out in the newspaper.

Getting back to the workshop I was talking about, I am always surprised at how few people use the newspaper for job leads in places other than the want ads. The newspaper can be a rich source of job leads if you know what you are looking for and where to look.

National and Local News

In these sections you will find stories that may reveal job opportunities, or at least solid networking leads. You may read a story about a company that is rolling out a brand new product. It is possible that this company may soon need individuals to help manufacture, package, sell, or service those products. You may also read a story about a company that has been awarded a major contract. Perhaps it's a government purchase agreement or an ad firm that has won the right to market a product. In these cases, it's possible that the existing staff at that company will be insufficient for this new activity.

Business Pages

In the business section you will find a wealth of information, including networking contacts and job leads. In this section you may find profiles of successful businesses, giving you insight into the operations of that company, as well as contact names. You will also find announcements of major expansions that will likely result in new jobs. Many communities have local economic development agencies that use tax incentives to lure new businesses to their area, or to keep them there. Announcements of these awards may not always make it into the major stories, but are usually included in stories that report the meetings of those governmental economic development agencies.

Business/Social Pages

Often the newspaper will carry a section that reports on promotions and new appointments. These stories often include a photograph of an individual and information like:

> Michelle Bewley has been named liaison for the Pan American Exposition Centennial for the XYZ Foundation. Ms. Bewley previously was employed by M. Moore Inc., where she served as a Benefits Analyst.

This is good news for Ms. Bewley, but it is also good news for anyone who would like to be the benefits analyst at M. Moore, Inc. Although these stories may take a few weeks to make it into the papers, they still will probably appear before an ad is placed.

Tax Liens, Mortgages, DBAs

In some newspapers you will find a section that lists the businesses that have had tax liens filed against them. This information will tell you that although the company is not necessarily going out of business, they may be in a bit of financial difficulty. So, these companies are less likely to be hiring people. Often, near the same section you will find a list of companies that have incorporated, or filed that they are "Doing Business As." You may also find information about companies that have been issued mortgages. This type of information lets you know when a new company may be opening.

Other Sections

You can find job leads throughout the newspaper. I remember a line from the movie *When Harry Met Sally…*, in which Billy Crystal suggests to Meg Ryan that the obituaries should be combined with the real estate pages so that you might find out when an apartment opens up as the result of someone's death. Perhaps only in a comedy would someone be able to suggest the same for the want ads and the obituaries.

Less cynical, and marginally less depressing, you might peruse the wedding announcements. They usually list where people work and where they will be residing. If you note that the groom is going to have to give up his job because he's moving to San Francisco with his wife, there's a lead.

The key to using the newspaper for leads is to always be thinking about how what you are reading might relate to your job search. If you read a story about a company that sounds like a great place to work, send a letter to the person interviewed for the story to try to set up an appointment. At the very least it will help you extend your network.

Another positive thing about reading the newspapers, and conducting other research on companies in which you have an interest, is that you will be prepared in the event that you receive a job interview. This goes for researching the bad along with the good. If you read a story that troubles you, better to have your concerns addressed *before* you take the job than to take the job and find out about it later.

Employment Agencies

Another traditional source of job leads is employment, temp, and executive-search firms. These organizations serve as brokers between individuals who are seeking work and companies that have positions to fill. They try to match the appropriate people with the jobs that fit their skill set.

Some agencies receive their fee from the employer. With this type of arrangement, the agency works for the employing company. They are paid their fee when the position is filled. To be successful, the agency must screen out applicants and forward a manageable number to the hiring company, at which point they are interviewed and a hiring decision can be made. Keep in mind that it's the employer who pays the bills in this scenario, so it's the employer's interests that will be primary.

Other agencies charge the job seeker a fee to place them in a position. Usually these agencies charge a percentage of the first year's or first six months' salary. Because you are paying the bills, the agency will have a higher level of motivation to find a position that will be a good fit for you, because you will be paying only as long as you remain employed there.

There are also some agencies that will help you on a flat-fee basis. These agencies receive their fee up front, or over time, regardless of whether you find employment with them. The drawback with using this type of agency lies in the fact that when you are unemployed, you are not in a good position to pay this type of fee.

Although employment agencies are a valuable resource to job seekers, it's not the method that is most likely to land you the job that you are looking for. In general, only a small minority of job seekers find their jobs through employment agencies. If you choose this method, choose the agency carefully, and remember that you are still the person responsible for choosing the right opportunity for you.

For the person with a disability, employment agencies carry an added risk. Earlier in the book I discussed the fact that people with disabilities face discrimination as they look for work. By using an agency, the potential for discrimination is doubled. If you choose to use an agency, ask around to see if they have a good track record of helping people with disabilities.

You should not rule out using an employment agency, however. Nearly five percent of all jobs are filled through employment agencies, including temporary employment agencies.

Temporary Agencies

Scott Adams, the cartoonist who chronicles humor in the modern workplace, gives us glimpses into the next millennium in his book *The Dilbert Future* that ring true to me. He suggests that in the future, more and more people will be "contract employees"—people who are paid by a person or an organization to perform a function or complete a project. When they have successfully completed that project, they will move on and sell their services to someone else who has a project that needs to be completed. Signs of this are already upon us, as employers who hire staff for a project, but who do not necessarily need that staffing for the long term, turn to temporary agencies for help. These temp firms send competent individuals to the employer's site to handle a mailing, reorganize a filing system, or convert records into an electronic format. When that project is completed, the worker will wait for the next call from the temp agency to see where the next assignment is.

This type of arrangement is attractive to the employer because they get the work they needed done, and they do not have to pay benefits or make a long-term salary commitment. It is good for the temp firm, because they earn a fee for solving the company's problem. And it is good for the temp, who earns a paycheck and is exposed to an employer who may decide to ask them to stay on permanently. The worker gains practical experience performing a function that they may be asked to perform by a future employer, and can put this experience on a resume.

U.S. Department of Labor

Another traditional source of job leads is the Department of Labor (DOL). Each state has an office that helps people who are unemployed. In addition to processing paperwork for unemployment insurance benefits, these agencies usually carry job listings. These listings come from large corporations and from small storefronts. Many employers turn to the Department of Labor because they know that the people who use the DOL services are likely to be potential candidates for their positions. The DOL is particularly attractive to the smaller employer because there is usually no fee to post a job with the DOL.

The DOL is also a great place to find information on government jobs. In addition to information on civil service examinations, the DOL often will have information on nonclassified positions as well.

College Career Centers

If you are a college graduate, your alma mater's office of career planning will be a great resource for you as well. In addition to having some job listings that come directly to them, they may collect and catalog jobs from other sources.

Most college career centers offer some level of service to their alumni. Besides the job listings, they are likely to have a great collection of books, videos, and assessment instruments (such as tests to determine your skills and interests) that can help you with the various steps of the job search.

If you have relocated since college, ask the career center at your alma mater if they would be willing to send a letter of reciprocity to a school close to where you live now. Usually, one college or university will be willing to extend services to the alumni from another institution with the notion that a member of their alumni would receive the same kind of services at the school making the request.

To find information about a career center near you, visit the Web site at:

```
www.utexas.edu/world/univ/alpha/
```

This site, sponsored by the University of Texas at Austin, has links to the Web pages of regionally accredited U.S. universities.

State Vocational Rehabilitation Offices

Each state has an office that handles vocational rehabilitation. These offices often work with people with disabilities to help them locate the resources necessary to find employment. Sometimes this involves providing support for education or other formalized training necessary to pursue a career in a certain field.

Many companies post their job openings with the vocational rehabilitation office in addition to posting them with the Department of Labor. This is a very good source for job leads for a number of reasons. The most important reason is that companies that post their jobs with the vocational rehabilitation office are probably less likely to discriminate against people with disabilities.

Business Leadership Network

A business-led initiative of the U.S. Chamber of Commerce in collaboration with the U.S. Department of Labor, this group assists businesses in accessing potential employees among the disability community. The group's focus is on education and assisting employers in the area of hiring people with disabilities, and its Web site is at

```
http://www.usbln.com
```

The site contains resources for people with disabilities as well. Perusing the membership info will provide you with leads as to which employers in your area may be more inclined to hire people with disabilities.

Internet Leads

One of the newer, and possibly richest, sources of job leads is the Internet. A multitude of sites is available to a job seeker, and there are even some that are particularly geared toward people with disabilities. Many of these sites have a national or international constituency; as a result, they allow you to search for jobs across the world.

If you do not have access to the Internet from home, go to your public library or your college or school district to find out about accessing it through their sites.

Once a refuge for the "techies" among us, the Internet has truly gone mainstream in the last couple of years. Commercial providers like AOL, AT&T, CompuServe, and others have marketed heavily to homes with personal computers. At the same time, direct computer sellers like Gateway and Dell and retail brands such as Hewlett-Packard and Compaq have made owning your own PC affordable. These hardware and software companies have even collaborated to make it easy to take a PC out of its box, plug it in, and get connected to the Internet.

Nowhere has this democratization of computer technology had a bigger impact than on the online job-search resources. As recently as ten years ago, the Internet was a great tool to use to look for jobs if you were a computer programmer, a database designer, a systems analyst, or an electrical engineer. Today you can go to a mega-site like America's Job Bank, HotJobs, or Monster.com and find hundreds of thousands of jobs. These sites still list plenty of information on technology positions, but you can also find jobs from receptionist to package handler.

You should use your own judgement as you look at some of the sites that feature job-search information. Some of the sites will be more helpful to you in your situation than will the others. Some, like Monster.com, are for-profit organizations that have been around for a while (in Internet terms) and have established themselves as quality sources of job openings. Others, like America's Job Bank, are run by government agencies and have quality openings and links to excellent publications. Others, like the *Chronicle of Higher Education*, are trade-specific and contain job openings somewhere amidst their trade content.

Another good source for job openings is via your local college or university's Web page. More and more schools are posting on their home pages the thousands of job listings they receive.

Many of these sites add an extra feature for the job seeker. In addition to including a database of jobs that you can search by job title, geographic area, salary, or other criteria, many of them allow you to post your resume and fill out some background information about yourself. This gives interested employers the opportunity to search the database by what *they* are looking for, and find *you*.

Disability-Related Sites

The following are just a few examples of the many disability-related Web sites that can provide job leads. To find more, type "disabilities employment" at any search engine.

Gateway Café

`http://www.gateway-cafe.com/jobsDisabilities.html`

Focusing on the Canadian market, this site offers links to multiple Ontario and other Canadian resources.

Careers and the DisABLED **Magazine**

`www.eop.com/cd.html`

This is the site for the nation's first and only career-guidance and recruitment magazine for people with disabilities. The site has sample articles from the magazine, job postings, a list of companies that are actively recruiting, and a database where you can post your resume.

JobAccess

`www.jobaccess.org`

This site, affiliated with CareerBuilder, specializes in opportunities for people with disabilities.

National Business and Disability Council

`www.business-disability.com/`

The NBDC is an organization for companies that recruit people with disabilities. Its site includes a section for job seekers where you can post your resume and search job listings from NBDC member companies.

Office of Disability Employment Policy

`www.dol.gov/odep/`

The ODEP is a small federal agency whose mission is to communicate, coordinate, and promote public and private efforts to enhance the employment of people with disabilities. Among the many resources on this site is the Job Accommodation Network, which provides information and support to individuals and companies looking for appropriate workplace accommodations for disabilities (see Chapter 13 for more information on JAN).

United Cerebral Palsy Employment and Training

`http://www.ucpnct.org/employment_services.html`

Look here for information about this organization that trains and places people with Cerebral Palsy. This site enables employers to post job leads.

Government-Sponsored Sites

America's Job Bank

`www.ajb.dni.us`

This site is the largest single source of job leads in the United States. It's run by the United States Department of Labor, in cooperation with job service offices from across the country. At the time of this writing, this site had close to 1.3 million job openings listed. America's Job Bank has very elaborate search options, including by job category (including military and other government opportunities), salary, state, or even within a specified distance of a certain ZIP code. This site also enables the job seeker to post a resume or brief background description that individual companies can search. At the time of this writing, this site contained the resumes of over 1.1 million job seekers.

DisabilityInfo.gov

`www.disabilityinfo.gov/`

This site was created by order of President George W. Bush as part of his New Freedom Initiative, which directed federal agencies to work together to build a one-stop interagency Web portal for people with disabilities, their families, employers, service providers, and other community members. This Web site provides a one-stop shop for disability-related information and programs available across the government on numerous subjects, including employment, education, housing, transportation, health, income support, technology, community life, and civil rights.

For-Profit Sites

These are commercial sites that offer job listings. Usually they are free for the job seeker to explore. They are supported through advertisements and through the fees paid by employers to list their openings.

CareerBuilder

`www.careerbuilder.com`

Begun as CareerMosaic, this site was one of the earliest for-profit organizations to begin offering services for job seekers over the Internet. This site gives the job seeker several different job-search–related articles, brief profiles of some individual employers, job postings, and an opportunity to post your own resume. You can search for openings by company, geographic area, and employment category.

FlipDog

`www.flipdog.com`

Billing itself as the Web's largest collection of jobs, FlipDog searches the employment pages of individual employer's sites, collects the postings, and allows you to search for them by category, geography, and keywords.

MonsterTrak

`www.monstertrak.com`

This service is marketed primarily through colleges and universities. It serves as an excellent source of job openings for people with a college education.

Monster.com

`www.monster.com`

Like CareerMosaic, Monster.com was an early entry into the online job bank game. They also provide job search information and the opportunity to post a resume or search for a job.

Trade Publications

Many professions are served by associations that publish information of mutual interest. In addition to journals that present research and express opinions, many of these professional associations also publish newsletters. These newsletters may carry stories of recent developments in the field, profiles of successful members, and other news. Often these newsletters also include a section in which job openings are advertised. Usually this is a vehicle to recruit people who have experience in the field; however, sometimes they will include an ad for an entry-level position. Here is a list of some professional associations for a few selected careers. For a more exhaustive list, ask a career counselor, or check the *Occupational Outlook Handbook* in print or at

www.bls.gov/oco/

Near the bottom of the listing you will find the heading "Sources of Additional Information." Here you will find a list of professional associations and trade publications.

Accounting

American Institute of Certified Public Accountants
Harborside Financial Center
201 Plaza III
Jersey City, NJ 07311-3881
www.aicpa.org

Auto Mechanics

Automotive Service Industry Association
25 Northwest Point
Elk Grove Village, IL 60007-1035

Purchasing

American Purchasing Society
30 W. Downer Pl.
Aurora, IL 60506
www.american-purchasing.com

Secretarial

Association of Administrative Professionals
P.O. Box 20404
Kansas City, MO 64195-0404
www.iaap-hq.org

Welders

American Welding Society
550 NW Lejeune Rd.
Miami, FL 33126-5699

CHAPTER 8

Managing Your Job Search

One of the great benefits of conducting a well-organized job search is that it prepares you for some of the demands that will be placed on you as a new employee. You need to be able to manage multiple tasks, maintain meticulous records, and carefully keep track of your own time. If you can do all of these things, you greatly increase your chances of finding the job that you are seeking, and of doing it in less time.

Tracking Contacts

Like all sales professionals, one of your greatest challenges will be to effectively manage the contacts that you have established. In Chapter 6, I showed you a sample contact management card for keeping track of your networking referrals. The same kind of card will also work for managing your other job-search contacts. If you choose to use these cards, put them in alphabetical order in a card-filing box. Create a second card for each organization at which you have a contact (purchase colored index cards for this purpose). This will enable you to find a person by their company name in the event that the person's name escapes you.

Your best bet is to complete these cards right after you get off the phone or leave your contact. This way you will be best able to capture and record the essence of the conversation. By logging the information on the card and on your contact log, you will be able to find the information you need later.

This kind of record-keeping is really quite easy if you are disciplined enough to do it right after each contact. This way you can easily transfer the information on the cards onto your calendar to remind you of when your next follow-up with that contact should be.

The frequency of contact for each individual will vary according to your relationship with them. You want to find the best time frame in which to stay in regular contact, but to not wear out your welcome. The best way to do this, of course, is to ask that person what they prefer. They will probably be happy to tell you how often they would be willing to speak with you, based on their perception of how likely it is that they will be able to help.

Time Management

In addition to the need to carefully manage your contacts, you also have to be very disciplined in terms of how you manage your time. Each person has different constraints on their time, but you need to make a conscious decision about how much time you are going to spend on your job search, and then stick to it. If at all possible, you should plan on spending at least forty hours a week looking for a job. This isn't always feasible, as you may already be employed. There is no easy substitution for the time spent on a task, however. If you spend only twenty or so hours a week on the job search, it may take you twice as long to find what you are looking for.

How you spend that time is at least as important as how much time you spend. Once you have set your time commitment, plan your week accordingly. For example, if you are currently working part time but you are pursuing full-time work, you will need to plan around your work schedule. Ideally, your part-time job would be flexible enough to allow you to search for jobs during the day, and then work nights. This is not always the case, however. So whatever your work schedule, that will necessarily be the first thing to go on your calendar.

Copy the following pages and put them in your binder. These forms will help you track your job-search–related activities. They will also give you an easy way to determine where you are in terms of the goals you have set for yourself.

APPOINTMENTS AND INTERVIEWS

	Monday	Results	Tuesday	Results
8:00am				
8:30				
9:00				
9:30				
10:00				
10:30				
11:00				
11:30				
12:00pm				
12:30				
1:00				
1:30				
2:00				
2:30				
3:00				
3:30				
4:00				
4:30				
5:00				
5:30				
6:00				
6:30				
7:00				
7:30				
8:00				
8:30				
9:00				
9:30				

continues

APPOINTMENTS AND INTERVIEWS

	Wednesday	Results	Thursday	Results
8:00am				
8:30				
9:00				
9:30				
10:00				
10:30				
11:00				
11:30				
12:00pm				
12:30				
1:00				
1:30				
2:00				
2:30				
3:00				
3:30				
4:00				
4:30				
5:00				
5:30				
6:00				
6:30				
7:00				
7:30				
8:00				
8:30				
9:00				
9:30				

APPOINTMENTS AND INTERVIEWS

	Friday	Results	Saturday	Results
8:00am				
8:30				
9:00				
9:30				
10:00				
10:30				
11:00				
11:30				
12:00pm				
12:30				
1:00				
1:30				
2:00				
2:30				
3:00				
3:30				
4:00				
4:30				
5:00				
5:30				
6:00				
6:30				
7:00				
7:30				
8:00				
8:30				
9:00				
9:30				

JOB-HUNTING ACTIVITIES

	Goal	Mon	Tue	Wed	Thur	Fri	Sat/Sun	Total
Phone calls made								
Information interviews								
Referrals gained								
Job interviews								
Resumes sent								

TIME USAGE IN HOURS

	Goal	Mon	Tue	Wed	Thur	Fri	Sat/Sun	Total
Classes/ studying								
Prospecting								
Personal/ social								
Job interviews								
Other specific activities								

RESUME/CORRESPONDENCE LOG

Date	Company	Contact	Source	Response	Follow up

continues

RESUME/CORRESPONDENCE LOG

Date	Company	Contact	Source	Response	Follow up

RESUME/CORRESPONDENCE LOG

Date	Company	Contact	Source	Response	Follow up

PHONE LOG

Date	Name/title	Company	Results	Follow-up date	√

PHONE LOG

Date	Name/title	Company	Results	Follow-up date	√

Goal Setting and Record Keeping

For advice on how to best approach the goal-setting process, ask any salesperson how *they* do it. Most successful salespeople follow a few simple rules that help them accomplish their goals:

- **Have a goal.** This goal should be something you are striving for, something concrete.

- **Visualize that goal.** Picture yourself successfully accomplishing your goal. How do you feel? What are you doing? What do you see around you? What do you hear?

- **Break down the goal into the steps that you need to take to accomplish it.** Be conservative in your estimation. For example, if a salesperson wants to sell a vacuum cleaner, he or she may have to sit down with 50 people to show them the product. To sit down with 50 people, the salesperson will need to get 150 people to return cards that offer them a free rug cleaning if they agree to see a demonstration. To get 150 people to send back the card, the salesperson may need to make 1,000 calls and send out 2,000 letters with the cards enclosed.

- **Have a deadline.** Have a realistic yet aggressive time frame in which to achieve your goal. In the above scenario, if the salesperson sets a goal of selling one vacuum cleaner a week, he or she needs to mail 400 letters and make 200 phone calls a day.

- **Plan your work and work your plan.** Once you have broken down your goal into the steps you need to take to meet that goal, you need to follow that plan. If you do not meet your day's numbers, don't get discouraged. Just increase your effort the following day. If you focus your attention on the details, the big things will fall into place.

- **Recalibrate along the way.** Engineers will tell you that "smart bombs"— those missiles that can be aimed toward a chimney a continent away—are off course 90 percent of the time. What makes these bombs so successful is that they are constantly being recalibrated: If they are off by a hair to the north, they will readjust for a hair to the south, and so on. You need to do the same thing. Experiment. If you find that you are not succeeding in the interviews you get, practice (more on this in Chapter 10). If your cover letters and resumes are not generating interest, look for feedback from your mentor and/or networking contacts and adjust them accordingly.

Time Management and the Job Search

Use a calendar like the one presented on pages 141–143, or use one of the time-management software packages such as Outlook, Lotus Agenda, Day-Timer, and so on. These packages are great because they integrate your contact information with the calendar functions you need to have—eliminating the need for index cards.

Break down your goal into what it's going to take to get you there. You may receive two offers from less-than-perfect matches before you get the offer you want. It may take you 20 interviews to get one offer. You may need to send out 50 resumes to qualified leads to get an interview. That adds up to 3,000 resumes sent to get you the job you want. Now, before you get discouraged, the more time you spend on networking and qualifying your leads, the more you can whittle these numbers down to something manageable. Still, it is best to set a manageable goal and strive to achieve it. If you achieve your end result sooner, all the better for you!

It may take, on average, in the neighborhood of three to eight months to find a job, depending on the field and the region in which you live. Assuming that your search takes six months, this translates to 500 resumes and 10 interviews a month. This breaks down further to around 125 resumes and between two and three interviews a week.

The two hardest parts about this effort will be generating these *qualified* leads and staying upbeat throughout. Looking for a job can be physically and mentally draining. It's easy to feel down on a day that you don't generate an interview. It's even easier to feel down if you have an interview that doesn't go well. Feeling down, of course, only hinders your ability to generate leads and to perform well in interviews, and you begin a vicious cycle.

To stay upbeat, you have to look at this as a long-term process. If you need to send out 3,000 resumes and make 3,000 phone calls in order to get to the 60 interviews you need, that means that you may experience 2,940 responses of "No." So, make up a tally sheet that starts with 2,940 and goes down to zero. For each "No" you get, cross off a number. This way, each time you receive a negative reaction, you have a positive feeling because you know it is bringing you closer to your goal.

Beat the Odds

As I said before, the odds can change in either direction, depending on a lot of factors. The odds will be against you if you write a poor resume or if you do not do well in interviews. You need to keep on top of these skills by working with a career counselor or people in your network, role-playing interview situations, and reviewing your resume and cover letters. These activities can shift the odds in your favor.

Don't Overlook the Smaller Companies

Your choice of job-search methods can also improve your odds. Many people conduct their job search in the same way. They will seek out contacts and look for opportunities with the major employers in their area. Someone from Detroit, Michigan will look first to the automobile industry and to some of the major banks in town and focus their efforts there. It stands to reason that a company with 5,000 employees will be more likely to have an opening than a company with 50 employees.

While this may seem to be true, it is a statistical fact that most new jobs are created in small to medium-sized companies. The majority of people in the economy work for employers with fewer than 500 employees. In fact, more than two-thirds of Americans work in companies with fewer than 250 employees, according to the Department of Labor. This trend may only grow in the coming years, as the hottest companies today include many that were not even in existence five years ago. Companies like Amazon.com, Yahoo!, and others were, very recently, start-ups with only a few, if any, salaried employees. Many smaller companies, when they are successful, grow at an exponential rate. Bigger, Fortune 500 companies tend to grow at a much smaller (percentage-wise) and slower pace.

Don't Forget the Not-for-Profits

Looking at the potential for jobs in sectors of the economy that you had not considered can help your prospects immensely. Many job seekers overlook the not-for-profit sector altogether. The higher profiles of the larger, for-profit companies tend to obscure the not-for-profit organizations in an area. Most not-for-profits do not spend a great deal on advertising, and many do not have flashy offices or high visibility within the general community. The fact is, however, not-for-profits are a significant portion of the employment market within most communities. They hire specialists in their area, as well as receptionists, accountants, secretaries, executive directors, and people from various backgrounds.

Check your local United Way office to get a listing of not-for-profit community-service organizations in your area. Most community-service agencies are more "person-centered" and are also more likely to be able to see past a disability to the person inside.

Consider Government Jobs

Another overlooked part of the economy is the government sector—federal, state, and local. Although there has been pressure in recent years to change this fact, government is the largest single employer in many communities across the country. The fact that the government hires people to fill jobs from every employment group imaginable (auditors, barbers, marching band conductors, curators, registrars, librarians, and so on), and the fact that there are so many different levels of government and types of governmental agencies, makes this sector too good to ignore.

It is also true that government has consistently been more likely to hire people with disabilities, often aggressively pursuing people with disabilities for various positions.

CHAPTER 9
Applying for Jobs

There are four basic ways to apply for a job, three of which have already been discussed in this book. The most effective way is to speak face to face with the person who is making the hiring decision and ask for the job. The second way is to write a cover letter and resume and send them to someone at the organization where you want to work. The third way is to apply online. The fourth way is to fill out a formal job application from the employer.

Networking

As was discussed earlier, if you can get someone you know to introduce you to a hiring manager, or to give his or her permission to use his or her name when speaking to a hiring manager, you will increase immensely your chances of being hired.

Whenever you can eliminate a middleman, it will be to your advantage. Each person who has to look at your application before it is passed on to the hiring manager is in a position to remove you from consideration. Each person who conveys a message will likely filter that message somehow before they pass the message along to the next person. You may have written an excellent cover letter, but it may be separated from the resume by the first person who sees it, only to end up in a pile of papers to be discarded. When that middleman works for human resources, you face the additional challenge of overcoming their misinformation about the position, as well as their own preconceptions and prejudices about you as a candidate.

By going directly to the person who will make the ultimate decision of whether or not to hire you, you can remove those obstacles to your success. That's one of the reasons why people are generally far more successful using networking methods than by replying to ads in the newspaper. Employers value those employees who network as well. Some companies will post "bounties" (cash rewards) for their employees to collect if they suggest a person as a potential employee, and that person is hired. From the company's perspective, if they feel good about having you work for them, the odds are pretty good that they will feel good about having your friend work there, too.

One great opportunity designed to help people with disabilities in their networking is Disability Mentoring Day. Co-sponsored by the Business Leadership Network, the American Association of People with Disabilities, and the U.S. Department of Labor Office of Disability Employment Policy, this event connects people from business and industry with people with disabilities who aspire to obtain employment. The event is held in the fall of each year. Check the Web site of any of the organizations mentioned above for details.

Sending a Resume and Cover Letter

A well-written cover letter and resume can be very helpful in getting you an interview for a job. It is a bit of a numbers game, because depending on the type of position and the job market in that area, there could be anywhere from a dozen to several hundred resumes submitted for any given position. Still, if you have the qualifications that they are looking for, and if you have a background that would be appropriate for the position, there is a chance that you will be invited to at least have a phone interview with the organization.

Obviously, it doesn't always work out that way. If there are a hundred applicants for a position, there may be 20 to 40 who don't meet the minimum qualifications for the position. That leaves 60 to 80 people who *are* qualified. Obviously, the company will not interview every qualified candidate. At this point the employer will go through the remaining resumes and decide which ones are *most* qualified. This might mean that someone with three years experience will be chosen over someone who has two years. It may mean that someone with a degree from Canisius College will be passed over in favor of someone with a degree from Notre Dame. Or, it could mean that someone with a degree from Harvard will be passed over for someone with a degree from the University of Scranton if the person screening the resumes has a degree from the University of Scranton.

The point is that you just never know what's going to happen to your resume. In fact, you may never know. Chances are, however, that if you went to school with the daughter of the president of the company, you will increase your chances of being in the "to be interviewed" pile if she puts in a good word for you. You will also increase your chances if you list a well-respected employee of that company in your references or refer to that person in your cover letter. This is the point at which "who you know" pays off most. At this point, any single intangible can tip the scales in your favor.

Applying Online

Many companies give you the opportunity to apply for a job directly on their Web site. You fill in a brief form outlining your qualifications for the position and click on the Submit button. At that point, your information is sent along to a human resources or personnel office to be evaluated and forwarded in the appropriate way. Usually you will receive some sort of automated response via e-mail to acknowledge that your application was received.

You can sometimes apply for positions on some of the job banks described in Chapter 7. By using that sort of site, you are going through an intermediary who will then forward all the applicants in one package to the employer. Unless the site belongs to an employment agency, it is unlikely that they would screen your application and discard it.

Filling Out a Written Application Form

Many larger organizations will have printed application forms that will seek to collect certain information about your background and your qualifications for the position. These forms are usually available at the company's office or can be requested via the mail.

The same rules that apply when you're writing a resume apply when you're filling out an application. In fact, filling out a job application can be even more demanding than preparing a resume. With this in mind, it's probably to your advantage to have the application mailed to you, or to pick it up in person and then take it home to fill it out. This may not be possible in all situations, so be prepared by bringing one or two black pens (preferably the erasable kind).

There is one thing you should keep in mind as you fill out an application: They are written exactly the way they are for a reason—to easily quantify who should be selected (or not selected) for a position. Having said that, the following are some guidelines for filling out applications.

Be Meticulous

If you write like I do, it is definitely to your advantage to take the application home and type it. Poor handwriting can obscure what you are trying to communicate, and that can never be to your advantage. Also, be sure that you read the application carefully. Any error at all can take your application out of the running.

Don't Be Too Wordy

Applications have limited space available for you to answer each question. Because of this, you need to really "sharpen your pencil" and make sure that you are including only the absolutely most important information.

Beware of Traps

Some questions are more likely to rule you out of a position than others. One of those is "Salary Requirements." As we will discuss in Chapter 11, salary negotiations are a delicate dance. It is usually the person who blinks first, by mentioning a figure, who loses. If your requirement is too high, you might cost yourself the opportunity to show the employer why you would be worth such a figure. If your number is too low, you lose out on those dollars, and you might eliminate yourself from consideration because of the "Kmart factor": If your price is that low, you can't possibly be worthy of our company. I would suggest answering this question with a response like "Open for discussion."

Other traps include questions about criminal history, health conditions, and reasons for leaving a previous employer. It should go without saying that you should never be dishonest—not on your resume, and not on an application. If that weren't reason enough, lying on an application can be grounds for dismissal in and of itself. I recognize that there are times, however, when a simple yes or no answer cannot adequately explain your situation. Perhaps you have a conviction for disorderly conduct because you were one of a hundred people who "failed to disperse" after your hometown team won the Stanley Cup. If you caused no damage, and were just waiting for the team to leave the building to show your appreciation, it is unlikely that an employer would hold it against you. In a case like this it may be to your advantage to write "see attached" or "see other side" and then either ask for a sheet of paper or write on a blank side of the application form the circumstances surrounding your criminal record. Keep in mind that you are not required to disclose an arrest record, only a criminal conviction.

In the case of questions about your health, you need to have considered the requirements for the position as well as your abilities to perform those functions. If these two variables are a match, respond "Excellent" to any query regarding your health. Regardless of whether you have diabetes or high blood pressure, if it will not interfere with your job, and if it's currently mitigated with medication or other means, you will not put yourself in danger by responding that your health is excellent. The question itself is not only ambiguous to the point of being meaningless, it may also, depending on how it is used, be an illegal question to ask.

Describing the circumstances under which you left your previous employer can also be quite difficult. Simply listing "wanted more money" will not put you in the most favorable light with a potential employer—and it may suggest that you would be well served by an appointment with a career counselor. Nor, of course, will listing "fired" too many times on an application. Instead, write that a position was not a good fit for you, and then describe the circumstances in greater detail in an interview if necessary. Keep in mind that at some point the prospective employer may make inquiries with past employers before making you a firm offer, so avoid saying things that your employer would be able to contradict.

Improving Your Chances of Getting the Job

There is no reason to avoid any of the four ways to apply for a job. Although the "closing percentage" (the likelihood of your getting the job) increases if you use the first method, plenty of people have gotten jobs using the other three methods as well. In fact, you would be well advised to use every method at your disposal. Time permitting, anything that you do to get your candidacy known by an employer is time well spent.

The fact remains, however, that too many people think of their career as an object that you can have, rather than as what it really is—a series of connections with people. People hire people the same way they choose baby-sitters, hairstylists, stockbrokers, etc.: They pick those people they are comfortable with. It's only natural to feel more comfortable if you can take into account the opinion(s) of those you trust. There is absolutely nothing wrong with using this fact to your advantage if possible.

If your friend or networking contact gives you a great recommendation, it may help you get an interview with that organization. Once you get the interview, however, it's up to you. You will win the job yourself, or they will decide that some other candidate is more qualified. If you use networking, and if you hone your interviewing skills (see Chapter 10), you will be in a much better position to win the job.

CHAPTER 10

Preparing for the Interview

Your hard work will eventually begin to show results in the form of invitations to interviews. Now you can breathe easily because you've finally made it, right? Of course not. There are several chapters left in the book! This is the time when you need to redouble your efforts in order to succeed. When you get an interview, this usually means that you have made it into a small group of three to twelve people who are being considered for the position. Even under the best of circumstances, those are not the kind of odds that you can use as collateral at the bank. Because you have been invited to interview, you know that you have shown that you are qualified for the position. Now you need to prove that you are the *best* person for the position.

At this point the stakes are raised, because you know that the other two or eleven people are also qualified for the job. The decision about who will get the job will now come down to who the interviewers believe will be the *best fit* for the organization—who is the best prepared, who is the most likeable, who seems the most capable, and who is most likely to have the kind of personality that will mesh with the people who already work there.

Several times in this book I have compared the job search to a marketing or sales effort. Here it comes again! What makes you feel most comfortable buying a product? Some of the factors relate directly to the product itself, and some relate to the way that the product is sold. There are hundreds of brands of cigarettes, most made by just a handful of companies. With the exception of a billionth of a milligram of menthol here, or a charcoal versus a plain filter there, the ingredients of cigarettes are pretty much the same. You couldn't tell that by watching smokers purchase them, however. How many commercials have you seen in which a construction worker ambles up to the counter and requests a carton of Virginia

Slims? Or a debutante saunters up to the counter in a ball gown and asks for a pack of Luckies? Or some guy in a Mercedes offers his lady one of those generic cigarettes? Each brand is specifically targeted to a particular segment of the population. How a product is marketed makes all the difference in the world in how it is sold.

I'm no techie, but friends who are swear that in the early days the Apple computer had a far superior operating system than the PC did. Everyone seems to agree that Beta was superior technology to VHS. The moral of the story is that the superior product is not always the one that sells the most, and the corollary is that the best person for the job does not always get the job. Usually the person who is best prepared for the interview does.

Doing Your Research

By doing your homework, you can prepare yourself for the interview. You should become familiar with the major trends that are occurring in the field. You will want to know if the field is growing or contracting, as well as which companies or organizations have been doing well and which have not. You also need to research the individual company. How are things going for them? And whenever possible, it helps to know a little something about the person who will be conducting the interview. What are her priorities? What is her background? By answering as many of these questions as you can, you will be more confident and more prepared during your interview.

Researching the Field

Way back when you were in the midst of your self-exploration and assessment, and when you were exploring the world of work, you did a great deal of research into various jobs and career fields. You looked through the *O*NET Dictionary of Occupational Titles* and the *Occupational Outlook Handbook,* you contacted professional associations, and you spoke with individuals who were employed in the field. Go back to your notes and refresh your memory. If it's been a while since you initially did this research, use the Internet to see if there is any new information out there on this topic. Reread enough so that you feel confident in your understanding of the field in which you want to work.

You should also go back to those people whom you interviewed as you were gathering information. Let them know that you have been granted an interview, and see if they have any suggestions for you. They may be able to update you on significant new developments in the field that would be helpful for you to know and perhaps make reference to during the interview.

Researching the Company

I'm assuming that you have already done some amount of research on a company if you have applied for a position there. Hopefully you have kept your notes, because they will be a good starting point for you. You will now need to switch into full "fact-finding" mode. It is to your advantage to go into an interview with as much information about a company as possible. There are many sources of this kind of information, all with different values.

Company Public Relations Literature

Almost all organizations produce some sort of literature that is intended to inform the public about that organization or the products or services that they offer. Larger companies that are publicly held (their shares are sold on a public stock exchange) will publish an annual report that is sent to stockholders to update them on the recent developments within the company.

If the company doesn't publish an annual report, they may at least be required to file financial disclosure agreements with the Securities and Exchange Commission. You can view these reports at most public libraries. When looking at these reports, or at an annual report, there are certain things that you should be looking for. Has the company been growing in terms of sales, revenues, or earnings? Is the company's market share growing in their product areas?

If you find that a company is in a stagnant period, or even if they have experienced recent losses, that should not necessarily scare you off. Some of the hottest companies to work for and to own stock in are companies that have yet to post a profitable year. It is advisable to have an understanding of how the company is doing, in the event that this comes up in an interview.

Besides the financial statements, a company's sales brochures can provide a wealth of information as well. These publications will give you the key selling points that distinguish a company's goods or services from those of other companies. They will inform you of what new products or services are being launched, improved, or replaced. You can get these by simply calling the sales department and having them mailed to you.

Public Relations Materials from Competing Organizations or Product Lines

It will also be worth your while to collect what information you can about the competition. If the company you are interviewing with makes a nondairy creamer, look around and see what other products are available that serve the same need. Collect whatever information you can about the companies that make those products. How are those companies doing? Are they growing? Are they launching any new products or improving the existing ones? The better you understand the interviewer's business, the better able you will be to frame your answers within the context of the actual circumstances under which you would be working.

News Accounts

It is quite possible that the organization with which you will be interviewing has been in the news, either locally or in a national publication, in the recent past. If you visit your local public library, you should find back issues of the local newspaper, as well as an index of stories that have appeared in the past year. Most big-city newspapers will have a Web page where you can search back issues of the paper online. The same is true for most major magazines. This service is sometimes limited to subscribers, in which case the library would be your best bet.

Third-Party Publishers

There are many organizations that publish directories of information on hundreds of corporations. These publications usually offer an abbreviated collection of information about many companies. At the very least, this information will give you a broad overview of the type of business the company is in, the performance of the company's stock, recent developments, and who some of the key players are. While these books can be helpful for giving you a thumbnail sketch of a big corporation, you usually cannot find information about smaller companies in these kinds of publications. One excellent resource that many libraries subscribe to is CareerSearch. This online database provides information on the company (sales, revenues, number of employees, etc.), lists key contacts within the company, and also lists major competitors. Check your local library or nearby college career center to see whether they subscribe.

Some other sources for this kind of information include the following:

Dun & Bradstreet's Million Dollar Directory

Fortune Magazine's 500

Hoover's Handbook (various editions)

Macmillan's Directory of Leading Private Companies

Standard & Poor's Reports

Vault Reports

On the Internet

Many Web sites on the Internet provide information about various companies. In addition to some of the on-line versions of the resources mentioned earlier, check out the following site:

Hoover's Online

`www.hoovers.com`

Also, many *search engines* are available for you to search the Internet by company name, which will possibly help you discover the company's own Web site, if they have one:

AltaVista

`www.altavista.com`

Excite

`www.excite.com`

Google

`www.google.com`

Infoseek

`www.infoseek.com`

Lycos

www.lycos.com

Yahoo!

www.yahoo.com

After you have used these search engines, you will begin to get more comfortable with some of them than with the others. Choose one or two and get to know them well. Focus on how to use their search procedures to limit your searches and make the site most useful for the way you think.

Networking Contacts

Obviously, a great source of information about a company is a person who currently works for the company. If you have a networking contact who works for the company you will be interviewing with, contact that person and let them know that you have been granted an interview. The contact may be willing to spend a little time with you and give you some inside information that will make you better prepared for the interview.

If you don't have a networking contact within the organization, now is a good time to establish one. Make contact with some of your first ring of supporters and let them know that you have an interview. Ask if they know anyone in that company whom you might be able to call. The person does not have to work in the same department in which you are applying for a job to be able to give you valuable information. Any employee who works with the organization will be able to give you a feel for its culture and what you will need to know to survive in it.

Researching the Recruiter/Interviewer

One of the things that your networking contacts can help you with is information about the person or people who will be conducting your interview. Just knowing whether it is likely to be an interview with an individual or with a group is helpful as you prepare for the interview. After you have been invited to interview, it's a good idea to make a point to gather some specific information. You should find out exactly what time you need to be there. You should also see if you can get an estimate of how much time you should plan to be at the site. (Some interviews last a half hour, while others can last several hours over a couple of days.)

You should find out where they suggest that you park. If they suggest a lot that is part of the organization, ask if you will need a guest permit, or if there are particular spots dedicated to visitors. The trend of having visitor spaces close to the door may answer your need for close parking without indicating that fact prior to the interview. Having asked these simple questions, you might then ask if the person can give you the name of the person who will be conducting the interview. You may also ask if it will be with just that individual, or if it will be with a group. (If the interview will last longer than an hour, it is likely that there will be other people involved in the interviewing process.)

Accessibility Issues

If you believe that your disability may impact your ability to physically get to the interview, or if you will need any accommodations in order to do your best *in the interview,* I believe that it is to your advantage to raise the issue while you are asking the questions above.

If you use a wheelchair, the last thing you will want is to arrive at the site and find that you can't get to the interview location because it is inaccessible. Remember, human resources offices are often involved in the scheduling of interviews, and their location is not always central in an organization. If you raise this issue directly, the employer will be able to make the appropriate a rrangements ahead of time. This ensures that you won't end up wasting precious interview time trying to figure out a way to get up a loading dock.

You may want to bring up other issues as well. I believe that you will be better off by informing the employer up front that you use a guide dog or some other form of assistance. You have already secured the interview, and they are going to learn this information soon, so it's better to have them receive the information in a way over which you have more control. You could say "Just so you know, I have a guide dog named Jessie. She is a beautiful yellow Lab, but some people are a little thrown off when they see her. If you could let Ms. Interviewer know ahead of time, I would appreciate it. I don't want her to feel caught off guard." This approaches the topic gently, and doesn't make a huge deal out of it. Having addressed it already will take away some measure of the awkwardness of the first few minutes of the meeting. And it's during those first few minutes that so many lasting judgements are made.

You have to feel comfortable with what you are going to say to the employer, but in most cases I counsel people with visible disabilities to share that information in some way at the point when they have been invited to interview and are making arrangements for that visit. I have worked with many clients who have been happier handling it this way. I had a client with significant scarring from facial burns who informed the employer ahead of time: "I just want to let you know that I was in a major car accident last year, and I got banged up pretty badly. I had some pretty severe burns. I don't get mistaken for Christie Brinkley, but everything has healed, and I am anxious for the chance to get to work for a company like yours."

Another client asked the secretary who was setting up his interview if the person conducting the interview had a moustache. The secretary hesitated and replied "No…." He then explained that he had a hearing impairment, and that sometimes it was hard for him to understand what a person was saying if they had a moustache. He had a great self-deprecating sense of humor, and he seemed to win this secretary over right away. When the interview came, the interviewer reacted the way many people do when they encounter a person with a disability: He spoke more slowly and more loudly. As time went on, he spoke more and more normally, and it was then that the client knew that he had won the interviewer over. The interview was for an internship, which he got. It turned into full-time employment when he finished his schooling.

Most people I have worked with have had to spend some time building up their assertiveness in order to do this. Some people have tried it and failed, mostly because of the difficulty in addressing this issue directly. In most cases, however, clients have told me that discussing it up front, although tough at first, was far better than getting "that look" when they first met their interviewer. No one has told me yet of an instance where an interview offer was rescinded after they disclosed their disability in a conversation about the specifics of their interview date, etc.

This advice is strongly suggested really only for those people whose disability is likely to at least have the potential to impact the interview itself. It is somewhat less emphatically suggested for those people whose disability is visible but is not likely to impact the interview directly. As I mentioned before, however, even if the disability is only visible (loss of a limb, and so on), there still is some advantage to allowing the interviewer to assimilate that information before the interview, so that you can reduce the awkwardness of those first few seconds.

Rehearsing for the Interview

There are a few things you should do before you actually enter your job interview, all of which should help prepare you and eliminate some of your anxieties. If possible, take a drive to the interview site. See if there isn't a place nearby where you will be able to relax before the interview, like a coffee shop, fast-food restaurant, or even one of those bookstores with comfortable chairs. See how long it takes you to get there, and then plan to arrive 45 minutes early on the day of the interview and spend a little time at the coffee shop composing your thoughts and relaxing. This way, if you run into a little bit of traffic, you will know that you have a cushion, and you can relax.

The same is true if you are going to use public transportation. Get a copy of the schedules for the trains or buses you will need to take. Plan your schedule so that if each train or bus you need to take is one behind, you will still make it there thirty minutes ahead of time. Make sure that paratransit is available if appropriate.

The last thing that you want is to go into an interview frazzled, and nothing will upset you more than waiting in construction traffic as you watch the seconds tick away, knowing that you are going to be late. It starts you out on the wrong foot, and it puts you in a frame of mind that doesn't come across well in an interview.

Practice, Practice, Practice

If you have done all of your research into the company, the field, and the recruiter, and if you took seriously the challenge of assessing your own skills and abilities, you will be able to go into the interview knowing that you would be a great fit for this position. The next most important thing you can do to increase your chances of doing well in a job interview is to practice your skills ahead of time. Know what it is that makes you a great candidate for this position, and be prepared to state that in as many ways as possible. Remember, everyone who is interviewing is presumably qualified to do the job. The question on the interviewer's mind is going to be twofold: Who can do the job best, and who is the best fit?

Of course, if your disability is visible to the interviewer, there is an additional question, which puts you at a disadvantage. Quite often, the interviewer will begin to question our first assumption—that everyone who is interviewing is qualified for the position. Consciously or subconsciously, the interviewer may begin to wonder *how* you can do the job. You will definitely need to perform much better than the other candidates just to be considered at par with them. We don't have to look far for inspiration, however. Spud Webb was a great NBA player at 5'7". Jim Abbott is a great Major League Baseball pitcher with one arm. And heck, Lyle Lovett was married to Julia Roberts! Chances are, however, that you don't have to look too far past yourself, and to the obstacles you may have already overcome, to get yourself where you are today. Focus on giving examples of how you have already performed many or all the functions that will be required of you in this position— either in past positions, internships, or in other settings.

In addition to the ability question, a person with a visible disability will also have to deal with a magnified version of the second overarching question: Will this person fit in? Your ability to put the interviewer at ease quickly and to focus on you rather than on your disability will be the key to your success. This is no small challenge, and it is why it's imperative that you perform extremely well in the interview.

With that in mind, you have to prepare yourself to answer questions that you can anticipate being asked. Write out responses if it helps you, but be ready to use each question as an opportunity to sell yourself to the employer. When you are actually in the interview, just as important as your answers to the questions will be how much you really understand what the questioner is asking. While some questions may seem fairly straightforward, most questions have at least a couple of sub-questions built into them. As you shape your answer, pay as much attention to addressing the sub-question(s) as you do to the question itself.

The best way to prepare yourself for your interviews is to practice. The best way to practice is in front of a video camera in the presence of either a career planning professional or a person who conducts interviews on a regular basis. This is particularly helpful the nearer you are to the interview. Prior to this, you can practice on your own with a tape recorder. The earlier practice sessions will give you the opportunity to hone your answers. The videotaped session will give you a feeling for how you appear during the interview.

This objective viewpoint can help you determine whether you appear relaxed, confident, and engaging, or whether you appear nervous, introverted, and bashful. You can then repeat the exercise, this time being conscious of your mannerisms and nonverbal cues. As you practice your interviewing skills, your confidence will become more and more evident, and you will be able to position yourself in the most positive way possible.

Disclosing Your Disability

If your disability is visible, your interviewer may have questions about your ability to do the job. You should be prepared for these questions, and you can do that by first making contact with the Job Accommodation Network. With information about the nature of the job and your disability, the professionals at the Job Accommodation Network can help you determine which accommodations will be helpful to you in performing the functions of the job. We'll discuss job accommodations and the JAN in more detail in Chapter 13.

If your disability is visible, it is best to address it directly early on in the interview. Because human nature is what it is, a failure to disclose the visible disability may result in the interviewer going through the motions, trying to be careful not to break any laws, but focusing less on your answers. It is better to address the disability up front, point out that it will not impact your ability to perform the functions of the job, or that it will require only minimal accommodations. Although there is no guarantee, this approach is your best bet at getting the interviewer's attention focused where you want it—on your ability to do the job.

If your disability is not visible, it is up to you as to when or if you ever disclose it. In most cases, I have advised clients to wait until after an offer is extended to disclose any disability. After you have agreed upon the terms of employment and have established a starting date, you should mention any accommodations you may need so that the employer can have them in place for you when you start. If your disability is not visible and you do not need any accommodations at this point, there is no reason to discuss the disability at all. While some clients have felt "dishonest" about this approach, the truth is that, unfortunately, discrimination still exists, and the more you give the people around you the chance to get to know the real you, the less likely they will hold on to prejudicial attitudes when they do find out about your disability.

Guidelines for Interviewing

Regardless of the questions asked, there are a few guidelines you should follow that will help you present a more positive answer to any question.

Listen Closely

If you are unsure of what the exact question is, restate it for the interviewer to see whether you understand it correctly. You don't want to restate every question asked, but you are better off restating the question than answering a question that was not asked.

Keep It Short and Simple

I mentioned the Dale Carnegie method of public speaking before. I have seen people give great, memorable talks that lasted less than two minutes. Only the most elaborate or technical competency-based question should take you the full two minutes or longer.

Have a Pre-Planned Message

Before you begin the interview, try to determine the two or three things that make you the best candidate for the position. Then make sure you drive home those points throughout the interview.

Use Examples

It's one thing to say that you have excellent leadership skills; it is far better to describe how you were the captain of the rugby team that won the state finals, or that you organized and led a Habitat for Humanity corps at your last place of employment that rehabbed three properties in the past year. An example paints a picture in the interviewer's mind, as opposed to a simple answer that may even risk sounding like a cliché—"I'm a *people person.*"

Find a Way to Work Your Message into the Answer

Take a page from the playbook of the politicians (but not the full page). Pay attention to the next political debate you see between two or more candidates. They are, in fact, interviewing for the same job, and the voters are the search committee. The successful ones usually answer a question with a mini-speech that they have given before. It may or may not have anything to do with the question that was asked. They may start out as if they are going to answer the question but quickly segue to their memorized speech.

That method actually can be quite irritating, and it wouldn't work well in a real interview because the interviewer would then just follow it up with the same question. What does work well is to answer the question in full, but then use a rehearsed example that illustrates the point you made. When possible, use an example that also underscores one of your theme messages.

Don't Be Afraid to Pause!

Although it may seem like minutes if you are nervous, take a good breath and wait about five seconds before launching into your answer. It will give you a chance to synthesize the question and begin formulating an answer. It will also show that you are thinking about your answer and not giving some memorized response. If you are having trouble formulating a response, don't be afraid to take a somewhat longer pause. Some people jump right into speaking before they know what they are going to say, and it seems forced and is often rife with fillers such as um, you know, and uhhh. You are much better off pausing and knowing what you want to say than demonstrating that you don't. Pauses in speech are quite natural, but in the pressure of an interview, every second feels like five. Relax!

Resist the Urge to Start Formulating Your Answers While the Interviewer is Still Asking the Question

This is really only a slight variation on the *listen closely* guideline. Too many people begin to tune out when they *think* they know what question is going to be asked. This is usually the result of nervousness manifesting itself as overeagerness. The problem is that if you are right, and you did know exactly what the interviewer was going to ask, you still appear impatient and give the interviewer the feeling that you aren't listening. Think of how many times you have talked with people and gotten the feeling that they were waiting for you to take a single pause so that they could respond—not to what you were saying, but with some point that *they* wanted to make. Worse, if you were wrong, and the interviewer was going to ask a different question, you will seem less intelligent as you answer a different question. Then you will take up precious interview time as the interviewer asks the same question a different way. Either way, you are worse off than if you just waited.

Sample Interview Questions

Although each interviewer is different, with different styles, some questions are common in job interviews. By practicing these, you will feel more confident in the event that the interviewer asks a variation of one of them.

Standard, Commonly Asked Questions

- Tell me a little about yourself.

- Why should I hire you?

- What kind of leader are you?

- What kind of team player are you?

- What is your greatest strength?

- What is your biggest weakness?

- Tell me about your most recent position.

- Why did you leave your last job?

- What makes you interested in this position?

- What do you know about our organization?

- Where do you see yourself in five years?

- What would your dream job be like?

- What kind of salary are you looking for?

Not as Common, but Asked Frequently Enough to Include

- Who are your heroes?

- What book do you have on your nightstand?

- What was the last movie you went to see?

- Tell me about a time when you had to break the rules to get something done.

- Which three adjectives would your friends use to describe you?

- Which three adjectives would your past employer use to describe you?

- Tell me how you deal with irrational people.

Competency-Based Questions

- If you have a cleaning solution of ammonia and bleach, what agent should be added as a grease cutter?

- If you were building a bridge across a river with a swift current, would you use a suspension design or concrete pilings?

- Which theory provides the basis for how you do your work?

- If a patient presents an arrhythmia with no sign of myocardial infarction, what diagnostic steps would you take?

Problem Questions

- How will you be able to do the job?

- Why are you interested in (qualified for) this job at this stage of your career?

- Can you explain this gap on your resume when you were not working?

Most of the questions in the commonly asked section seem pretty straightforward. However, they too have a subtext that gets to a question that the interviewer wants to ask but that is either illegal or uncomfortable for them to ask. It's up to you, then, to decide how much information you want to share with them.

Sample Answers for the Most Commonly Asked Questions

Although you shouldn't rehearse these answers to the point that you have them memorized, it may help to consider how the questions *could* be answered. Obviously, your answers will be different, depending on your background, but focus on the elements of the answer for clues as to how you might approach the question.

Tell me a little about yourself.

This question is part icebreaker, part opportunity for the interviewer to see how you handle yourself and ambiguity. Hidden in this question are questions like "How confident is this individual?" "What does he or she value?" "How does he or she present himself or herself?"

One possible answer might be:

> *I have a degree in accounting and five years experience as a tax preparer with H&R Block. My wife and I have been married for ten years and we are both very*

active in the community. I have been the chair of the church finance committee for the past two years, and the volunteer coordinator for the Cystic Fibrosis walk for the past three years. We live in Bloomington with our two children.

This answer shows that the respondent is well-rounded and contains a combination of information of a personal, professional, and community nature. It also stresses a few positive traits: education, longevity at a place of employment, stability, volunteerism, and leadership. And all in under 30 seconds!

Why should I hire you?

This question gives you the chance to convince the interviewer that you are the person for the job. It also gives a good indication of your self-confidence, your understanding of yourself and of the position, and some idea of how much you want the position.

You might respond:

I believe that I have a great combination of an excellent education, where I earned outstanding grades, as well as a record of directly related work experience, in which I have received glowing evaluations for working hard and being a constant and eager learner. When you couple these assets with the fact that I have overcome considerable adversity in order to get where I am today, the result is a can-do guy with the tools and the attitude to make a positive impact right from the first day.

This question is almost certain to be asked in one form or another, and usually toward the end of the interview. Answering like this is a great way to present a memorable thirty-second commercial for your candidacy. This sample answer spells out some significant strengths and also helps turn a potential perceived negative into a positive.

What kind of leader are you?
What kind of team player are you?

"Yes-men" come pretty cheaply, but a more valuable find is a person who can take on a project and see it through to a successful completion. Employers look for signs that you will be able to work in a way that gets results. Sometimes this calls for a person to exert leadership and bring the work of many toward a common goal. Other times it means listening closely to the directions of others, sharing their vision of that common goal.

You might respond:

> *I believe that I am a strong leader, and an excellent follower as well. Perhaps more importantly, I have a good sense of when the situation calls for a leader, and when it calls for a strong team player. A good example of this was when I was working on the Cystic Fibrosis Walk three years ago. My job was to be sure that we had enough supplies at the registration desk. Two hours before the event was to begin, the volunteer coordinator still had not arrived. Rather than bother the overall walk coordinator with this problem, I found someone who could work in my assigned area, which I already had pretty much under control. I then filled in assigning volunteers to projects where there was a staffing shortage. By the time the volunteer coordinator arrived, via a tow truck, the walk had been under way for 20 minutes. I filled her in on what I had done, gave her the list of who was assigned where, and went back to my job stocking supplies. The next year, I was asked to assume the position of volunteer coordinator.*

This answer addresses the leader question as well as the team player question. It also shows that you do not seek out leadership roles for the sake of holding them, but that you will not wait around for someone to solve your problems for you.

What is your greatest strength?

This question is a little more straightforward than most. It, along with "Tell me a little about yourself" and "Why should I hire you?", is perhaps one of the most obvious chances you will get to sell yourself. You should be prepared for this opportunity if it presents itself.

You might say:

> *My greatest strength may be my determination to succeed. As you may have noticed, I have a slight hearing impairment. This has made it quite difficult, as you might imagine, to learn to speak clearly. Throughout my school years I went through training with a speech and language pathologist. Although the insurance stopped paying for it when I turned 18, I used the money I earned at my part-time job to pay to continue my training through college. Although I don't have any desire to go to Broadway, one of my proudest moments was when I auditioned for and won the role of Frankie in our college production of Grease. It was then that I realized how long a road it had been, but how great the rewards were.*

This is another example of taking something that might be perceived as a weakness and showing how the weakness is not what it might appear to be, and how your strengths have more than made up for it.

What is your biggest weakness?

This question is the one that frightens the most job seekers. It is also the one that has led the most career-planning professionals to offer ill-founded advice. The suggested answers to this question can range anywhere from total honesty to an attempt at humor to using a strength and talking about it as if it were a weakness. I don't think that this is the time to discuss how lousy your handwriting is, or how you can't hit a nine iron, or how you can sometimes take on multiple projects, thereby working yourself to death.

Chances are, the interviewer has asked this question before. They have heard the sad stories of the perfectionists who are never happy until all the details are taken care of on a project, and of the workaholics who put in endless hours, often forgetting to eat while involved with a project. A decent interviewer will either see right through such a response or will take it at face value. Who hasn't worked with someone who is such a perfectionist that the work piles up while they neurotically triple-check every comma? Who hasn't worked with someone who is always talking about how hard they work and how tired they are? It's like those pathetic adolescents who feel the need to tell their peers exactly how many drinks they have consumed. Neither makes for a pleasant coworker, and nobody wants to hire someone who thinks they are smart enough to pull one over on the interviewer.

So what can you do? Well, since the death of Mother Theresa, my guess is that everyone reading this book has a weakness or two. Also, because you spent the time doing your self-assessment, you have identified what some of those weaknesses are. Perhaps you have had the opportunity to begin addressing those weaknesses by continuing your education, by reading self-help books, or through practice, practice, practice.

You could respond like this:

> I guess my biggest weakness has been my fear of public speaking. In school I would sometimes freeze up if I had to give a class presentation. I knew that I would occasionally have to give presentations to small groups if I were to enter this field, and so I have joined Toastmasters. I have been going for a month

now, and while I am still not a spellbinding speaker, I feel a lot more confident. This past week I was called on to give a presentation on the decision to remove the bald eagle from the endangered species list. I did the research, and even brought along some color transparencies that were breathtaking. As is their custom, everyone gave me a nice round of applause, but several people came up to me afterward and asked me questions. It really felt great. I can't wait until my next turn.

First of all, this is a relatively "safe" weakness, because as I mentioned before, most people aren't too crazy about speaking in public. It is also not a weakness that is central to the job the way some other weaknesses might be. Also, by admitting an honest weakness and taking concrete steps to overcome it, you show a maturity that is attractive to an employer. Also, by having already taken steps to address the weakness, it is less a weakness than it had been, and may soon be no weakness at all.

Tell me about your most recent position.
Why did you leave your last job?

The first question is used to gather information about your experiences at your most recent job. It also will help the interviewer get a feel for why you left that position. The interviewer will be looking for signs regarding how you got along with your coworkers and your supervisor. Like the second question, anything you say that sounds at all negative will reflect more poorly on you than it will on the previous employer. In either case, you may be better off, depending on the circumstance, talking about what you learned and accomplished in that position, and then either describing your position as no longer providing you with an opportunity to be challenged, or that it wasn't the best fit for you.

You could respond:

For the last five years I have worked as a machinist with Hoodmaker Tool and Die. I held a number of different positions while I was there, as you can see from my resume. I was hired as a temp in a clerical assignment while I was still finishing my degree. I was then hired as a full-time clerical worker. I moved up the ranks after receiving my degree, through the position of office manager, and into my current position of bookkeeper. I have really enjoyed my time there. Bridget and Claire, my last two supervisors, have been great to work for, and they have taught me a lot. I would be happy to stay there forever if it were not for the fact that there is no opportunity to grow with the company. Because it is a family-owned company, it's unlikely that I will have the opportunity to move into Barb's position as the controller, and I have no real interest in learning how to use the machinery, so the plant manager position is out of the question, too. That's one of the reasons why I am excited about the possibility of this position. Your organization is growing. And not only is this position sure to offer an exciting challenge, it seems likely that there will be opportunities to grow with the company later in my career.

This response shows that your leaving the company will be amicable, and that you weren't forced out for embezzlement or some other problem that your interviewer will not want to inherit. It also exhibits a genuine interest in the position for which you are interviewing—one of your main goals in the interview.

What makes you interested in this position?
What do you know about our organization?

Both of these questions give you the opportunity to show that you have done extensive research into the company and that you have a thorough knowledge of your own strengths, weaknesses, and potential. This is a great chance to show how, based on your research, you believe that you would be the best candidate for the position.

You could respond like this:

Everything I have read or heard about your company has shown it to be truly dynamic and an exciting place to work. I am excited about the possibility of getting in on the ground floor of your new EM50 Project. Everyone I have talked to, from people at the parent company to folks down at the Chamber of Commerce, are excited about the future of your company.

Although those people's comments were impressive, I am even more impressed by the financial backing your project has received from giants like Microsoft and Reuters. With backers like that, I am sure that this project will have the support to succeed. Working for your company, and the possibility of working in support of this project, seems frankly like the chance of a lifetime. I am sure that I would be able to make a significant contribution given my background in software development and my experience in the area of e-commerce.

This kind of response gives an indication of your enthusiasm, interest in the company, and the value you could bring to the organization.

Where do you see yourself in five years?
What would your dream job be like?

These questions are asked to measure your focus. Is this a job you are applying for to fill a short-term need, or is this the type of field in which you would like to establish your career? It measures, to some extent, your self-understanding as well. No interviewer will be foolish enough to assume that you will apply for this position and then retire from it some thirty years later, so you don't have to make them think that's your plan.

When answering the question, you want to show primarily that you are interested in the position for which you are applying. Beyond that, you should show an interest in the company, rather than in the industry that the company is in. No employer wants to spend a great deal of money training someone only to see that person leave and go to work for a competitor.

You could respond to the first question like this:

> *I see myself at a point where I will be firmly established in my career. I will be challenged in my work, taking on new projects and challenges as I prove my worth to the company. I don't know what my job title will be in five years, mostly because I am not too caught up in titles. It's much more important to me that whether it is my first year on the job or my twenty-first, the job holds challenges and an increasing area of responsibility.*

A response to the "dream job" question could be somewhat similar:

> *I don't know what the title of the dream job would be, but I can tell you what it would be like. I will wake up every morning excited about getting to work. When I get there, I will see a group of bright, energetic people. Some may be coworkers, supervisors, or subordinates. All will support and be a part of a shared vision for the company. There will be excellent communication in every direction.*

> *Personally, I will feel valued by my supervisor, and it will show in the responsibilities and challenges I receive. I will be given the support to carry out those responsibilities and the freedom to be creative and resourceful in how I go about fulfilling them. And, of course, I will bat cleanup for the company softball team!*

These responses allay any fears that you will be caught up in superficial ego items like titles. It shows that you will be motivated by the opportunities you will be given. Nowhere in the responses is there a mention of salary, benefits, time off, or keys to the executive washroom.

What kind of salary are you looking for?

This is one of those good news/bad news questions. The good news is that it's not a question that is asked of everyone. Chances are, the employer has a real interest in you. The bad news is that it is a bit of a lose/lose question. If you have not yet been offered the job, you can say a number that is too high and be eliminated from consideration, even though you would have accepted less. You could be afraid to say a number that might be too high, and end up with a salary that is less than what you are worth (a better result, but not the best, because they may also think that because of your low number they might be better off with someone who wants more money).

You might respond:

> To be honest, I would have to learn a lot more about the job. If I were offered the job of starting shortstop for the New York Yankees, I would gladly do it without pay. If the job were changing light bulbs on the poles in Yankee Stadium, you couldn't pay me enough. What sort of pay range do you have in mind for this position?

In sales training, there is a little game called "pass the ball." The idea is to be able to gather as much information as you can from a prospect, so that whenever a question is asked of you, you quickly slide past the question to ask a question of your own. There will be a more detailed discussion of salary negotiations in Chapter 11.

Sample Answers for Problem Questions

These questions may or may not be asked, and they may or may not provide you with any particular difficulty or challenge. Regardless of the likelihood that they will be asked, if they would be hard to answer, you should be prepared with an idea of how you would answer them.

How will you be able to do the job?

This question borders on being illegal, but it's framed in such a way that the interviewer might be able to get away with it. This question may be asked regardless of whether or not you have a visible disability (but is most likely to be asked in this way if you do have a visible disability). The question shows the anxiety that the interviewer has about your disability and the way in which it may impact your ability to do the job. If you have not done so already, you will want to address this question head-on.

You might respond like this:

> *I have complete confidence that I could do this job and do it very well. Throughout college and in my part-time jobs, the fact that I did not have the use of my left hand has presented some challenges, yet I have been able to be successful in spite of this. The job, as I understand it, requires very little typing, and even my typing is respectable with the help of a shareware program I have been using for years.*
>
> *I can assure you that if I am selected for this position, you will be very satisfied with your choice.*

Why are you interested in (qualified for) this job at this stage of your career?

This question can be asked in one of two ways. It can be asked of an inexperienced job seeker who finds him- or herself in the familiar Catch-22 where you can't get a job without experience, and you can't get the experience without a job. This is one of those cases where a volunteer or internship experience would help. The question is also asked of older job seekers as they look to make a career change or to compete for a promotion.

You might respond to the first question like this:

> *I realize that often these positions go to people who have been in the field for some time. I also know that many of these people continue their education while employed, and that the company supports this through tuition assistance programs. Because I already have the academic qualifications that these people seek, accompanied by eight months of experience as an intern, I think that I will be able to make an immediate impact here.*

For the second question you might respond like this:

I feel that I have learned what I can from my current position. While many people hit their 40th birthday and begin to count down to retirement, I am 43 and I am still looking for a challenge in my work. I believe that this position would be a challenging one. I also believe that I would be very successful here. I have a track record of being a quick study, a hard worker, and an enthusiastic leader. I believe that I will be a great fit for this position.

Both of these answers show that age is just a number, but that what is really most important is talent and attitude. A 35-year-old with a poor attitude is not nearly as valuable as a person with a good attitude, regardless of whether that person is 28 or 58.

Can you explain this gap on your resume when you were not working?

This question can mean different sorts of trouble for different reasons. For a person who is returning to the workforce after raising children, there is a question of how you were able to remain current, although the question is hidden in the text. For a person who was fired or laid off, and who had not anticipated this possibility, it means something different. For this person the time between jobs may be much longer because of the slow start to the job search. For other people, the gap in employment may be for medical or illness reasons.

Regardless of the source of the gap, you need to approach the question honestly, but at the same time allaying the fears that lie beneath the question. If you were raising children, say that, but say that they are now off to college (or high school, or pre-kindergarten), and that you are ready to be back in the work world full time. If you lost your previous job, tell them that when you left that position you wanted to make sure that your *next* job would be a better fit for you, and that took a bit more time. Mention that you think that it was time well spent, because it brought you to this job, which you believe will be a great fit. Finally, if the gap was related to an accident or an illness, state that you had some medical problems, but also add that you have been given a clean bill of health and that you have no reason to believe that any such circumstance would affect you in this job.

None of the answers here is meant to be memorized and used word-for-word. The idea is to see the logic behind the answers, and to personalize them and shape them to fit your circumstances. Again, if you listen carefully to the words and the body language of the interviewer, and the context within which they are used, you will hear both the question and the hidden question. If you find a way to answer the question and to put to rest the fear or uncertainty that underlies it, you will most likely find success at the end of the interview.

Questions They Can't Ask You

The following is a list of some of the kinds of questions that are discriminatory, and illegal to ask in an interview. If someone asks you questions like these, you don't have to answer them. If they are asked in a rhetorical way, you can shrug them off. If you are pressed for answers, politely tell the interviewer that you think it might be an illegal question to ask.

- Do you have a disability?

- Have you ever been arrested?

- Is that a Spanish name?

- Are you married?

- Do you have children?

- How old are you? (But it's OK to ask "Are you over 18?".)

- Chris? Is that a girl's name or a boy's name?

- Ryan, eh? Is that Orange Irish or Green Irish?

Interviewing Styles

Each interviewer will have his or her own style, even though they may follow the same general script. You should observe the interviewer and the surroundings carefully as the interview begins. If it takes place in the interviewer's office, take a look around. What sorts of pictures are hanging in the room? Certificates? What kinds of memorabilia or knick-knacks are displayed? Is there music playing? What sort of computer equipment is being used? These will all give you clues to the personality of the interviewer. Those clues can help you shape your answers.

Also, throughout the interview, observe the body language of the interviewer. If she is leaning forward in her chair, that is usually a sign that you have her full attention. If she is glancing at her watch or over your shoulder toward a door or window, you may need to make some alterations to your tone or delivery.

Reading the interviewer is a challenge for all job seekers. There is an added dimension of challenge for people with visible disabilities, however. In addition to looking for nonverbal indicators of your performance, you need to be looking for indicators of how the interviewer is responding to your disability. Again, the goal is to have the person see past the fact that you have a disability as quickly as you can. If you can bring the focus of the interview to what you *can* do, you will have a chance at succeeding.

The Interviewer's Emotions

You are likely to encounter several different emotions in the interviewer that relate to the presence of your disability. The following sections discuss them in more detail.

Some of these issues are well beyond your control. You certainly cannot change in five minutes what has been ingrained in someone since childhood. From Captain Hook to *The Fugitive's* "One-Armed Man" to "Two-Face" from *Batman*, the public is bombarded with negative images of people with disabilities that are not balanced by many positive images. You need to focus your energy and attention to make you and your abilities the focus of the interview, rather than your disability and the interviewer's perception of people with disabilities.

Curiosity

Most people are naturally curious about disabilities. They may wonder how it occurred—is this congenital, or was it something you acquired later in life? If you have a guide dog, you already know this: People love to pet them. Things like the Braille and Speak also fascinate them. You may detect some curiosity in the interviewer. The best way to get past that curiosity to is to address your disability early in the interview, perhaps with the first icebreaker-type question—"Tell me a little about yourself." By working that information in, and discussing anything that you anticipate they will be curious about, you can move on to the things that you need to discuss if you are going to be successful.

Guilt

Although it is more difficult to detect, one other natural emotion experienced by people who see people with visible disabilities is guilt. The expression "There but for the grace of God go I" has a particular resonance for people who encounter people with a visible disability. There is little you can do to deal with this emotion, because it will never come too close to the surface. You should be aware that it might be there, however. It is often present along with pity.

Pity

For the most part, people feel sure that they would not be able to cope if they had a disability. Even some well-meaning exercises that are used to raise awareness, like making a person use a wheelchair for a day, or blindfolding someone so that they can "experience blindness," do much more harm than good. When people see the challenges of a disability as insurmountable, they are moved by real pity. While they often believe that they are better people for experiencing this emotion, their actions often are far worse than a crass person who isn't fazed by a disability and expects the same results from anyone regardless.

If you detect feelings of pity in the interviewer, you will have your work cut out for you. In this case, you want to focus the conversation on how little the disability impacts you in relation to the tasks that are required by the job. The more they feel sorry for you because of what you *can't* do, the more likely they will be to lose focus of what you *can* do.

Prejudice/Ignorance

Most of the people that you encounter are likely to be ignorant of disability issues. Unfortunately, they are also likely to have misperceptions regarding the limitations that may be associated with a disability. Sometimes these misperceptions are worse than having no opinion at all, because you first have to disabuse the person of the prejudices they have that are based on misinformation, and then educate them.

Differentness

Some people simply have a fear of the unknown, and tend to shy away from those who are different from them. This is true in cases of ethnicity, religion, nationality, as well as disability status. This heightens the need for you to bond with the interviewer on a more personal basis. Making the disability issue secondary, and establishing a level of comfort in interacting with the interviewer, needs to be done early on in the interview.

The Day of the Interview

As I mentioned before, you should be prepared to arrive at your interview a half hour to forty-five minutes early so that you can unwind and get your thoughts together before the interview begins.

As you get ready for the interview, focus on being your most presentable. Again, there are plenty of suggestions for how to dress for an interview. Some of them will seem pretty basic for a lot of people. Others will find the suggestions "way repressive." In general, the idea is to keep the focus of the interview on the *content* of what you are saying. Anything that distracts the interviewer's attention from that content works against you.

That means that nothing should be visibly pierced other than one ring per ear. At the time of this writing, this is still more acceptable for women than for men; however, earrings for men are far more mainstream than they were even five years ago. It also means that if you wear a fragrance, keep it subtle. You want the interviewer to remember you long after you have left, but not necessarily every time they walk into their office for the next week. Be sure you get rid of the gum before you enter the building, and hold off on the cigarettes until after the interview, even if offered. Your clothing choices should be tasteful, if not necessarily colorful. It won't matter if your wardrobe is dull if you are not. For best results, scope the organization out and see how the employees dress. If they are dressed casually, be sure to go back again another day to be sure it wasn't a "dress down" day. At any rate, it's still a good idea to dress better than you expect your interviewer to dress.

What to Wear

For a man, the style rules have changed to include much more variety. You still cannot go wrong with a basic dark suit. Lighter-color suits are fine, particularly for the summer, but you are probably still better off with a darker color. Consider a white dress shirt, although light blue is also fairly common. You should wear well-polished cordovan or black laced shoes and coordinate your socks with the shoes. Choose a tie that makes you feel confident. Bring along a valise or briefcase with an extra copy of your resume. Don't have anything bulging in your pockets (directions to the building, copies of the job description, etc.). Get a haircut during the week before the interview. And don't work on the car, weed the garden, or do anything else that will make your hands or nails look dirty.

For women, there is the classic matching jacket and skirt worn over a white blouse. Women are allowed a little more latitude if they choose to wear a tasteful bit of jewelry or a colorful scarf. Stay away from high heels, and be sure that you have skin-colored hosiery with no runs. This isn't the time to get those fake nails with the flags of your ten favorite states painted on them. Nor is it the time to get that fortune teller thing going with the rings on every finger, or the makeover by the overly aggressive cosmetics salesperson. It is also a good idea to leave your purse at home and bring a valise or briefcase instead.

If you don't have clothes that you feel would be appropriate for an interview, check with some of the organizations in your community and see if they have a lending program. Also, Dress for Success is a national organization that provides suits for low-income women who have job interviews. You can contact them at:

www.dressforsuccess.org

Arriving at the Interview Site

Remember that you are interviewing for the job from the minute you arrive at the employer's place of business. Too many people make the mistake of waiting to go into interview mode when the interviewer comes into the waiting area to shake your hand and bring you to the room where you will be interviewed. The danger in this mistake is that you may not make a favorable impression on some of the other employees. Too many people make the mistake of treating the receptionist or the secretary as if that person would not impact their chances of being hired. The fact is that in most cases the interviewer (particularly if the interviewer is a hiring manager rather than a human resources professional) will ask the secretary or receptionist what they thought of the candidate.

Take the time to learn the greeter's name, and try to establish a bond. This can help you relax and slowly raise your comfort level as the interview is about to begin. You may also learn a lot from this small talk, including information that you probably would not find out any other way. This does not mean that you should grill the greeter, but using casual conversation to gather information is completely acceptable. Be careful as you are asked questions, because you don't want to share anything at this stage that you would not want to share later.

At some point you will be directed to the room where the interview will take place, or the interviewer will come out and greet you. If you can, it is appropriate to stand as the interviewer asks your name. Look the recruiter in the eye, smile, and shake the interviewer's hand. If you do not have use of your right hand, grasp the interviewer's hand with your left hand. If it is only recently that you have lost use of this hand, practice this maneuver until it becomes second nature. When you shake his or her hand, remember that it's not a strength demonstration; but you do want to use a firm, confident handshake if possible.

You should have some notepaper in your folder or valise, along with several copies of your resume, as well as references if they are not listed on your resume. Use the notepaper to record the names of those you encounter, starting with the secretary. They may give you their business cards; if they don't, feel free to ask them to repeat their names or to give you the correct spelling. Jot down a note about their positions if you can. As you shape your answers to their questions, try and keep in mind the perspective from which the question was asked. An auditor may be looking for a different type of answer than an engineer or public relations specialist.

Make eye contact with the questioner, but if it's a group interview, attempt to make some eye contact with the other members of the interview team as well. Try to look at each person for a few seconds, and then move on to the next person. You don't want to get into a stare-down with anyone, but you also don't want anyone to feel ignored. You may want to spend a little more time with anyone who does not seem to be engaged in the interview. You don't want to make that person uncomfortable, but if they "zone out" on you, you have lost them.

Smile. I teach a course in vocational counseling to Master's students who are studying to become counselors. In this class, we always do a segment on helping clients prepare for job interviews. As part of this session, I usually pull two students aside. I tell the first person that he will read a prepared script in response to the question "Tell me a little about yourself." I then give the second student the same script and directions, only I ask that student to smile while reading it. I then ask the two students to sit in the front of the classroom, with their backs to their classmates, and to read their response. I then poll the class to see which person's response they liked better—who, if they were an employer, they would be more likely to hire. Invariably the results are overwhelmingly in favor of the second student, the one who smiled, even though the students couldn't see the smile.

Then we take the exercise further. I ask the students in the audience what it was that made the second candidate more likely to be hired. The answers are not surprising. "The second person sounded much friendlier." "The second person seemed more confident." "The second person was more enthusiastic." As any speech pathologist will tell you, the way we physically shape our mouth is equally important as where our teeth or tongue are placed to produce the sounds. By smiling, we know that we *look* friendlier, more enthusiastic, and more self-confident. This exercise shows that it also makes us sound friendlier, more enthusiastic, and more self-confident. Surely you can't have a fake smile frozen on your face throughout your interview. Nor would you want to. However, if you make a conscious effort to smile as much as you can where it is appropriate, you will find that you fare much better in the interview.

Toward the close of the interview, it's usually customary to give the candidate a chance to ask a few questions. This is a great chance for you to clarify any information that you are unsure about. This is not the time to ask about salary, benefits, time off, or other extraneous things. It is a good time to find out what the rest of the process will be like, or what the time frame is for the position to be filled. A great question to ask is "What exactly is it that you are looking for in a _____ (position name here)"? Once they have responded, it gives you a chance to sum up. In your summation, you want to express your appreciation for the opportunity to interview for the position. You also want to reiterate any points that you feel you may not have driven home to your satisfaction, and then to frame your candidacy within the parameters of how they described what they were looking for in a candidate.

As the interview draws to a close, you want to again show your personality and enthusiasm. Smile, shake the hand(s) of the interviewer(s), and once again offer your thanks. As you leave, be sure to say good-bye to anyone you pass that you met when you came in. If possible, use their name when you say good-bye. Nothing shows that you care and that you listen like using a person's name.

Second Interviews

Many organizations use a series of interviews before determining who they want to hire. The first interview may produce one to three front-runners for a position. These individuals are often invited to return for a second round of interviews. These interviews sometimes include groups of coworkers, supervisors, or team members. These interviews may be somewhat less formal, and their purpose is usually to determine the extent to which the others in the organization will get along with the candidate. It is also possible that this interview will be your first chance to meet the hiring manager or someone from the hiring unit.

The Lunch or Dinner Interview

As part of this second round, there is sometimes a lunch or other meal, and the interview is meant to be an informal conversation. Although the atmosphere may be more relaxed, this is not the time to let your guard down. Plenty of people have done well in initial interviews, only to blow their chances at the lunch table.

In many ways, the sit-down meal is really a social phenomenon. The typical family uses their dining room more often to put together jigsaw puzzles than to have a formal dinner. This trend has let our etiquette skills atrophy over time. Unfortunately, employers use the interview meal to measure the extent to which a person exhibits poise in social situations, knowing that the candidate may have to perform in such a setting for their job. Here are a few tips to remember if you are invited to a lunch or dinner with your employer or an interviewer:

- **The table setting:** The setting is designed so that you can use your utensils from the outside in. For example, the salad fork is usually on the far left, followed by a dinner fork and a desert fork. If you drop a utensil, ask a server to bring you a new one.

- **Napkin:** Place your napkin on your lap when you sit down. Use it sparingly, to dab the corners of your mouth during the meal. If you need to leave your seat for any reason, gently lay the napkin at the side of the table setting.

- **Ordering:** Keep in mind that you can always eat later if you have to. Your main purpose here is not eating; it is to sell yourself to the interviewer as a person. If your host orders first, feel free to follow his or her lead. If the interviewer orders alcohol, take a pass. Order an iced tea instead. It seems a bit more mature than a soda pop. Keep away from messy foods or foods that you need to eat with your hands. A good interview meal is a grilled chicken Caesar salad. It's usually reasonably priced and fairly easy to eat. But by all means, hold the anchovies! Just use your discretion; however, it's particularly advisable to stay away from French onion soup au gratin, fried chicken, and spaghetti.

  Also, because it is the host who is paying for the meal, try to choose a reasonably priced meal. And by no means should you ask to "Supersize it"!

- **Smoking:** Even if smoking is permitted, refrain. This suggestion goes for whether or not your host smokes. Gently decline; but, if you feel comfortable, suggest that your host feel free to do so if he or she chooses.

- **Beginning the meal:** Don't pick up a utensil until your host does. Normally, you should not eat anything until all parties have been served their food.

- **Elbows:** If you hear your grandmother's voice, that will be no surprise, but sit up straight and keep your elbows off the table. The chair is not meant to be a Barcalounger. Keep your feet on the floor and your back against the chair back. You can lean forward and let your arms touch the table, but they should not support you.

- **Soup:** Before your main course is served, you may be served soup. (You should refrain from this added course, unless coaxed by your host. You don't want to be the only one having this course, and it adds to the host's bill.) If you are served soup, use the soup spoon provided. Don't fill the spoon completely, and move it away from you in the bowl, before bringing it up to your mouth. This is the fancy way to do it, but it also makes sense. If you scoop toward yourself, you increase the chances of having soup on your lap.

- **Eating:** This is not your goal. Hopefully you will have had something to eat earlier in the day, because you usually will not be able to truly enjoy your meal. It is likely that your host will be asking a lot of questions, and you will be answering them between bites. Accept this fact, and be careful that your bites are small enough that you can easily stop chewing, swallow, and answer the question.

- **Passing foods:** If you are eating with a group, there may be a need to pass food to others. If the bread is placed in front of you, pick up the basket, offer a piece to the person at your left, take a piece, and then pass it to your right. If someone asks for the salt, take the salt and pepper and pass them in the direction of the person who requested it. Formal etiquette suggests that you not *hand* anything to anyone, but rather that you set items on the table near the individual. To me, this seems a bit extreme; however, if the person next to you is occupied, set the item down and call the person's attention to it. By the way, if the person to your right asks for the salt and the person on your left trusts you to give it to the person on your right, it is improper to "steal" some of the salt while it is in transit.

- **Gristle:** Depending on your luck, you may have a situation where you take a bite of meat that cannot possibly be chewed. Usually it is suggested that you remove the item from your mouth with your fork and place it on your plate. I would suggest that you consider feigning a subtle wipe of your mouth, and capture the culprit with your napkin, where it can remain hidden. Although it is not what Emily Post would suggest you do, I can't imagine how it can be such a great idea to leave a half-chewed piece of meat on your plate in view of the rest of your party.

- **The check:** Unless otherwise specified, it is usually the responsibility of the person who is hosting or who invited the other person to lunch to pick up the check. You should thank the host after the lunch as the bill is being paid, or as the lunch is ending. If the host wants you to contribute to the bill, you will be asked. At that point, do not hesitate to chip in.

- **The rest room:** It is perfectly acceptable, once the order has been placed (or while you are waiting to be seated) to ask to be excused. This will give you an opportunity to wash your hands, collect your thoughts, use the facilities, and check your appearance in the mirror.

- **Doggie bags:** Because you will be on the receiving end of most of the questions, it's likely that you will not finish your meal. I would suggest that you hit the drive-thru on the way home if necessary, but don't ask to wrap up what you don't eat.

- **Dessert:** If it is offered, suggest that your host(s) go ahead, but suggest that you would prefer not to have dessert. It adds to the bill, and it is just as likely that you won't have a chance to finish it. And it is far more difficult to walk away from a piece of chocolate cake that you haven't finished than to leave some poached salmon!

If you still feel like you need more help, check out:

`www.cuisinenet.com/digest/custom/etiquette/manners_intro.shtml`

Some Online Interviewing Resources

Several sites offer help in the area of interviewing. Some of the sites include sample questions as well as answers.

The U.S. Department of the Interior

`www.doi.gov/`

William and Mary

`http://staff.wm.edu/career/02/Student/Interview/InterviewIndex.cfm`

For a good book on interviewing, check out:

Why Should I Hire You?

`www.jist.com`

CHAPTER 11

After the Interview

When you return home from the interview, take a few moments to write down your thoughts about the interview while they are still fresh in your mind. Make note of any questions that were asked that were particularly difficult, or that caught you off guard.

Writing Thank-You Letters

The next thing you want to do is to begin writing your thank-you letters. Hopefully you took the time during the interview to collect the business cards of the people you met, or to at least make a record of the names and their correct spellings. This will enable you to personalize your letters, rather than sending a letter addressed to "Dear Interviewer" or "Dear Search Committee Member." If you are unsure about the spelling or the correct title of any of the people you met with, call the organization and check. It is far better to do it this way than to send a letter with an error, particularly an error in the spelling of a person's name.

In the letter, you want to start out by thanking the person for taking the time to meet with you. In many cases, particularly if you are meeting with a human resources professional, it's just part of their job. But it's still advisable to recognize that their jobs are not easy ones.

In a second paragraph, you want to accomplish one or two things. You may want to settle any unfinished business you left in the interview. If you were asked a question and you didn't have the answer, you may have responded that you would get back to the interviewer with the information. Sometimes you may feel that your answer was not strong enough in the interview, and you want another opportunity to address that question. Don't overuse this method, though. It's only natural that you will say to yourself "I wish I had said…." If what you said was clearly not understood, or if you really feel that they didn't get your point, it may be worth addressing it in your thank-you letter.

The second thing you may want to do in the second or third paragraph is to reiterate one or two of the points you think are most important and that put you in the most positive position for the job. This is a good time to summarize what you said in your closing at the interview. It's also a good time to restate your confidence that you will be able to perform the functions of the job. This is particularly important if you believe that there are any questions at all relating to your disability. You may want to interject some information you gathered through the Job Accommodation Network (see chapters 10 and 13) if you did not mention this during the interview.

Finally, in the last paragraph, you want to reiterate your thanks and make yourself available in the event that the person has any new or additional questions or requests for specific information.

To the extent that you can, it's good to personalize each thank-you letter if you are writing to several people (and you should write one to each person who met with you, including the receptionist). This will give you a chance to address those issues that you think will be of particular interest to each individual. And just in case everyone you met compares the letters you sent them, they'll see that you took the time to make each one individual—very impressive indeed.

People often start out with good intentions about writing thank-you letters, but too often they just never get around to writing them. Sometimes they get caught up in whether they should hand-write it or type it. Or they are out of the paper they used for their resume, so they wait until they get to the store.

Regardless of how you write it, or what you print it on, the key is to write the letter, and to send it within a few days of the interview. It shows several things that can help set you apart for the others. It shows that you have a genuine interest in the position and that you weren't just going through the motions. It gives you the opportunity to reinforce a point that you made during the interview. It gives you a chance to clarify anything that may have been misunderstood during the interview. And it gets your name in front of the interviewer once more. If they sort through the pile to attach the letter to your resume, you will have gotten yourself to the top of the pile, if only physically.

Sample Thank-You Letters

Here are a couple of sample thank-you letters. The first one was written in an attempt to address an issue that the interviewee may not have had the chance to cover during the interview. The second letter takes the opportunity to clear up an issue that arose during the interview.

Thank-You Letter Making a New Point

20 Lyndhurst
Batavia, NY 14565

July 15, 2005

Heather Holmes
Director of Human Resources
Geneseo Health Care Affilliates
1610 Oak Avenue
Geneseo, NY 13045

Ms. Holmes:

Thank you for taking the time to meet with me this Monday. I know that you have many demands on your time, and I truly appreciated the opportunity to talk with you about the phlebotomist position.

As I mentioned in the interview, I believe that my experience in the Serology department at Strong Memorial Hospital, coupled with my internship in the Health Science Lab at the University of Rochester, gives me just the kind of hands-on ability that you said you are looking for. I also believe that the fact that I will complete my coursework for my Bachelor's degree this August makes me an ideal candidate and puts me in the position to hit the ground running.

Although it was not directly mentioned, I detected the possibility that my disability was of concern to some of the members of the search committee. To allay that fear, and to find out for myself, I contacted Steve Harvey, the salesman from Harvey Instruments in Tonawanda. He explained to me that the Sero 9000 Cyclotron that I used at the lab at the U of R was quite similar to the Sero 8500 that you have at GHCA. In fact, he said that the LCD readout is identical in both models, and that my vision difficulties should not play a role in my ability to excel at this job.

Again, I thank you for giving me the opportunity to meet with you and discuss this position. I would be more than happy to answer any additional questions that you or any of the other committee members may have, either in person or on the phone. I can be reached at 716-445-8610. I look forward to hearing from you.

Sincerely,

Katherine R. Bartolotta

Thank-You Letter Clarifying a Point

490 Taunton Place
Brooklyn, NY 10023

July 18, 2005

Ms. Cheryl Incorvia
Vandelay Architects
2500 Koehler
New York, NY 10011

Dear Ms. Incorvia:

Thanks for taking the time to meet with me this morning, and for the opportunity to discuss my qualifications and learn more about the position of Office Manager at your firm.

During our meeting, I told you that I was unsure which software packages I was familiar with. The AppleWorks software with which I have had extensive experience was V 6.2.5, while the Adobe PageMaker version was 7.0. The Peachtree Accounting package was version 2004. I am sorry that I was unable to tell you that during the interview, but as I said, I would be uncomfortable with the possibility of unknowingly misrepresenting myself.

I am very excited about the prospect of joining you at Vandelay. Your work there is very well regarded, and it would truly be an honor to be able to make a contribution there. I believe that my experience as an office manager, as well as my accomplishments in the area of graphic design, will enable me to make an immediate contribution to Vandelay.

I understand that you expect to make a decision sometime in the next two weeks. If you have any questions about my background during that time, or if you would like to speak with any additional references, please let me know.

I look forward to hearing from you.

Cindy Suffoletto

Following Up Via the Phone

If the interviewer gives you a time frame within which a decision is expected to be reached, you will be well-advised to sit tight during that period of time. By sending the thank-you letter, you will have distinguished yourself from most of the other candidates. Calling during the period of deliberation is unlikely to do anything in your favor. On the other hand, any contacts that you may have—either within the organization, or networking contacts who also know the interviewer—can help you out during this period. With discretion, these individuals will be able to drop one or two good words about you to the interviewer while deliberations are under way. If those comments reinforce good feelings that the interviewer already had, that's great. If the good words do not mesh with the interviewer's memory of the meeting with you, it may cause the interviewer to look back over his or her notes.

When the anticipated decision date has come and passed, it is acceptable to call and ask where the process is. This call, if handled professionally, should not hurt you, because it is reasonable that you might call if you haven't heard by a date specified by the interviewer. It's likely that the reason you haven't heard can be explained in one of a few ways:

- Your letter is in the mail.

- They have hired someone, and they were too unprofessional to let you know.

- They have offered the position to someone, and they are waiting to hear whether their offer will be accepted.

- They offered the position to someone, and that person declined, bringing them back to the decision stage.

- They just haven't moved as quickly as they had expected.

In the first two cases, your call in and of itself does nothing to help you in your pursuit of the position. It does help, however, to know the status of your candidacy so that you can focus your efforts on your other prospects. In the other three scenarios, you have once again communicated your interest in the position. That can't hurt. You will also find out what the new time frame is for the decision.

Sometimes You're the Windshield; Sometimes You're the Bug: Handling Rejection

Through the mail, through the grapevine, or in your follow-up phone call, you may find that you were not given the job. As was discussed in Chapter 8, it is possible that you could go on as many as 59 interviews before you are offered a job that you will want to accept. You need to be able to accept this fact if you are going to get through the almost inevitable experience of having your hopes dashed.

There are a few tips that can help you gain some competitive advantage from every negative interviewing experience. The following sections give more details on these tips.

Send a Thank-You Note

Although this suggestion sounds a little masochistic at first, it makes sense when you think about it. If you genuinely appreciate the fact that you were considered for the position, why not say so? I guarantee that this tactic will help separate you from the competition. Who knows what will happen with the person who was selected? It may not work out. The person hired may not like the job and quit. If you distinguish yourself from the other runners-up, you may be the first person the employer thinks of in the event that the first candidate does not work out.

I have benefited firsthand from a second possible scenario. Even if the first person does work out, there may be a second position that is available at the same organization later. By distinguishing yourself from the other candidates, you may find that you may be considered for other opportunities.

Even if it doesn't pay off immediately, you can be certain that the employer will remember you. It may be several years down the line, and it may not be a position that you would still be interested in, but you might put yourself on their short list. If not, it cost you only a postage stamp and the time it took to write the letter.

Here is a sample thank-you letter in response to a rejection.

23 Blantyre Road
Seattle, WA 89564

January 18, 2005

Raymond A. Smith
President
Smith Office Supplies
2220 Sea Mist Place
Tacoma, WA 88765

Dear Mr. Smith:

Thank you for taking the time to speak with me on the phone yesterday. I realize that you are a busy man, and I can imagine how difficult it is to deliver disappointing news.

I just wanted you to know that I really did appreciate being considered for the position. I also appreciated the chance to learn more about your company.

I also wanted to thank you for giving me input regarding my performance in the interview and my background. I want you to know that I have taken your feedback to heart. Yesterday after I spoke with you I contacted Gonzaga University and inquired about the spreadsheet certificate they offer as part of their continuing education department. I start on Monday!

Thanks again for your help. I hope that you will keep me in mind in the event that any other opportunities arise at Smith Office Supplies.

Sincerely,

Richard J. Gruber

Ask for Feedback

That letter hints at a second reason to follow up with the employer. If you ask in the right way, you just might get the employer to give you a better understanding of why some other candidate was selected. The other candidate may have had more experience, or perhaps had expertise in a certain area.

If that is not the case, ask if perhaps you did not present yourself well in your interview. By bringing up the possibility yourself, you may make the interviewer comfortable enough to share such sensitive information. If they do, it gives you something to focus on in your next practice interviews.

Don't expect the interviewer to come out and say anything about your disability. It's likely that there will already be a certain amount of fear or paranoia regarding this issue, and so it's unlikely that the interviewer will bring it up. You may consider approaching the topic gingerly, by asking the interviewer if there were any concerns relating to your ability to perform the job. Simple fear of a lawsuit, however, along with common sense, will probably prevent anyone from answering that question.

You should note that you need to ask these questions in person or on the phone. It's unlikely that anyone will put into writing anything that is critical about you or your performance during an interview. You may find that the questions are a dead end, leading to responses like "Nothing that I can think of" or "It is not our policy to discuss the qualifications or interview performance of any of our candidates."

Ask if You Can Stay in Touch as a Networking Contact

If nothing else, you may at least be able to include this interviewer in your list of possible networking contacts. They may be able and willing to stay in touch, and to discuss the possibility of openings either with other departments within their organizations, or positions with other organizations in the same line of work.

If this person agrees to allow you to stay in contact, it will be a huge plus for you. It shows a certain level of commitment to you as an individual. It also signifies an investment in you by someone who is also a potential employer. That certainly gives you an advantage in the event that another position becomes available within the same organization.

Even if none of these activities is successful immediately, they are all good "risk/reward plays," because if they do work, they can be extremely helpful. If they do not work out immediately, they have not cost you much.

The key through this period, when you may begin to experience a heightened sense of disappointment on a more regular basis, is to remain in a positive, upbeat state of mind. Being out of work, or simply looking for a new job, can translate into a lot of disappointment. If you do not get an offer at a place where you were really interested in working and where you felt you did pretty well on the interview, it's easy to feel a little depressed. If you begin to feel depressed for any period of time, it will be more difficult to perform the tasks that will generate leads, like sending out resumes, networking, and so on. The fewer job-seeking activities you perform, the longer it takes you to land interviews. The longer it takes you to land interviews, the more depressed you can become. The more depressed you are, the more difficult it is to perform well in an interview. The worse you perform in the interview, the worse your chances are for getting the job, and so on....

The Uneven Playing Field

Sometimes you may strongly suspect that the reason you did not get the job was because of your disability. Sometimes it is a conscious decision made by the employer, not based on any real understanding of the issues, but because misinformation and stereotypes have clouded his or her judgement. Sometimes it's even more subtle than that. Stereotypes can be subconscious as well, with the employer not even realizing that the disability is what took you out of consideration.

Prejudice against people with disabilities is not a new phenomenon. In ancient Greece, the Spartans used to sacrifice children with disabilities by throwing them off of Mt. Taygetus. In the more enlightened Athens, children with disabilities were left in earthen vessels that were put on an altar as an offering to the gods that had punished them. Since that time, having a child with a disability has evoked pity, disdain, and accusations of devil worshiping.

The strides that society has made may appear significant given that history, but we are still far from the day when someone will be viewed as a person first and as a person with a disability second. In fact, as recently as 1974, there was a city ordinance in Chicago that imposed fines on persons appearing in public who were "diseased, maimed, or in any way deformed, so as to be an unsightly or disgusting object."

Legislation in the latter half of the 20th century started to open up doors to people with disabilities in the United States. Perhaps the most significant piece of legislation, from an employment perspective, is the Americans with Disabilities

Act of 1990 (ADA). This law, signed by President Bush, was intended to usher in "a bright new era of equality, independence, and freedom." The results of this legislation can be seen all around us. Curbs have been cut to make it easier for people with mobility impairments to cross the street. Malls have elevators for the same reason. Restaurants provide picture menus and Braille menus. Theaters provide assistive listening devices. And TVs come equipped with closed captioning decoders.

These architectural and equipment changes are far easier to implement, however, than breaking down the more pervasive barriers—those of attitudes. Unfortunately, no one has yet been able to find a way to build a ramp to a closed mind. Polls show that most Americans feel awkward around people with disabilities. Unfortunately, those people are the same ones conducting job interviews.

The ADA has provisions that specifically address job discrimination. Like any discrimination case, an ADA claim can be difficult to prove. Unfortunately, the case law is not too helpful, because not many cases have been successfully argued. It helps to have some understanding of the law, however, so that in the event you feel you are discriminated against you will be able to make an informed decision about how to proceed.

Employment Provisions of the ADA

- Title I of the ADA protects against discrimination by an employer of 15 or more people. (29 C.F.R. Part 1630)

- Title II of the ADA protects against discrimination by any state or local institution, including educational institutions. (28 C.F.R. Part 35)

Who Is Covered?

An individual with a disability under the ADA is a person who has a physical or mental impairment that substantially limits one or more major life activities, has a record of such an impairment, or is regarded as having such an impairment. Major life activities are activities that an average person can perform with little or no difficulty, such as walking, breathing, seeing, hearing, speaking, learning, and working.

Additionally, to be qualified, an employee or applicant must be able to prove that they can perform the essential functions of the job with or without reasonable accommodations. Excluded from coverage by the ADA are those individuals who pose a direct threat to themselves or to others.

Now, if you haven't already picked out a number of "problem words or statements" in the above, you aren't watching enough episodes of *Law & Order* or *Court TV*. Right from the start, we have the word "qualified." A qualified employee or applicant with a disability is someone who satisfies skill, experience, education, and other job-related requirements of the position held or desired, and who, with or without reasonable accommodation, can perform the essential functions of that position.

Recently the Supreme Court in the U.S. ruled that a person with poor eyesight that is mitigated by using glasses is not "qualified" under the ADA. How "mitigation" legally impacts other disabilities will be seen in the years to come.

Next we come to "substantially limits." This is viewed as when the condition, manner, and duration of performance are different than for a nondisabled person.

A "major life activity" could include learning, working, breathing, seeing, hearing, walking, or speaking.

"Essential functions" should be defined beforehand and should be a part of the written job description. This means that if there are two people in shipping and receiving who can refill the bottled water dispenser, it can't be considered "essential" that the receptionist, bookkeeper, or computer operator be able to do it.

A reasonable accommodation (referred to as a "reasonable modification" under Title II) may include, but is not limited to, making existing facilities used by employees readily accessible to and usable by persons with disabilities; job restructuring; modification of work schedules; providing additional unpaid leave; reassignment to a vacant position; acquiring or modifying equipment or devices; adjusting or modifying examinations, training materials, or policies; and providing qualified readers or interpreters. Reasonable accommodation may be necessary to apply for a job, to perform job functions, or to enjoy the benefits and privileges of employment that are enjoyed by people without disabilities. An employer is not required to lower production standards to make an accommodation. An employer generally is not obligated to provide personal-use items such as eyeglasses or hearing aids. These accommodations need not cause an undue hardship on the employer.

And, going into the bonus round of legal jargon, "undue hardship" means an action that requires significant difficulty or expense when considered in relation to factors such as a business' size and financial resources, and the nature and structure of its operation. (So whereas a corner florist with fourteen delivery people on the payroll might not be obligated under the law to provide an employee with a delivery van equipped with a wheelchair lift at a cost of $40,000, General Motors would be obligated to provide that equipment if it were providing company vehicles for its other employees in the same job category because of the size of the company.)

Finally, there are four factors impacting whether or not someone is considered to be a "direct threat." These include:

- The duration of the potential for harm

- The potential for lethality or the severity of the harm

- The likelihood that the harm will occur

- The imminence of the harm

Types of Discrimination that Are Covered Under the ADA

Prohibited Inquiries and Examinations

Before making an offer of employment, an employer may not ask job applicants about the existence, nature, or severity of a disability. Applicants may be asked about their ability to perform job functions. A job offer may be conditioned on the results of a medical examination, but only if the examination is required for all entering employees in the same job category. Medical examinations of employees must be job-related and consistent with business necessity.

Discrimination under the ADA also includes:

- Hiring and firing

- Compensation, assignment, or classification of employees

- Transfer, promotion, layoff, or recall

- Job advertisements

- Recruitment

- Testing

- Use of company facilities

- Training and apprenticeship programs

- Fringe benefits

- Pay, retirement plans, and disability leave

- Other terms and conditions of employment

Under the ADA, it is also illegal to discriminate in any aspect of employment, including:

- Harassment on the basis of race, color, religion, sex, national origin, disability, or age.

- Retaliation against an individual for filing a charge of discrimination, participating in an investigation, or opposing discriminatory practices.

- Employment decisions based on stereotypes or assumptions about the abilities, traits, or performance of individuals of a certain sex, race, age, religion, or ethnic group, or individuals with disabilities.

- Denying employment opportunities to a person because of marriage to, or association with, an individual of a particular race, religion, national origin, or an individual with a disability.

Employers are required to post notices to all employees advising them of their rights under the laws EEOC enforces and their right to be free from retaliation. Such notices must be accessible, as needed, to persons with visual or other disabilities that affect reading.

What to Do If You Think You Have Been Discriminated Against

If you feel that you have been discriminated against, document everything that you can. Write down what encounters you have had, and with whom. Reconstruct, to the best of your abilities, any event that you can recall, leading up to an interview. Document the questions that were asked in the interview, as well as your responses to those questions. Chronicle the demeanor of the interviewer, along with the words that were used. Include information about what you were led to expect that the following steps would be.

You then need to gather any other information that you can about the rest of the hiring process. Was someone hired? What were the qualifications of that person? Were they asked the same kind of questions that you were (were the hiring practices applied uniformly)?

You can also bolster your case if you can collect any information about the company's past practices as they relate to interviewing or hiring people with disabilities. This information can help determine whether your experience was an isolated one or part of a pattern of discrimination.

Once you have collected all of this information, you may consider filing a formal complaint with the Equal Employment Opportunity Commission (EEOC). The EEOC is the agency to approach if the employer has fifteen or more employees.

The EEOC'S Charge Processing Procedures are as follows (taken from the EEOC Web site at www.eeoc.gov/):

Who Can File a Charge of Discrimination?

- Any individual who believes that his or her employment rights have been violated may file a charge of discrimination with the EEOC.

- In addition, an individual, organization, or agency may file a charge on behalf of another person in order to protect the aggrieved person's identity.

How Is a Charge of Discrimination Filed?

A charge may be filed by mail or in person at the nearest EEOC office. Individuals may consult their local telephone directory (U.S. Government listing) or call 1-800-669-4000 (voice) or 1-800-669-6820 (TTY) to contact the nearest EEOC office for more information on specific procedures for filing a charge.

Individuals who need an accommodation in order to file a charge (e.g., sign-language interpreter, print materials in an accessible format) should inform the EEOC field office so appropriate arrangements can be made.

What Information Must Be Provided to File a Charge?

- The complaining party's name, address, and telephone number.

- The name, address, and telephone number of the respondent employer, employment agency, or union that is alleged to have discriminated, and the number of employees (or union members), if known.

- A short description of the alleged violation (the event that caused the complaining party to believe that his or her rights were violated).

- The date(s) of the alleged violation(s).

What Are the Time Limits for Filing a Charge of Discrimination?

All laws enforced by EEOC, except the Equal Pay Act, require filing a charge with EEOC before a private lawsuit may be filed in court. There are strict time limits within which charges must be filed:

- A charge must be filed with EEOC within 180 days of the date of the alleged violation, in order to protect the charging party's rights.

- This 180-day filing deadline is extended to 300 days if the charge also is covered by a state or local anti-discrimination law. For ADEA charges, only state laws extend the filing limit to 300 days.

- To protect legal rights, it is always best to contact EEOC promptly when discrimination is suspected.

What Happens After a Charge Is Filed with the EEOC?

The employer is notified that the charge has been filed. From this point there are a number of ways a charge may be handled:

- A charge may be assigned for priority investigation if the initial facts appear to support a violation of the law. When the evidence is less strong, the charge may be assigned for follow-up investigation to determine whether it is likely that a violation has occurred.

- EEOC can seek to settle a charge at any stage of the investigation if the charging party and the employer express an interest in doing so. If settlement efforts are not successful, the investigation continues.

- In investigating a charge, EEOC may make written requests for information, interview people, review documents, and, as needed, visit the facility where the alleged discrimination occurred. When the investigation is complete, EEOC will discuss the evidence with the charging party or employer, as appropriate.

- The charge may be selected for EEOC's mediation program if both the charging party and the employer express an interest in this option. Mediation is offered as an alternative to a lengthy investigation. Participation in the mediation program is confidential and voluntary and requires consent from both charging party and employer. If mediation is unsuccessful, the charge is returned for investigation.

- A charge may be dismissed at any point if, in the agency's best judgment, further investigation will not establish a violation of the law. A charge may be dismissed at the time it is filed if an initial in-depth interview does not produce evidence to support the claim. When a charge is dismissed, a notice is issued in accordance with the law, which gives the charging party 90 days in which to file a lawsuit on his or her own behalf.

When Can an Individual File an Employment Discrimination Lawsuit in Court?

A charging party may file a lawsuit within 90 days of receiving a notice of a "right to sue" from EEOC, as stated above. Under Title VII and the ADA, a charging party also can request a notice of "right to sue" from EEOC 180 days after the charge was first filed with the Commission and may then bring suit within 90 days after receiving this notice. Under the ADEA, a suit may be filed at any time 60 days after filing a charge with EEOC, but not later than 90 days after EEOC gives notice that it has completed action on the charge.

Under the EPA, a lawsuit must be filed within two years (three years for willful violations) of the discriminatory act, which in most cases is payment of a discriminatory lower wage.

What Remedies Are Available When Discrimination Is Found?

The "relief" or remedies available for employment discrimination, whether caused by intentional acts or by practices that have a discriminatory effect, may include:

- Back pay
- Hiring
- Promotion
- Reinstatement
- Front pay
- Reasonable accommodation
- Other actions that will make an individual "whole" (in the condition s/he would have been but for the discrimination)

Remedies also may include payment of:

- Attorneys' fees

- Expert witness fees

- Court costs

Under most EEOC-enforced laws, compensatory and punitive damages also may be available where intentional discrimination is found. Damages may be available to compensate for actual monetary losses, for future monetary losses, and for mental anguish and inconvenience. Punitive damages also may be available if an employer acted with malice or reckless indifference. Punitive damages are not available against state or local governments.

In cases concerning reasonable accommodation under the ADA, compensatory or punitive damages may not be awarded to the charging party if an employer can demonstrate that "good faith" efforts were made to provide reasonable accommodation.

An employer may be required to post notices to all employees addressing the violations of a specific charge and advising them of their rights under the laws EEOC enforces and their right to be free from retaliation. Such notices must be accessible, as needed, to persons with visual or other disabilities that affect reading.

The employer also may be required to take corrective or preventive actions to cure the source of the identified discrimination and minimize the chance of its recurrence, as well as discontinue the specific discriminatory practices involved in the case.

To contact the EEOC, look in your telephone directory under "U.S. Government." For information and instructions on reaching your local office, contact:

Equal Employment Opportunity Commission
1801 L Street NW
Washington, DC 20507
(800) 669-4000 (Voice)
(800) 669-6820 (TDD)
(202) 663-4900 (Voice—for 202 Area Code)
(202) 663-4494 (TDD—for 202 Area Code)

or visit their Web site at:

www.eeoc.gov

More Questions and Answers About the ADA— From the Department of Justice Web Site

`www.usdoj.gov/crt/ada/adahom1.htm`

Q: *Is an employer required to provide reasonable accommodation when I apply for a job?*

A: Yes. Applicants, as well as employees, are entitled to reasonable accommodation. For example, an employer may be required to provide a sign-language interpreter during a job interview for an applicant who is deaf or hearing impaired, unless doing so would impose an undue hardship.

Q: *Should I tell my employer that I have a disability?*

A: If you think you will need a reasonable accommodation in order to participate in the application process or to perform essential job functions, you should inform the employer that an accommodation will be needed. Employers are required to provide reasonable accommodation only for the physical or mental limitations of a qualified individual with a disability of which they are aware. Generally, it is the responsibility of the employee to inform the employer that an accommodation is needed.

Q: *Do I have to pay for a needed reasonable accommodation?*

A: No. The ADA requires that the employer provide the accommodation unless doing so would impose an undue hardship on the operation of the employer's business. If the cost of providing the needed accommodation would be an undue hardship, the employee must be given the choice of providing the accommodation or paying for the portion of the accommodation that causes the undue hardship.

Q: *Can an employer lower my salary or pay me less than other employees doing the same job because I need a reasonable accommodation?*

A: No. An employer cannot make up the cost of providing a reasonable accommodation by lowering your salary or paying you less than other employees in similar positions.

Q: *Does an employer have to make non-work areas used by employees, such as cafeterias, lounges, and employer-provided transportation, accessible to people with disabilities?*

A: Yes. The requirement to provide reasonable accommodation covers all services, programs, and non-work facilities provided by the employer. If making an existing facility accessible would be an undue hardship, the employer must provide a comparable facility that will enable a person with a disability to enjoy benefits and privileges of employment similar to those enjoyed by other employees, unless doing so would be an undue hardship.

Q: *If an employer has several qualified applicants for a job, is the employer required to select a qualified applicant with a disability over other applicants without a disability?*

A: No. The ADA does not require that an employer hire an applicant with a disability over other applicants because the person has a disability. The ADA only prohibits discrimination on the basis of disability. It makes it unlawful to refuse to hire a qualified applicant with a disability because he is disabled or because a reasonable accommodation is required to make it possible for this person to perform essential job functions.

Q: *Can an employer refuse to hire me because he believes that it would be unsafe, because of my disability, for me to work with certain machinery required to perform the essential functions of the job?*

A: The ADA permits an employer to refuse to hire an individual if she poses a direct threat to the health or safety of herself or others. A direct threat means a significant risk of substantial harm. The determination that there is a direct threat must be based on objective, factual evidence regarding an individual's present ability to perform essential functions of a job. An employer cannot refuse to hire you because of a slightly increased risk or because of fears that there might be a significant risk sometime in the future. The employer must also consider whether a risk can be eliminated or reduced to an acceptable level with a reasonable accommodation.

Q: *Can an employer offer a health insurance policy that excludes coverage for pre-existing conditions?*

A: Yes. The ADA does not affect pre-existing condition clauses contained in health insurance policies, even though such clauses may adversely affect employees with disabilities more than other employees.

Q: *If the health insurance offered by my employer does not cover all of the medical expenses related to my disability, does the company have to obtain additional coverage for me?*

A: No. The ADA only requires that an employer provide employees with disabilities equal access to whatever health insurance coverage is offered to other employees.

Q: *I think I was discriminated against because my wife is disabled. Can I file a charge with the EEOC?*

A: Yes. The ADA makes it unlawful to discriminate against an individual, whether disabled or not, because of a relationship or association with an individual with a known disability.

Q: *Are people with AIDS covered by the ADA?*

A: Yes. The legislative history indicates that Congress intended the ADA to protect persons with AIDS and HIV disease from discrimination.

Negotiating the Offer

Not everyone is going to discriminate; in fact, there are many employers who have had great success with people with disabilities in their workplace and, as a result, proactively promote their opportunities to them. A list of these employers can be found in the appendix at the back of this book.

After a successful series of interviews, you may be offered an opportunity. Sometimes that offer will come in a letter, and sometimes it will come in a phone call. Usually there will come a time when you will be invited to discuss the particulars of the job, including salary.

Negotiating the terms of an offer can be a tricky business. It is in the best interest of the employer to try to offer you the least that you will accept. You, on the other hand, will be looking to negotiate the most attractive package that the employer will be willing to provide. Somewhere in the middle is where most negotiations will usually end up. Your goal is to reach a number that is closer to your goal than theirs.

In order to successfully negotiate an offer, you need to be particularly well informed. You need to collect as much information as you can, and then you need to do some soul-searching to decide exactly how you will proceed. The factors you will want to consider include the following:

- **What do you need?** Some jobs are worth a great deal more than they pay because of the opportunity to learn and grow in the position. This is why many people volunteer or take unpaid internships with companies. If you could afford not to be paid, and if this opportunity is worth taking regardless of the pay, you should consider that going in. That is not what you will be shooting for, but it helps give you perspective as you go through the negotiations.

- **What are you worth?** Do the research to find out what the going salaries are for this kind of job. Factor in your years of experience. That should give you a ballpark number for what you might expect or ask for. You can find information about salaries from your local office of the State Department of Labor. You can also visit your college career center, where they have information on starting salaries, as well as information on salaries broken down by area of study. You can also check out Jobstar California on the Web at www.jobsmart.org/tools/salary/index.htm.

- **What is the cost of living in the area where the job will be?** If you are offered a job in New York City, and are offered the same job in Dubuque, Iowa, it is likely that the starting salary for the New York job will be higher. The reason for this differential is the fact that the cost of living in New York is considerably higher than it is in Dubuque. To determine whether you should modify your salary expectations to reflect the cost of living in that city, look at the cost-of-living comparisons like the one at Homefair (www.homefair.com).

- **How is the company doing?** If the company has been growing, and if they have been having trouble recruiting qualified people, they may be more willing to pay higher salaries. On the other hand, if your research indicates that an organization is struggling, they may be more resistant to a higher salary request.

- **What issues are most important to you?** What are your values? If you are willing to put in a lot of extra work, and if you already have health coverage, perhaps the salary offered will be your most important consideration. Perhaps you will decide that the money is important, but not nearly as important as a flexible work schedule, the opportunity to telecommute, or the retirement package. These variables are up to you, and sometimes the employer may have more flexibility in one area than another. Don't make the mistake of focusing on only one variable.

- **What will your new expenses be?** Parking, tolls, the time you spend commuting, and any new clothes or uniforms you may have to purchase can add up.

- **Are there disincentives to working, based on your disability?** If you receive any government benefits related to your disability (SSI, SSDI, medical insurance), check with your rehabilitation counselor to see what impact working full time will have on those benefits.

Once you have gathered all of this information, you will be prepared to negotiate your offer. You may be asked what kind of salary you were looking for. If you can, put this question back on the employer by asking if they had a range in mind, or what they have historically paid people in this position. This lets you know what the parameters are early on.

You may decide, based on those parameters, that you are being "lowballed," or offered something far below what you are worth. If you have done the research, you should feel comfortable providing that information to the employer. "To be honest, that seems a little low. I know that the median salary for that position is $24,000 in this state, and that people coming right out of college, without my experience, are making in the low- to mid-twenties nationally. Is it possible that the salary could be revised upward based on my experience?"

That kind of response is quite assertive, but it may impress the employer that you know what you are talking about. When you ask about *revising* the salary, by taking into consideration your *experience,* you are also leaving the employer with a bit of an out. This puts the employer in a position to increase your offer if they choose to, while still saving face.

If you absolutely feel boxed in by this request, answer by using a range. "I would be looking for something in the high teens to mid-twenties, depending on the rest of the package" is a response that gives you and the employer a little wiggle room. If the employer balks, you may decide that you want to firmly stand behind your expectation, even at the risk of not working for that company. You may also decide that you would prefer to take the job. If you decide the latter, you should try to leave the door ajar for future salary negotiations. "Well, I am really excited about this opportunity, and I don't want to let it pass by because of a few thousand dollars. If I were to take the position, would we be able to review the salary in six months (or a year)? In that time, I am sure I can show you that I am worth even more!"

The negotiations do not end with the salary figure being finalized. There may be an opportunity to negotiate issues like a signing bonus (these are becoming quite prevalent in the highly competitive technical fields), the number of vacation days, the health-care package, as well as working arrangements (these are usually settled with the hiring manager, not with the human resources manager). If you lost the salary argument, or if the employer feels that they may have gotten you at a bargain price, he or she may be more willing to give in on some other issues.

There are plenty of other areas where you may be able to negotiate. Some employers offer discounts to their employees on the goods or services produced by the organization. Other employers offer partial or full tuition reimbursement for approved continuing-education courses. Sometimes this includes college and/or graduate coursework. Sometimes there is the opportunity to have the use of a company vehicle. Many companies offer stock options.

It's never too early to think about the other end of your career, either. Excellent pension and retirement benefits can make a lower up-front salary much more palatable. If the industry is volatile, it may even be worth your while to discuss what involuntary separation/severance policies there are.

If accepting this position means that you will have to relocate, you should discuss these policies up front. Some companies pay all expenses; you just provide the receipts. Other companies actually handle the arrangements with the moving company, and they are billed directly. Some companies provide a lump sum that they will pay for these expenses, regardless of what costs you actually incur. And of course, some companies will give you a map and suggestions for where you can find some good boxes to use for packing.

Phone, Get Out of the Booth, or Ask for a New Number

Once you have all of this information, you will be asked to make a decision. Don't be afraid to ask for twenty-four hours to think it over. This is not a decision that you should enter into lightly. Seek out the opinions of those who matter. If you feel like the offer is too low, you may want to say that up front. "I am going to need a little time to think this over, and to talk with my wife. I have to admit that while the other benefits are quite attractive, the salary is not quite what the position seems to be worth. I don't want to respond hastily, however, and so I would like to talk it through with my wife. At the same time, if you could go back and see if there is any possible way that the salary number could be adjusted, that would be great."

When you come back the next day, you need to have made a decision, considering the risks that are involved. On one hand, if accepting a salary that is lower than you believe you are worth is going to make you miserable and resentful, you may be better off sticking to your principles, even at the risk of having the offer rescinded. On the other hand, if you push a little too hard, and the offer is withdrawn, and you are miserable because you are still unemployed, you may decide that it would have been better to take the offer and try for a salary upgrade later.

Each case will have a different answer, but consider these variables carefully and adjust their weights according to your own values:

- Is the offer *unreasonably* low, or just lower than you believe it should be? (If it is unreasonably low, score 1 for turning it down; otherwise, score 1 for accepting.)

- Do you have other offers you are currently evaluating? (If yes, weigh them against each other and choose the best; if not, score 1 for accepting.)

- Do you have any other hot prospects that you have interviewed for and are waiting to hear from? (If yes, score .25 for turning the offer down for each hot prospect; score 2 for accepting if the answer is no.)

- Does the position offer good potential for advancement? (Score 1 for turning it down if the answer is no; score 1 for accepting if the answer is yes.)

- Are you currently fully employed and considering a switch, or are you unemployed? (Score 1 for declining the offer if you are fully employed; score 1 for accepting if you are unemployed.)

- Ask yourself the Clint Eastwood/Dirty Harry question: Do I feel lucky? (Score 1 for decline if yes; score 1 for accept if no.)

If the numbers add up to a yes, the employer may give you a letter outlining your agreement. If that letter does not arrive close to your start date, you should consider writing a thank-you letter to the employer. In that letter you should outline your excitement about the new position, and spell out what you understand the terms of the agreement to be. Suggest that if there are any questions before you start, they should let you know.

This strategy will formalize your agreement to some extent. Sometimes a hiring manager exceeds his authority when making an offer. If there is no formal response to your letter, you will be in a better position to ask for what you negotiated if you have your request in writing than if it was all just verbal.

Turning Down an Offer

There will be times when those factors will add up so that the best choice you can make is to turn the job down. It may be because of the salary package, the work, or the working environment. Regardless of the reason, it is important that you decline the offer with a great deal of class.

Even if you tell the employer in person, you should write a thank-you letter to the employer. In the letter you should thank the employer for extending the offer, but state that given the terms of the offer, and your own personal circumstances, you must decline at this time. You may suggest that you still have a great deal of admiration for the organization, and wish the company and the employer well in the future.

Even if you have no intention of ever working there, you want to end this current relationship on positive terms. This is true for two main reasons. First, never say never. A new job could open up there tomorrow that would be perfect for you. Second, the manager who recruits you could leave that company tomorrow and end up interviewing you on Monday for a position with his or her new company.

PART IV

Succeeding at Work

Chapter 12: Keeping the Job

Chapter 13: Accommodating Your Disability on the Job

CHAPTER 12

Keeping the Job

Once you have accepted a job offer, feel free to celebrate your accomplishment. Take a few moments to look back over the past several months and make mental notes of your progress. If possible, write them down. You have a lot to be proud of, because too many job seekers with disabilities quit before you did. Hopefully, what you have done will serve as an example for others.

Don't pull any muscles as you pat yourself on the back, though. You have a lot of work left to do as you shift gears and focus on keeping your job. You do not want to be content with just getting the job. Your goal now, no matter what your job is, is to be the best possible _____ in your organization and, in fact, to be the best _____ there is.

Several factors will ultimately determine the extent to which you will accomplish this goal. You will need to show the right attitude on the job. You will need to establish positive working relationships with coworkers, supervisors, and subordinates. You should learn all that you can about your position, the organization, and the industry. Also, you will need to look for projects that will give you an opportunity to show all this off.

You will also need to find ways to minimize the extent to which your disability impacts the relationships that you establish. You will need to be aware of the attitudes of others, and, when appropriate, you will need to find ways to educate those you work with about your disability. You will also need to determine what kind of accommodations—special equipment, flexible hours, and so on—your disability necessitates. Chapter 13 covers this topic in detail.

Finally, you will need to remind yourself that the days of an employee working 35 years at the plant, retiring, and receiving the gold watch are well behind us. You need to always be looking for the next appropriate opportunity. Sometimes that opportunity is with the same employer, and sometimes it may be elsewhere.

Having the Right Attitude

Just like when you were interviewing, you need to remember that first impressions are very important. The same rules should apply for your first several months on the job. For starters, practice your route to work during the morning rush hour to get a feel for what time you will need to leave in order to get to work early.

On your first day, you will want to be just a little early—10 minutes or so. But once you have gone through orientation and you have a key to get into the office, and you know where your work space is located, there is almost no such thing as "too early." At the very least, you want to be at your work space before your supervisor gets there, and stay for at least fifteen minutes after he or she has left. This way, your boss will never know for sure that you ever go home!

This isn't just about schmoozing the boss, either. The fact is, you will find out that you can be much more productive in that hour before your colleagues get to work than you can in three hours after they are there. Between the people stopping by your work space, the phone calls, the e-mail, the voice mail, and the fax, you can quickly get caught up in a reactive mode instead of a proactive mode. Regardless of the nature of your job, just getting there early, clearing your head, and planning your day will give you a noticeable mental edge.

Another way to show that you have the right attitude is to remain eager to grow. Earlier in the book we discussed the process of identifying your weaknesses. Perhaps you will notice a few more after you begin your new job. Whatever they are, try to take a few minutes each day to focus and work on those weaknesses. If you have a half hour per day, that's great. But even if you can set aside only ten minutes a day, do it. Over time you will find that even if you don't eliminate your weakness, you will have lessened it. In the effort, you are bound to find ways to use your other skills to ameliorate your weaknesses.

You should remain eager to continue learning about your job and your company. If you are on a production line, try to see what you can learn about how the products are designed. How does the company handle quality-control issues? How do they incorporate design changes? How are the production units stored? Sold? Shipped? The more you know about the bigger picture, the better you will be able to do your own job, as you will have a better grasp of where your job fits into the grand scheme of things.

This commitment to personal growth should not stop at the gates of the factory, either. After you have been on the job for a while, you may want to reacquaint yourself with the tuition-reimbursement program at your company. You may find that it will be in your best interest to pursue additional formal education, either by working toward an additional degree or by taking additional courses in an appropriate area.

Succeeding at Office Politics

In the last several years, the term *politics* has taken on increasingly worse connotations. People who get involved in politics are smeared with the same brush as those who have betrayed the public's trust. The term *office politics* has a similarly negative connotation. In its most negative form, it is used by people who have failed to succeed at the rate they believe they deserve to describe how people they perceive as being less qualified have succeeded. Other times it is used by people who attempt to explain things that they don't understand in the workplace.

Promotions, like jobs, do not usually go to the person who is best qualified. The fact is that they usually go to someone who is qualified, but who is particularly good at the art of office politics.

First of all, notice that I do not cast the term *office politics* in a negative light myself. Like gravity, it is a fact of life. It is rather futile to be "for" or "against" something over which you have no control. The best thing to do, in my opinion, is to recognize that it exists, protect yourself from it, and do what you can to use its power for your own benefit.

It's worth noting that there is a huge difference between learning to be good at office politics and being a "brownnoser." People who succeed at the former are much more likely to advance than those who attempt the latter. The "brownnoser" is also more likely to earn the disdain of his or her fellow workers. You will impress both your boss and your coworkers much more by working hard and keeping your mouth closed than by "tooting your own horn" or by being a "yes man."

There are a few things you can do to help yourself navigate the politics of your workplace:

- **Study the organizational chart.** Get a copy from your supervisor or from human resources; or, if necessary, try to construct one yourself. This will give you a good idea of how the organization is set up on paper—who reports to whom, where each division lies, and so on.

- **Figure out what the "real" chart looks like.** After a period of time, you will see that regardless of how it looks on paper, power is distributed in a different way. You may find that the secretary to the president has more real power than a vice president.

- **Be a good person.** Sometimes people overlook this simple principle. By treating people with respect—regardless of whether they are above you on the organizational chart, in the next cubicle, or reporting to you—you will earn their respect.

- **Be a good listener.** Sometimes your coworkers will just need an ear. They may want to vent about that jerk in accounting, or they may want to complain about how the step-up in production is going to create problems on the assembly line. Regardless of the issue, pay attention to what they are saying, and show them that you have heard them and understand what they are saying. That doesn't mean that you should chime in with your two cents about the people in accounting. Your best bet is to speak no ill of anyone else in the workplace. Just having you listen to them nonjudgmentally is enough to make your coworkers think you are "on their side."

- **Gossip is inevitable,** but don't believe it unless you see it yourself, and even then don't be so sure. Even Machiavelli would be unable to keep all of the plots straight, with twelve different versions of each story, all containing a certain amount of truth, twelve different motivations for sharing the story with you, etc. Don't get caught up in it. If someone tells you that Stephanie from the other territory is trying to steal your account, don't act on it unless that action is going directly to Stephanie and asking her. If a person tells you such a story, in fact, suggest that the two of you approach Stephanie right then. More often than not, the person who brought you the message will back down quite a bit from his or her assertions.

- **Don't let the gossip get beyond you.** I know a lot of people who are well respected who have been made to look foolish by passing on a story that was not true. This is also true for passing on urban legends and Internet hoaxes. It's worse when the message was gossip that turned out to be untrue. In those cases, the once well-respected people look malevolent and end up being less trusted.

- **Build relationships.** Every new worker figures out that they need to please their boss. This is a given, although you should be aware of the possibility that you will be perceived as a brownnoser. Just as important as building those relationships with those above you, you must strive toward building relationships with those beside you and below you on the organizational chart. I know of a person who was pretty well respected in their field who applied for a lateral job with a better organization. Unfortunately for this person, the secretary for the person doing the hiring had worked for the applicant a couple of years before. I say unfortunately because the secretary had left because she had not been treated very well. This person made it through the first round of interviews but never really stood a chance of getting the job, because the secretary had a chance to give her input on the situation. You just never know who might have the chance to help or hurt you in the future, so you should be consistently decent with everyone.

- **Do not be too provincial.** It's very easy to get into set patterns at work. Before too long you can be hanging out with the same people after work, on breaks, and at lunch. Break those patterns. Set aside at least two days a week where you eat your lunch with people from another department. Get involved in activities that involve people from outside your department. Softball and bowling teams are a great way to meet new people, establish new relationships, and relax at the same time.

- **Seek out a mentor.** As you move around the organization, keep an eye out for those people who have been successful. Try to establish contact with these people, and choose one with whom to establish a deeper relationship— maybe someone with whom you have something in common or have a particular rapport. Ask this person for their advice on topics that are puzzling you. Over time this person can help you as you make the decisions that will determine whether you move up within the organization.

- **Manage your boss carefully.** Outside of the world of Dilbert, no two bosses are the same. Try to determine what motivates your boss. Remember that the bottom line is that if you look good (but not too good), they look good. If you look bad, they look worse. Try to find that balance where your boss still thinks of you as a "self-starter" but also as a person who is smart enough to seek advice from her or him.

- **Ask a lot of questions.** If you tell your boss "We should stop painting the flange first and then adding the rivets; we should paint the flange after we put in the rivets," your boss may dismiss your suggestion without even thinking about it. If you ask "It seems we spend a lot of time repainting the flanges after the rivet gun hits them; do you think we could paint the flanges after they are riveted?", the response you get may be quite different.

- **Don't get caught up in seeking credit.** In the above scenario, the result is likely to be that your boss will announce that she has had a breakthrough: From now on, you will paint after the riveting is completed. The fact is, the boss may actually believe that it was her idea. That really doesn't matter. Again, if it helps your boss and helps the company, it helps you.

- **Communicate bad news and criticism verbally; communicate good news in writing.** E-mail is considered writing. Both are more permanent than the spoken word, and your words on paper will be associated with you long after spoken words melt away. This way, people will remember the good news much more clearly than the bad news.

Looking for Projects

It's essential that you have a good understanding of the politics of your office; however, politics alone will seldom carry you the distance. In order to accomplish the goals you have set for yourself, you will eventually need to have a track record of accomplishments on which to stand. Establishing that track record should be your priority from your first day on the job.

You need to seek out the opportunities that will give you the chance to establish a track record. You don't always get them handed to you as a part of your job description. Your supervisor is also probably so busy that sometimes it may seem easier to just perform a task herself than to delegate that task to you and shepherd you through it. Given that scenario, you should be on the lookout for the opportunities, and ask your supervisor if you can get involved in them. Sometimes a project may not even exist; you need to create it.

Often there are a few tasks that have to be done but that do not attract volunteers. These may include organizing the office holiday party, the United Way or charitable giving drive, or even the annual inventory effort. These can be great projects to sink your teeth into. You can quickly establish yourself as a well-known quantity throughout the company by adding a bit of pizzazz to these projects. Create a theme for the office party. Dress up like Dracula and pass out plastic fangs to all blood donors. Have a dunk tank or pie throw with senior staff members to raise funds for the charitable campaign. Bring in a live band or a disc jockey for an after-inventory party. If you put some creativity into these events, you can be sure that everyone will be talking about the fun they had, and your name will be on everyone's lips and minds for weeks.

If you are given a project that is more directly related to your job description, give it the same level of energy and creativity, and even more! If possible, seek out team members whom you don't normally work with. When you contact them, feel them out to see if they would be enthusiastic members of your team. If you can bring them on board, you will strengthen your relationship with them as individuals, as well as with their work units.

Once you have an energetic team in place, the sky is the limit. You will find that you can achieve amazing things if you have several people with energy who also share a common vision. If you make the goals challenging but attainable, and if you foster an environment where everyone feels like they are genuinely part of a team, it will mean a memorable and successful project for everyone.

The most highly valued employees are the ones who show some leadership and initiative. The most highly valued leaders are the ones who are also excellent followers. Sometimes it is going to be someone who approaches *you* and asks if you would be willing to come on board *their* team for a special project. If you join them, give it everything you've got. Give it the same energy and creativity that you would give the projects that you lead. In a true team environment, different people step up at different times and exert their leadership in a given situation, and then revert to a team member mentality when another leader steps up during another phase of the project.

Knowing when to follow and when to lead is a skill that comes in time, and with experience. The strongest leaders are those who lead by example. Anyone can be a leader by virtue of the position they hold. Usually that person is regarded more as a "boss" than as a leader. You will be far more successful, far more quickly, if you quietly lead by example, yet keep an eye out for opportunities where you can step up and use your leadership skills for a project over which you have some level of responsibility.

Fitting In and Succeeding with a Disability

It would be nice if once you had succeeded in getting hired, you no longer had to worry about the way your disability impacts your work. Unfortunately, that's not the case. You will need to remain cognizant of the ways in which your disability affects the way you do your job, as well as the way in which people perceive that your disability affects the way you do your job.

There are several aspects to this concern. First of all, you need to make sure that you have the necessary tools to perform your job effectively. Second, you need to be attentive to the perceptions and attitudes of those around you. You alone will never change their attitudes about people with disabilities, but you can be successful in changing their attitudes about *you*.

Normalizing Your Disability for Your Peers and Coworkers

It's not just the disabled employee who wants to appear "normal." It's true for the child in the schoolyard who wants to be asked to play kickball, and it is true for the new worker who wants to be asked to join the bowling league. Too often for people with disabilities, these invitations do not come right away.

With the support of the people in the human resources office, as well as from your hiring manager, you may want to take some proactive steps to educate your coworkers about your disability.

There are all kinds of tales of people overreacting when discovering that a coworker has a disability. People usually overreact out of ignorance, not out of malice. People who have AIDS or are HIV-positive have been almost universally feared in the workplace. Workers have raised concerns about catching the virus by using the same phone, by sharing a computer, or by using the same copy machine. With a little education (and assuming that everyone is using this equipment as intended), those fears dissipate quickly.

Sometimes people's first reaction is not fear, but rather a desire to help. This genuine caring spirit, when combined with misinformation, can have interesting results as well. Although not directly a workplace story, I recall attending a conference of College Disability Service Directors in New Orleans. A group of us went out to one of the city's hundreds of nice restaurants. One of our party was deaf and communicated using sign language. The hostess, seeing this, went out of her way to be helpful. That is to say, she talked v-e-r-y s-l-o-w-l-y. Then, to top it off, she handed out the menus. She was proud as a peacock as she handed our deaf friend a Braille menu. Our friend, who has a *great* sense of humor, looked at the menu, looked at us, then looked at the waitress with a straight face and began rubbing the menu against her ear. Then she said, "I think I'll have the special."

Most disability-specific organizations publish materials that educate people about that specific disability. For example, you can get information about what to do in the event that a person has a seizure at:

```
http://epilepsy.org.uk/info/firstaid.html
```

By providing your coworkers with this kind of information, you do several things

- You eliminate misinformation about your disability.

- You provide accurate information about your disability.

- You create an open dialogue with coworkers about your disability rather than having the only discussions take place at whisper level.

This may not be the first time you have encountered the need to educate people about your disability. If you use a service animal, you may have had to explain 1,000 or more times that it is a working animal, and that the well-meaning pats of strangers can actually cause harm. I have a friend who is blind. Once a month someone tries to drag him across the street, when in fact he is waiting for a bus, not waiting for someone to earn their next scouting badge. To get to this point, you must have a good sense of humor, and you have probably come to the understanding that people are usually well-meaning. By educating people, not only do you help break down their attitude toward you, but to some extent you poke a pinhole through their wall of ignorance. Over time, with enough pinpricks, the light of day will begin to shine through.

Being Ready for the Next Opportunity When It Presents Itself

As I said earlier, it's unlikely that you will stay in your current job until you get a gold watch and membership in the AARP. The skills you have developed as you have worked your way through this book are life skills—that is, they will be with you throughout your life.

Your main focus, especially in the first few years, should be on doing the best that you possibly can in your current position. At the same time, you should invest some time in your long-term career. Keep that binder or the disk you started as you worked through this book. At the end of every week, think back to any new challenges you faced. Did you get any new assignments? Did you have any accomplishments? At the end of the month, take a longer-term view. How has your job changed in the last month? The last six months? Add this information to your career autobiography.

With this information, you should also keep that "anthology," or long version of your resume, updated. What training sessions did you complete? What awards or commendations did you receive? What software have you learned? What productivity increases or cost savings have you been a part of?

By adding these pieces of information to your anthology resume, you make it possible to produce an up-to-date targeted resume at a moment's notice. You will be able to respond quickly to any opportunity you come across.

Make a point of staying in touch with your networking contacts. Now that you are employed, perhaps you will be in a position to help them in some way. Also, as you stay in touch with them, they will be able to appreciate your growth, and perhaps even take pride in it. At the same time, now that you are employed in the field, your network of people will grow considerably. If these new contacts or your old networking contacts see or hear of an opportunity that may be appropriate for you, they may think of you and let you know. This keeps you poised to take advantage of any opportunity that arises.

Being employed in your field of interest gives you a great advantage. You do not have to even entertain an opportunity if it doesn't seem to be much better than your current position. You will be able to pick and choose much more selectively. If you do that, your long-term results can be outstanding!

Knowing How to Handle Changes in Insurance

There are protections in place to keep your current health insurance in the event of a change in your employment circumstances. The following information is provided by the U.S. Department of Labor.

Who is entitled to benefits under COBRA? There are three elements to qualifying for COBRA benefits. COBRA establishes these specific criteria for plans, qualified beneficiaries, and qualifying events:

- **Plan Coverage.** Group health plans for employers with 20 or more employees on more than 50 percent of its typical business days in the previous calendar year are subject to COBRA. Both full- and part-time employees are counted to determine whether a plan is subject to COBRA. Each part-time employee counts as a fraction on an employee, with the fraction equal to the number of hours that the part-time employee worked divided by the hours an employee must work to be considered full-time.

- **Qualified Beneficiaries.** A qualified beneficiary generally is an individual covered by a group health plan on the day before a qualifying event who is either an employee, the employee's spouse, or an employee's dependent child. In certain cases, a retired employee, the retired employee's spouse, and the retired employee's dependent children may be qualified beneficiaries. In addition, any child born to or placed for adoption with a covered employee during the period of COBRA coverage is considered a qualified beneficiary. Agents, independent contractors, and directors who participate in the group health plan may also be qualified beneficiaries.

- **Qualifying Events.** Qualifying events are certain events that would cause an individual to lose health coverage. The type of qualifying event will determine who the qualified beneficiaries are and the amount of time that a plan must offer the health coverage to them under COBRA. A plan, at its discretion, may provide longer periods of continuation coverage.

The qualifying events for employees are

- Voluntary or involuntary termination of employment for reasons other than gross misconduct

- Reduction in the number of hours of employment

The qualifying events for spouses are

- Voluntary or involuntary termination of the covered employee's employment for any reason other than gross misconduct
- Reduction in the hours worked by the covered employee
- Covered employee's becoming entitled to Medicare
- Divorce or legal separation of the covered employee
- Death of the covered employee

The qualifying events for dependent children are the same as for the spouse with one addition: Loss of dependent child status under the plan rule.

CHAPTER 13

Accommodating Your Disability on the Job

To be successful in your job, you will need to have the appropriate tools to do your job effectively. You need to first determine what accommodations will be necessary. Then you will need to advocate putting them in place.

If your disability is readily apparent, it is quite possible that you discussed these issues with your new employer back when you were interviewed. If your disability cannot be easily discerned, and if you did not disclose it prior to being hired, you may need to approach your employer with the issue now.

Regardless of whether you have discussed this issue with your employer, hopefully you have given some thought to how you will be able to perform the essential functions of your job. The best resource for this is the Job Accommodation Network (JAN). JAN is a product of the Office of Disability Employment Policy, part of the U.S. Department of Labor. The Web site, at http://www.jan.wvu.edu/, points out the following facts:

- Job accommodations are usually not expensive.

- Job accommodations may be as simple as a rearrangement of equipment.

- Job accommodations can reduce workers' compensation and other insurance costs.

- Job accommodations can increase the pool of qualified employees.

- Job accommodations can create opportunities for persons with functional limitations.

Before calling JAN, you should organize your thoughts on paper regarding the exact nature of your disability, as well as the nature of the duties of the job, as you understand them. You should also be able to provide information about how those functions are currently performed at your place of employment.

When you call (800-526-7234, voice and TTY), you will be referred to one of the several talented staff members who specialize in an area related to your disability. When you share the information about the extent of your disability, the nature of the work, and so on, you will be given suggestions about possible accommodations to help you perform your job. They will provide the same service to your employer; however, it is probably to your advantage to make the first contact with JAN and then approach your employer with that information.

Real-Life Sample Accommodations

The Job Accommodation Network has helped thousands of people with disabilities as they seek to find the appropriate accommodations for their work settings. The accommodations can range from simple changes in the work schedule to modifications of the environment. Following are some sample accommodations suggested by the JAN staff.

Altering the Job Duties or Work Schedule

Sometimes the most appropriate accommodation is an alteration of the job duties or the work schedule. JAN provides these examples:

→ **Situation:** A data-entry clerk had agoraphobia and had difficulty traveling during peak hours of traffic.

★ **Solution:** The employee's working hours were changed from 8:30 a.m.–4:30 p.m. to 10:00 a.m.–6:00 p.m. Cost of accommodation: $0.

→ **Situation:** A highly skilled electronics technician who has AIDS was taking a large amount of annual and sick leave.

★ **Solution:** The employer provided a flexible work schedule and redistributed portions of the workload. The company also instituted AIDS-awareness training for employees. Cost of accommodation: $0.

→ **Situation:** As a result of diabetes, a productive employee in a retail business was experiencing fatigue and needed time during the day to administer medication. She was having difficulty performing her sales duties for a sustained period of time.

★ **Solution:** The employee's schedule was altered to allow for a longer meal break and periods during the day to administer medication. Cost of accommodation: $0.

Facility Modifications

Other times the company may need to modify the facility to accommodate your disability. Here's an example of this type of modification provided by JAN:

→ **Situation:** A computer programmer in a manufacturing company has cerebral palsy, which affects her fine motor control. The employee uses a wheelchair, and as a result could not access certain areas of the work site.

★ **Solution:** A bathroom stall was enlarged and safety rails installed. Her desk was raised several inches to enable the wheelchair to fit underneath, and computer space was made available on the first floor of the building. A ramp and automatic doors were installed, and a personal parking place close to the elevator was designated. Building owners provided materials and absorbed costs for building remodeling. Cost to owner of the building: approximately $5,000. Cost to the employer: $0.

Purchasing Adaptive Equipment

There are times when modifying the work space or altering the job duties will not be sufficient. In many of these cases, however, purchasing adaptive equipment or software can be an appropriate accommodation. Here are some examples of these types of accommodations provided by JAN:

→ **Situation:** A file clerk with no hearing needs to have effective communication in a training seminar held for all new employees.

★ **Solution:** The employer hired a sign-language interpreter for the employee's training, which lasted two days. Cost of accommodation: $500.

➜ **Situation:** An electromechanical assembly worker acquired a cumulative wrist-hand trauma disorder that affected handling and fingering. This decreased his ability to perform the twisting motion needed to use a screwdriver.

★ **Solution:** A rechargeable electric screwdriver was purchased to reduce repetitive wrist twisting. Electric screwdrivers were subsequently purchased for all employees as a preventative measure. Cost of accommodation: $65 per employee.

Developing Special Equipment

Sometimes there is no product that can accommodate your disability. In these cases, put your head together with your employer, and with JAN, to think whether there are other ways to accommodate your disability. Here is an example of these types of accommodations developed with the help of JAN:

➜ **Situation:** An elementary school teacher with hearing loss was having great difficulty hearing students due to the background noise of screeching tables and chairs on the tiled classroom floor.

★ **Solution:** The school system could not purchase carpeting for the classroom immediately, so the teacher was permitted to cut holes in tennis balls and place them on the legs of the tables and chairs. Although the tennis balls were not intended for this purpose, they eliminated the background noise of the screeching tables and chairs. Fortunately, the teacher had tennis-playing friends who were willing to donate their used tennis balls. As a result, the cost of the accommodation was $0.

Modifying a Product

Even the combined creativity of you, your employer, and the people at JAN isn't guaranteed to produce a great solution like the preceding one every time. Sometimes you will need to contact an appropriate professional to modify a product to meet your needs. The folks at JAN can help you identify which type of professional may be able to help you. The following are two success stories:

→ **Situation:** A catalog salesperson with a spinal cord injury had difficulty using the catalog due to finger-dexterity limitations.

★ **Solution:** The employer purchased a motorized catalog rack. When it was modified with a single-switch control, the employee could turn the rack to access the catalog using a mouth stick. An angled computer keyboard stand for better accessibility was also provided. Cost of accommodation: $1,500.

→ **Situation:** A custodian with decreased vision was having difficulty seeing the carpeted area he was vacuuming.

★ **Solution:** A fluorescent lighting system was mounted on his industrial vacuum cleaner. Cost of accommodation: $240.

Designing an Entirely New Product

Sometimes it's not that easy. Sometimes you may need to call on a professional to design a product that can meet your needs. The JAN Web site lists the following examples of new products that have been designed, as reported by the *Rehabilitation Engineering Tech Brief* published by the Cerebral Palsy Research Foundation of Kansas, Inc.:

→ **Situation:** A bicycle repairman was having difficulty bending down to work on bicycles as a result of a back injury.

★ **Solution:** The technicians at the Mobile Shop of the Cerebral Palsy Research Foundation designed and made an adjustable-height bicycle rack that could raise and lower the bicycle to a comfortable working height. Seventy staff hours were required for design, fabrication, and installation. Material and part costs for the modification totaled approximately $450.

→ **Situation:** A library clerk with a physical disability walked with crutches. She had limitations in shelving books that required climbing and reaching. Balance was also a problem for her.

★ **Solution:** A book-service cart with fold-up steps and handrails, with a place for her to stow her crutches, was designed and fabricated. Cost not identified.

Accommodations Don't Have to Be Expensive

One important point for you to keep in mind through this process is the fact that most accommodations in the workplace are inexpensive. In fact, 80 percent of all the accommodations recommended by JAN have cost employers less than $500. Many of the accommodations have been simple, and free, such as putting telephone books or bricks under a desk to enable a person who uses a wheelchair to fit his or her legs into the kneehole.

Software that allows the user to type by speaking into a microphone, although designed for people who could not use the keyboard, has become quite popular throughout the mainstream workforce and has increased productivity. As a result of the product's more widespread use, the price of the software has come down significantly. The same is true for "hands-free" telephone headsets. These devices are now worn by everyone from rock stars to drive-thru workers at fast food restaurants, as well as by telemarketers and people who have limited use of their hands. You can look around the highways and see people using them with their cell phones. (Either that, or they wear them because it allows them to talk to themselves without drawing attention!)

Sample Disability-Specific Accommodations from the Job Accommodation Network

Taken with permission from the JAN Web site:

        http://jan.wvu.edu

Accommodating People Who Are Deaf or Hard of Hearing

The accommodation process is one that must be conducted on a case by case basis. No two people will have the exact same accommodation needs. In order to implement accommodations for people who are deaf or hard of hearing, certain questions must be answered. Simply knowing a person has some type of hearing loss is not enough to assist one in providing accommodations. It is necessary to establish the individual's skills, abilities and limitations. Obtaining input from the individual with the disability is essential to achieving a successful accommodation process.

The following pages provide basic information regarding accommodations that can be implemented as well as information about legislation that affects people who are deaf or hard of hearing. The material is intended to be used for educational purposes only and should not be taken as absolute solutions to all accommodation scenarios. There may be additional accommodation options that are not listed in this material. Again, all accommodations must be provided on a case by case basis. Available resources are provided at the end of this document if further information is needed.

Accommodation Suggestions for People Who Are Deaf or Hard of Hearing Based upon Specific Limitations

Communicating One-to-One

One-to-one communication can be accomplished in a variety of ways depending upon the abilities of the individual and those around him/her. Suggestions include: written notes, e-mail messages, use of a computer terminal, use of assistive listening devices for people who are hard of hearing, interpreters, coworkers learning basic sign language, a communication board and the use of two TTYs connected without telephone lines.

Communication using a computer would involve two individuals taking turns typing their conversation for each to view on the monitor. This can occur in an immediate mode, where conversation occurs in real-time or in the more typical electronic mail format in which there are longer delays between sending and receiving messages.

Communicating Over the Telephone

Telephone communication is often of concern to employers and people who are deaf or hard of hearing. Traditionally, there are two different technologies that can be used for telephone communication: text telephone (TT) equipment and amplification. It is necessary to determine if the individual with hearing loss will benefit from amplification. If not, then text telephone equipment will likely be the chosen option. TT equipment is used when a person does not have enough functional hearing to understand speech even with amplification.

Amplification allows people who are hard of hearing to benefit from enhanced volume when using the telephone. Amplification can be provided through the handset, headset, in-line, portable additions and complete phone systems. Some assistive listening devices can also be used to provide telephone amplification. A person who uses a hearing aid may also have the option of using a T-coil for telephone amplification. Amplification can also be used with some cellular telephones.

In addition to amplification, clarity may help someone who is hard of hearing in using the telephone. For some people amplification is not so much the problem as is the need for clarity. Clarity can be achieved by adjusting the frequency of the incoming voice when listening on the telephone. Specifically designed complete telephone systems and in-line devices can be used to adjust voice frequency. For individuals who are deaf, a TTY or TDD will need to be used. With a TTY, the conversation is typed rather than spoken. Communication is direct with anyone who has a similar device or the telecommunications Relay Service can be used as a third-party communicator. Computers can be used to communicate with some TTYs. A TTY equipped with ASCII code allows communication with a computer. Most TTYs are equipped with Baudot communication code, but some are now equipped with both ASCII and Baudot. If the TTY does not have ASCII, the computer must have a modem that can translate Baudot code.

Communicating During Meetings

For individuals who are hard of hearing and benefit from amplification, there are various assistive listening devices (ALDs) which can be used during meetings, seminars or other group communication situations such as training courses. Options to consider include FM systems and infrared or induction loop technologies. The presenter speaks into a microphone or transmitter and the listener either uses a "T" switch on their hearing aid or wears a receiver designed to work with the assistive listening device chosen.

Qualified sign language interpreters can be used during group situations. According to the ADA, an interpreter must be qualified but not necessarily certified. A qualified interpreter is one who is able to sign what is said to the individual who is deaf and can voice to the hearing person what is said. The communication must be conveyed in an accurate, effective and impartial manner. A qualified interpreter will be familiar with any specialized vocabulary that is used during communication.

Computers and stenographic equipment can also be used to provide effective communication in group settings. Computer Assisted Note Taking (CANT) involves the use of a personal computer and possibly a PC projector. A person in a clerical support type position would need to sit in on the group activity. This person then types summaries of the communication taking place while the person who is deaf or hard of hearing either watches the computer monitor as s/he types or looks at the text projected on a wall or screen. CANT is a relatively inexpensive accommodation option but the information provided is not word for word.

If verbatim conversation is needed, Real Time Captioning (RTC) is a better option. RTC involves the use of a stenographic keyboard attached to a computer and special software to translate phonetic symbols entered by a stenographer into English. The same viewing methods can be used with RTC as with CANT. RTC offers word for word translation but is generally more expensive and requires someone who is trained in using the stenographic equipment.

It would be a good idea to have someone taking notes and to provide meeting minutes after each meeting. Prior to meetings or training courses, provide agendas or text materials to allow additional preparation time.

Environmental factors must also be considered in group communication situations. Be aware of background noise, lighting, seating and positioning. Allow the person with the hearing impairment to sit close to the speaker. Use a round table rather than a square or rectangular table to open up the lines of sight for people who might lip read. Hold meetings in a room that is carpeted, free of office machines and away from paths of heavy traffic (people and vehicles).

Responding to Fire or Emergency Alarms

Fire or emergency alerting systems can be modified for use by deaf or hard-of-hearing individuals. Visual or tactile alerting mechanisms can be substituted for the traditional audible signal. Alarms can be purchased which have lights, or lights can be hard-wired to an existing system. It may also be helpful to monitor the auditory signal and then transmit a visual or tactile cue to a strategically placed receiver in the individual's environment or one which s/he can wear. The individual who is deaf or hard of hearing can also be alerted to emergency situations through a vibrating pager system. Implementing a "buddy system" where a coworker alerts the employee with a hearing loss can also be appropriate, but only in conjunction with one of the above suggestions. The "buddy system" should never be relied on as the sole means of alerting a hearing impaired individual to emergency situations.

Responding to Other Sounds in the Environment

There may be other sounds in the work environment to which an individual needs to respond. What type of alerting system to use will depend upon what type of sound the person needs to be alerted to.

Computers often provide some type of auditory cue to alert a user when s/he makes an error, when e-mail has been received or when there is a problem with the equipment. The equipment may be able to be modified to substitute screen or cursor flashes for an auditory signal. Software is available that can perform this function. Windows 95 actually has this option built into the accessibility features: Sound Sentry. Macintosh computers have the option built in as well.

For other sounds that may need to be heard such as a telephone, doorbell, alarm clock, buzzer, or malfunctioning equipment, a substitution of a visual or tactile signal may also be used in place of an auditory one. This may be achieved by using a monitor/signaling device or by possibly hard-wiring a light to a sound source for a visual cue. A vibrating signal can be very useful in the work environment. Vibration can alert a worker to a sound in their environment with minimal distraction to other coworkers.

Another option to consider to assist a person with hearing loss in responding to various sounds might be the use of a specially trained hearing dog. A hearing dog can alert an employee to a telephone ringing, a person entering the room or maybe abnormal machinery sounds. Hearing dogs are trained to work and are not simply pets. When a hearing dog is "on duty," the dog is not to socialize and will not if properly trained. Never pet an animal who is "on duty" without first asking for permission from the owner.

At this time there is no national certification for service animals, but a service animal will typically wear a harness or cape of some kind which will indicate that the animal is a "working dog."

Difficulty with Extraneous Noises

Extraneous noises can be very difficult for a person who has a hearing impairment. Noise from radios, office equipment, traffic and employee conversations make it difficult for someone who is hard of hearing to focus on important sounds in their environment.

To block extraneous noise, use sound absorbing products such as carpeting, ceiling baffles, wall panels or cubicles. Discontinue the use of personal stereos or provide the employee with a space free from extraneous sounds from copy machines, faxes or printers.

Communicating with Workers in the Field

It is not uncommon for people to have to work from a location away from the main work site. Communicating with a worker in the field who is deaf or hard of hearing is often an issue of concern. In situations where two-way radios and CBs are normally used, a problem may arise. In order to reduce distance communication barriers, it may be necessary to consider other means of communicating. Cellular phones may be used in place of CBs and can be used with a portable TTY for people who are deaf, or with an amplification device for people who are hard of hearing. Some two-way radios might actually work with a portable TTY if the device has a separate transmitter and receiver so that the two-way radio can be hooked up acoustically with a TTY. Another option might be the use of a vibrating pager system. Many pagers operate over telephone lines while others are stand-alone units with a more limited range. Pagers can provide a full-length message and may allow the individual to respond directly using the pager through the use of programmed messages.

Responding to Vehicles in the Workplace

Employers often express concerns about people who are deaf or hard of hearing working around or driving forklifts or other heavy equipment. Past studies have shown that workers with hearing loss are at no greater risk for injury than workers with average hearing. However, in response to concerns, certain suggestions can be made. Set paths of travel should be established for forklifts, vehicles and heavy equipment. These paths might be marked off on the ground using tape or paint. Establish a rule that all forklifts and vehicles must stop at intersections. Place flashing lights and mirrors on vehicles to enhance the worker's visual cues of the environment. Mirrors might also be placed around the work environment. The individual with hearing loss may be willing to wear a hard hat or vest of a unique color to serve as a warning regarding his/her hearing limitation.

Some concerns involve the issue of wearing hearing protection in the workplace around heavy equipment. Employers become concerned that a person who is hard of hearing will not be able to hear coworkers speaking to them. Some workers might benefit from wearing electronic hearing protection, which allows the frequency range of the human voice (800 to 4000Hz) to be heard but filters out unwanted noise. Certain sounds can also be amplified with an adjustable volume control if desired.

Accessing Information from Videotape

If training videos are used for employment purposes, it may be necessary to caption the videos. Closed or open captioning displays printed text of the auditory information. Closed captioning requires the use of a decoder to view the captions, while open captioning displays the text automatically. The captions are just like captions displayed at the bottom of a screen in foreign-language films. No special equipment is required to view open captioning. Videos can be captioned in-house if the proper equipment is purchased, or the videos can be sent out to a captioning service for a fee.

Transcribing Information from Audiotape

Accommodation options for transcribing taped material are limited. A Pressure Zone Microphone (PZM) attached to the recording device can be used to increase the quality of tape so a transcriber with hearing loss can be better able to understand the recorded information. Such a microphone can be obtained from a local Radio Shack. Direct audio-input devices, in-line amplifiers or amplified headsets may also be helpful for the transcriber. Some individuals have success with using the T-coil in their hearing aid in conjunction with wearing the existing headset just in front of the ear.

Individuals Who Are Deaf or Hard of Hearing Telling You All About It!

- A carpentry supervisor who had no functional hearing was required as part of his job to order supplies from various vendors throughout the area. A text telephone was used in conjunction with the relay service to allow this job function to take place.

- A field geologist who works alone in remote areas needed to be able to report findings to the office. Two-way radio communication was not feasible due to hearing loss. Text telephone technology was used to allow the field geologist to communicate with the main office via a cellular telephone.

- A hard-of-hearing employee was required to participate in meetings with a number of coworkers. One microphone was not providing adequate amplification of all the participants' voices. It was recommended that microphones be placed in front of all participants or within three to four feet of each person and a mixer could be used to transmit the signals to one receiver. These microphones can be voice activated or self adjusting to increase volume and quality of sound while decreasing background noise.

- A top executive at a large U.S. company was required to participate frequently in meetings. The individual unexpectedly lost his hearing and needed a new way to be involved in the discussions. The company hired a court stenographer and purchased real-time captioning equipment to utilize stenographic captioning for the meetings.

- An essential function of the job of a postal employee was to monitor the performance of a sorting apparatus. The machine made a clicking sound when it was operating correctly. The machine was modified so that a light flashed to alert the worker if the machine failed to click as a piece of mail went through. The manufacturer of the metering machine used their design engineering group to adapt the equipment.

- A meter reader needed to be alerted to barking dogs. A device that vibrates in response to noise was purchased.

Accommodation Ideas for Persons with Epilepsy

The following are types of accommodations that might be appropriate for someone with epilepsy. As always, each situation needs to be considered on a case-by-case basis.

- Provide extra time to take an examination.

- Provide restructuring, such as redistributing a "nonessential or marginal" job task (driving a vehicle) to other employees.

- Install a safety shield around a piece of machinery.

- Install a piece of carpet to cover a concrete floor in the employee's work area.

- Ask a supervisor to give written rather than oral instructions for persons who experience memory loss as a side effect of their anti-epileptic medication.

- Schedule consistent work shifts to accommodate persons whose seizure activity is exacerbated by inconsistent sleep patterns.

- Allow an employee who experiences fatigue as a side effect of medication the opportunity to take more frequent breaks.

- Allow an employee to take an extended break or time off after they have had a seizure.

- Employee might require a reassignment to a vacant position (should be equivalent in terms of pay, benefits and status, if possible).

It has been found that in some cases, epileptic seizures can be triggered by blinking or flickering lights (by flash rates of 10 to 20 flashes per second). The following accommodation ideas might help in this area.

- Glare guards and/or tinted computer glasses may reduce/eliminate glare and decrease color intensity on the monitor.

- Not sit too close to the monitor and take time throughout the day to do something other than work with the computer.

- Adjust the display intensity on an employee's computer monitor; the blinking cursor can be reduced by changing the configuration of the DOS shell or by purchasing software that reduces, eliminates, or enlarges the cursor.

- If the employee is using a Windows application, slowing down the speed of the tabbing/flipping window below 3Hz (above 3Hz can trigger seizures) might help. To correct this, slow down the display speed by using a slower video adapter card so that the screen does not "roll" so fast.

- Changing the color of the monitor screen to a less bright color.

- Use a high-resolution VGA monitor/flicker-free screen (such as Motorola, Mitsubishi, or Magnavox monitors) to eliminate the flicker effect due to refreshing the screen.

- Replace a flickering light in an employee's work area; eliminate fluorescent lighting and replace it with incandescent or natural lighting. Full-spectrum lighting can be utilized (such as the Sun Box, Bio Light bulb).

- Reduce stroke lighting within the room to 3Hz or below. For example, if the fire alarm system includes stroke lighting, the strokes should operate at a minimum of 1Hz and a maximum of 3Hz (pg. 52, Federal Register / Vol. 56, No. 144 / Friday, July 26, 1991 / Rules and Regulations) to prevent triggering an absence (petit mal) seizure.

Actual Accommodations for People with Epilepsy, from JAN

The following accommodation examples are taken from returned input sheets to the Job Accommodation Network. These are accommodation solutions that have been successful in the workplace.

A person working as a line production operator needed accommodations in the workplace due to epilepsy. At times, this person was unable to be at work as a result of seizures. Two major concerns for this person were her attendance record as well as safety issues. The employer accommodated this individual by allowing absences resulting from seizures to not count against her attendance; these absences were excused. The work environment was also altered such that all safety precautions were considered. For example, hot solder and sharp corners were moved away from the individual. Accommodation was made at no cost to the employer.

In the case of a sewing machine operator who experienced grand mal seizures, safety issues were a major concern. To accommodate this individual, the sewing machine was moved so that when the employee had a seizure she would not fall into it or other objects. Also, a local epilepsy affiliate provided seizure first aid and education. Accommodation was made at no cost to the employer.

A quality-control inspector with epilepsy was unable to drive a forklift or work on elevated platforms. This individual was placed in another job that would not require him to drive a forklift or work on platforms. This accommodation has worked out well and was made at no cost to the employer.

A garage mechanic with epilepsy was unable to drive mobile vehicles. To accommodate the individual and to adhere to union specifications, negotiations with the union were settled by permitting any qualified employee, regardless of their job, to drive the mobile equipment as required for the garage mechanic to perform his duties. The accommodation was at no cost to the employer.

A person with epilepsy, employed as a "Burrer B"—an individual who removes burrs and rough edges from commercial and industrial machine parts—uses hand tools, files, burr knives, scrapers, and clampering tools. This individual was given work assignments that are all accomplished on ground level, do not include operating company vehicles, and are not around moving machinery. Cost was not given.

A plant operator was instructed by a physician not to work with heavy equipment or machinery or in height situations. He was offered a transfer at the same pay rate as an accommodation. Cost for this accommodation was not given.

APPENDIX

Job Links from the U.S. Department of Labor Office of Disability Employment Policy

The following employers have indicated interest in recruiting and hiring qualified individuals with disabilities for open positions within their company or organization. The address after each company or organization will take you to that company or organization's Internet page(s). From there, you need to navigate to the page that lists current job openings. If you see a position for which you believe you are qualified and wish to apply for it, please follow the directions given at that company or organization's Internet site.

Please note: This is a referral service only. Although every attempt is made to ensure that all information is accurate, we do not guarantee the accuracy, timeliness, or quality of the content of sources. Inclusion in this book does not indicate endorsement or certification of the information, products, or services offered by these sources. You can find links to these employers online at

http://www.dol.gov/odep/joblinks/joblinks.htm

However, many of the links at the government site may not function properly.

ALABAMA
AT&T
1715 6th Ave.
Birmingham AL 35203
http://www.att.com

Federal Aviation Administration
Southern Region Headquarters
Human Resource Management
Division, ASO-14
P.O. Box 20636
Atlanta, GA 30320
jobs.faa.gov

ALASKA
Federal Aviation Administration
Alaskan Region Headquarters
Human Resource Management
Division, AAL-14
222 West 7th Ave., Suite 14
Anchorage, AK 99513
jobs.faa.gov

ARIZONA
AT&T
Multiple locations across the state
http://www.att.com

Avnet, Inc.
2211 S. 47th St.
Phoenix, AZ 85034
http://www.avnet.com

Devereux
Richard L. Raskin Treatment
Network
11000 N. Scottsdale Rd.
Suite 260
Scottsdale, AZ 85254
http://www.devereux.org

Federal Aviation Administration
Western Pacific Region
Headquarters
Human Resource Management
Division, AWP-10
P.O. Box 92007
Los Angeles, CA 90009
jobs.faa.gov

ILEX Systems
Multiple locations across the state
http://www.ilex.com

Mesa, AZ Police Dept.
200 S. Center St., Building 1
Mesa, AZ 85201
http://www.ci.mesa.az.us

Northern Arizona University
Human Resources
Box 4113
Flagstaff, AZ 86011-4113
http://www.nau.edu

ARKANSAS
ALLTEL Corporation
11101 Anderson Dr.
Little Rock, AR 72202
http://www.alltel.com

Arkansas Department of Parks and
Tourism
One Capitol Mall
Little Rock, AR
http://www.arkansas.com

Federal Aviation Administration
Southwest Region Headquarters
Human Resource Management
Division, ASW-10
2500 Meacham Blvd.
Fort Worth, TX 76137-4298
jobs.faa.gov

CALIFORNIA
Analog Devices, Inc.
Silicon Valley
1500 Space Park Dr.
Santa Clara, CA 95054
http://www.analog.com

ARAMARK Uniform Services
115 North First St.
Burbank, CA 91502
http://www.aramark-uniform.com

AT&T
Multiple locations across the state
http://www.att.com

Avnet, Inc.
Multiple locations across the state
http://www.avnet.com

Bar Association of San Francisco
465 California St., Suite 1100
San Francisco, CA 94104
http://www.sfbar.org

Berkeley Policy Associates
440 Grand Ave., Suite 500
Oakland, CA 94610-5085
www.bpacal.com

Business for Social Responsibility
111 Sutter St., 12th Floor
San Francisco, CA 94104
http://www.bsr.org

California Department of
Rehabilitation Central Office
2000 Evergreen St.
Sacramento, CA 95815.
http://www.rehab.cahwnet.gov

California State Department of
Transportation (Caltrans)
Sacramento, CA 95814
http://www.dot.ca.gov

California State University, Fresno
Human Resources Office
5241 N. Maple Ave. (M/S TA55)
Fresno, CA 93740-8077
www.csufresno.edu

California State University,
Hayward
Human Resources, WA 615
25800 Carlos Bee Blvd.
Hayward, CA 94542-3026
www.aba.csuhayward.edu

California State University,
Los Angeles
5151 State University Dr.
Employment Services,
Administration Room 606
Los Angeles, CA 90032-8534
http://www.calstatela.edu

California State University,
Sacramento
Sacramento Hall
6000 J St.
Sacramento, CA 95819
www.csus.edu

Candescent Technologies
Corporation
16400 Lark Ave., Suite 100
Los Gatos, CA 95032
http://www.candescent.com

Canon Computer Systems, Inc.
Multiple locations across the state
http://www.canon.com/index.html

Centers for Medicare &
Medicaid Services
75 Hawthorne St.
4th Floor
San Francisco, CA 94105-3903
http://cms.hhs.gov/

Cisco Systems, Inc.
170 W. Tasman Dr.
San Jose, CA 95156
http://www.cisco.com

Community Development
Commission
County of Los Angeles
2 S. Coral Circle
Monterey Park, CA 91755
http://www.lacdc.org

Cox Communications, Inc.
Multiple locations across the state
http://www.cox.com

Data Focus Corporation Company
391 Taylor Boulevard
Pleasant Hill, CA 94523
www.data2020.com

Devereux
Multiple locations across the state
http://www.devereux.org

Disability Rights Education and
Defense Fund, Inc. (DREDF)
2212 Sixth St.
Berkeley, CA 94710
http://www.dredf.org

Federal Aviation Administration
Western Pacific Region
Headquarters
Human Resource Management
Division, AWP-10
P.O. Box 92007
Los Angeles, CA 90009
jobs.faa.gov

Hyperion Solutions Corporation
1344 Crossman Ave.
Sunnyvale, CA 94089
http://www.hyperion.com

Innovative Interfaces
5850 Shellmound Way
Emeryville, CA 94608
http://www.iii.com

Kensington Technology Group
2000 Alameda de las Pulgas
San Mateo, CA 94403
http://www.kensington.com

KLA-Tencor
160 Rio Robles
San Jose, CA 95134
http://www.kla-tencor.com

Lucent Technologies
Multiple locations across the state
http://www.lucent.com

Lucent Technologies NPS
NetworkCare Division
1213 Innsbruck Dr.
Sunnyvale, CA 94089
http://www.networkcare.com

Maintenance Warehouse (A Home Depot Company)
10641 Scripps Summit Court
San Diego, CA 92131
http://www.mwh.com

Mitchell International
Multiple locations across the state
http://www.mitchell.com

Mitsubishi Electric & Electronics USA, Inc.
Electronic Device Group
1050 E. Arques Ave.
Sunnyvale, CA 94085-4601
http://www.mitsubishichips.com

Perot Systems Healthcare Services
Multiple locations across the state
http://www.perotsystems.com

Raytheon Systems Company
Multiple locations across the state
http://www.rayjobs.com

SCO, Inc.
425 Encinal St.
Santa Cruz, CA 95060
http://www.sco.com

Sony Electronics Inc.
Multiple locations across the state
http://www.sony.com

SRI International
333 Ravenswood Ave.
Menlo Park, CA 940125
http://www.sri.com

Starz Encore Group LLC
Multiple locations across the state
http://www.encoremedia.com

The Stichler Group, Inc.
9655 Granite Ridge Dr., Suite 400
San Diego, CA 92123
www.stichler.com

TRW Inc.
Space & Electronics Group
One Space Park E1/4037
Redondo Beach, CA 90278
http://www.trw.com

Union Rescue Mission
Human Resources
545 S. San Pedro St.
Los Angeles, CA 90013
http://www.urm.com

VPA, Inc.
24025 Park Sorrento, Suite 200
Calabasas, CA 91302
www.VPAinc.com

Wells Fargo Bank NA - Orange County Phone Bank
Multiple locations across the state
http://www.wfjobs.com

COLORADO
AT&T
Multiple locations across the state
http://www.att.com

Career Service Authority
City and County of Denver
110-16th St.
Denver, CO 80202
http://www.denvergov.org

Centers for Medicare & Medicaid Services
1600 Broadway, Suite 700
Denver, Colorado 80202
http://cms.hhs.gov/

Colorado State Government
1313 Sherman St.
Denver, CO 80203
http://www.gssa.state.co.us

Devereux
Multiple locations across the state
http://www.devereux.org

Federal Aviation Administration Northwest Mountain Region Headquarters
Human Resource Management
Division, ANM-14
1601 Lind Ave. SW
Renton, WA 98055
jobs.faa.gov

HirePotential, Inc.
200 Fillmore St.
Denver, CO 60206
http://www.hirepotential.com

Loronix Information Systems, Inc.
820 Airport Rd.
Durango CO 81303
http://www.loronix.com

Lucent Technologies
Multiple locations across the state
http://www.lucent.com

Roaring Fork Transit Agency
51 Service Center Rd.
Aspen, Colorado 81611
http://www.rfta.com

Perot Systems-Recruiting
5990 Greenwood Plaza, Suite 350
Englewood, CO 80111
http://www.perotsystems.com

Starz Encore Group LLC
P.O. Box 6542
Englewood CO 80155
http://www.encoremedia.com

Qwest
Multiple locations across the state
http://www.qwest.com

CONNECTICUT
Aetna U.S. Healthcare
National Scanning Center
RSAA 151 Farmington Ave.
Hartford, CT 06156
http://www.aetna.com

American Eagle Federal Credit Union
417 Main St.
East Hartford, CT 06118
http://www.americaneagle.org

Devereux Glenholme
81 Sabbaday Lane
Washington, CT 06793
http://www.devereux.org

Federal Aviation Administration New England Region Headquarters
Human Resource Management
Division, ANE-14
12 New England Executive Park
Burlington, MA 01803
jobs.faa.gov

GE
3135 Easton Turnpike
Fairfield, CT 06431
http://www.gecareers.com

Goodwill Industries of Western CT
165 Ocean Terrace
Bridgeport, CT 06605
http://www.goodwillwct.org

The Hartford
Hartford Plaza
Hartford, CT 06115
http://www.thehartford.com

Pitney Bowes Inc.
One Elmcroft Rd.
Stamford, CT 06926
http://www.pitneybowes.com

Rogers Corporation
P.O. Box 188
One Technology Dr.
Rogers, CT 06263-0188
http://www.rogers-corp.com

Starz Encore Group LLC
181 Harbor Dr., Plaza-B
Stamford, CT 06902
http://www.encoremedia.com

United Technologies Corporation
1 Financial Plaza
Hartford, CT 06101
http://www.utc.com

DELAWARE
AstraZeneca
1800 Concord Pike
Wilmington, DE 19850
www.astrazenecacareers.com

E. I. du Pont de Nemours and Company
1007 Market St.
Wilmington, DE 19898
http://www.dupont.com

Federal Aviation Administration Eastern Region Headquarters
Human Resource Management
Division, AEA-10
One Aviation Administration
Jamaica, NY 11434-4809
jobs.faa.gov

PNC Financial Services Group
Multiple locations across the state
http://www.pnc.com

TruGreen ChemLawn
1350 First State Blvd.
Wilmington, DE 19804
http://www.truegreenchemlawn.com

DISTRICT OF COLUMBIA
AARP
601 E. St. NW
Washington, DC 20049
www.aarp.com

Academy for Educational Development
1825 Connecticut Ave. NW
Washington, DC 20009-1202
http://www.aed.org

Advanced Management Technology, Inc. (AMTI)
1101 15th St. NW, Suite 900
Washington, DC 20005
http://www.amti.com

American Council of the Blind
1155 15th St. NW, Suite 1004
Washington DC 20005
http://www.acb.org

American Institutes for Research
1000 Thomas Jefferson St. NW
Suite 400
Washington DC 20007
http://www.air.org

The Brookings Institution
1775 Massachusetts Ave. NW
Washington, DC 20036
http://www.brookings.edu

Burson-Marsteller
1801 K St. NW, Suite 901-L
Washington, DC 20006
http://www.bm.com

Centers for Medicare & Medicaid Services
200 Independence Ave. SW
Washington, DC 20201
http://cms.hhs.gov/

The Communitarian Network
2130 H St. NW, Suite 703
Washington, DC 20052
http://www.gwu.edu

Corporation for National and Community Service
1201 New York Ave. NW
Washington, DC 20525-0001
http://www.nationalservice.org

Devereux Children's Center
3050 R St. NW
Washington, DC 20007
http://www.devereux.org

Federal Aviation Administration
Human Resource Management
Division, AHR-19
800 Independence Ave. SW
Washington, DC 20591
jobs.faa.gov

Federal Bureau of Investigation
935 Pennsylvania Ave. NW
Washington, DC 20535-0001
http://www.fbi.gov

Federal Communications Commission (FCC)
445 12th St. SW
Washington, DC 20554
http://www.fcc.gov

The George Washington University
Human Resource Services
2033 K St. NW, Suite 220
Washington, DC 20052
http://www.gwu.edu

Health Systems Research, Inc.
1200 18th St. NW, Suite 700
Washington, DC 20036
www.hsrnet.com

Lucent Technologies
1450 G St. NW
Washington DC 20005
http://www.lucent.com

NAI Personnel
1725 K St. NW, Suite 1103
Washington, DC 20036
http://www.naipersonnel.com

National Aeronautics and Space Administration
300 E St. SW
Washington, DC 20546-0001
http://www.nasajobs.nasa.gov

National Association of Broadcast Employees and Technicians NABET-CWA
501 3rd St.
Washington, DC 20001
http://www.nabetcwa.org

National Journal Group, Inc.
1501 M St. NW
Washington, DC 20005
http://nationaljournal.com

Office of the Comptroller of the Currency
250 E. St. SW
Washington, DC 20219
http://www.occ.treas.gov

Overseas Private Investment Corporation
1100 New York Ave. NW
Washington, DC 20527
http://www.opic.gov

U.S. Coast Guard
2100 2nd St. SW
Washington, DC 20593
http://www.uscg.mil

U.S. Department of Education
Federal Building No. 6
400 Maryland Ave. SW
Washington, DC 20202
http://www.ed.gov

U.S. Department of Justice
950 Pennsylvania Ave. NW
Washington, DC 20530
http://www.usdoj.gov

U.S. Department of Labor
200 Constitution Ave.
Washington, DC 20210
http://www.quickhire.com

U.S. Department of the Navy
Human Resources Operations Center
Nebraska Avenue Complex
321 Somers Court, NW, Suite 40103
Washington, DC 20393-5441
http://www.donhr.navy.mil

U.S. Department of State
Personnel Management
1900 E St. NW
Washington, DC 20415-1000
http://www.stategov.com

U.S. Environmental Protection Agency
401 M St. SW, MC 1201
Washington, DC 20460
http://www.epa.gov

The Urban Institute
2100 M St. NW
Washington, DC 20037
http://www.urban.org

FLORIDA
AT&T
Multiple locations across the state
http://www.att.com

Bell Technologies, Inc.
6120 Hanging Moss Rd.
Orlando, FL 32807
http://www.belltechinc.com

CSX Technology
550 Water St.
Jacksonville, FL 32202
http://www.csxtechnology.com

Devereux
Multiple locations across the state
http://www.devereux.org

Federal Aviation Administration Southern Region Headquarters
Human Resource Management
Division, ASO-14
P.O. Box 20636
Atlanta, GA 30320
jobs.faa.gov

Harcourt Brace School Publishers
6277 Sea Harbor Dr.
Orlando, FL 32887
http://www.harcourt.com

Perot Systems-Recruiting
12320 Racetrack Rd.
Tampa, FL 33626
http://www.perotsystems.com

PNC Financial Services Group
3507 Frontage Rd.
Tampa FL 33607
http://www.pnc.com

SIRS Mandarin, Inc.
P.O. Box 272348
Boca Raton, FL 33427-2348
http://www.sirs.com

TRAK Microwave Corporation
4726 Eisenhower Blvd.
Tampa, FL 33634
http://www.trak.com

University of South Florida
4202 E. Fowler Ave.
Tampa, FL 33620
http://usfweb.usf.edu

West Central Florida Area Agency on Aging
5911 Breckenridge Pkwy., Suite B
Tampa, FL 33610
http://www.wcfaaa.org

WPBT
South Florida Public Television
14901 NE 20th Ave.
Miami, FL 33181
http://www.channel2.org

GEORGIA
Avnet, Inc.
Locations in Duluth, Smyrna,
and Norcross
http://www.avnet.com

Centers for Medicare & Medicaid Services
61 Forsyth St. SW, Rm. 4T20
Atlanta, Georgia 30323-8909
http://cms.hhs.gov/

Devereux
Georgia Treatment Network
1000 Cobb Place, Suite 360
Kennesaw, GA 30144
http://www.devereux.org

Federal Aviation Administration Southern Region Headquarters
Human Resource Management
Division, ASO-14
P.O. Box 20636
Atlanta, GA 30320
jobs.faa.gov

The Facility Group Inc.
2233 Lake Park Dr.
Smyrna, GA 30080
http://www.facilitygroup.com

Lucent Technologies
Multiple locations across the state
http://www.lucent.com

Six Continents Hotels, Inc.
3 Ravinia Dr., Suite 2900
Atlanta, GA 30346
http://www.sixcontinentshotels.com

Starz Encore Group LLC
775 Peachtree Dunwoody Rd., D-580
Atlanta, GA 30342
http://www.encoremedia.com

HAWAII
Federal Aviation Administration (FAA) Western Pacific Region Headquarters
Human Resource Management
Division, AWP-10
P.O. Box 92007
Los Angeles, CA 90009
jobs.faa.gov

IDAHO
Federal Aviation Administration Northwest Mountain Region Headquarters
Human Resource Management
Division, ANM-14
1601 Lind Ave. SW
Renton, WA 98055
jobs.faa.gov

ILLINOIS
Accenture
Multiple locations
http://www.accenture.com

ACSG, Inc
800 W. Fifth Ave., Suite 102A
Naperville, IL 60540
http://www.acsgconsult.com

**Alternative Resources Corporation
(A-R-C)**
600 Hart Rd.
Barrington, IL 60010
http://www.arcnow.com

AT&T
Multiple locations across the state
http://www.att.com

**Centers for Medicare & Medicaid
Services**
233 N. Michigan Ave., Suite 600
Chicago, Illinois 60601-5519
http://cms.hhs.gov/

The Chicago Board of Trade
141 W. Jackson Blvd., Suite 2080
Chicago, IL 60604
http://www.cbot.com

CHOICES Hospice Triage
932 N. Wright St., Suite 160
Napierville, IL 60563
www.hospicetriage.com

Construction Technology Labs
5420 Old Orchard Rd.
Skokie, IL 60077
www.c-t-l.com

corVISION MEDIA Inc.
3014 Commercial Ave.
Northbrook, IL 60062
http://www.corvision.com

Deere & Company
Corporate Headquarters
One John Deere Place
Moline, IL 61265
http://www.deere.com

Deloitte & Touche Tax Technologies
1751 Lake Cook Rd.
Deerfield, IL 60015
http://www.corptax.com

**Federal Aviation Administration
Great Lakes Region Headquarters**
Human Resource Management
Division, AGL-18
2300 East Devon Ave.
Des Plaines, IL 60018
jobs.faa.gov

W.W. Grainger, Inc.
Multiple locations across the state
http://www.grainger.com

Ingalls Memorial Hospital
One Ingalls Dr.
Harvey, IL 60426
http://www.ingalls.org

Lake County Government
Human Resources Dept.
18 N. County St., 7th Floor
Waukegan, IL 60085
www.co.lake.il.us

Lucent Technologies
Multiple locations across the state
http://www.lucent.com

McDonald's Corporation
One McDonald's Plaza
Oak Brook, IL 60523
http://www.mcdonalds.com

Morton College
3801 S. Central
Cicero, IL 60804
http://www.morton.cc.il.us

Motorola
Multiple locations across the state
www.motorolacareers.com

Opportunity Medical Complete
1200 Old Skokie Rd.
Highland Park, IL 60035
www.medpack.com

RR Donnelley & Sons
3075 Highland Parkway
Downers Grove, IL 60515
http://www.rrdonnelley.com

SBC
30 South Wacker Dr.
Chicago, IL 60606
http://www.sbc.com

Starz Encore Group LLC
111 E. Wacker Dr., Suite 918
Chicago, IL 60601
http://www.encoremedia.com

Towers Productions, Inc.
549 W. Randolph St., Suite 300
Chicago, IL 60661
http://www.towersproductions.com

TransUnion, LLC.
555 West Adams St.
Chicago, IL 60661.
http://www.transunion.com

INDIANA
The American Legion
National Headquarters
P.O. Box 1055
Indianapolis, IN 46206-1055
http://www.legion.org

**Federal Aviation Administration
Great Lakes Region Headquarters**
Human Resource Management
Division, AGL-18
2300 East Devon Ave.
Des Plaines, IL 60018
jobs.faa.gov

Purdue University
Affirmative Action Office
1066 American Railway Building
West Lafayette, IN 47907-1066
http://www.adpc.purdue.edu

Zimmer, Inc.
1800 West Center St.
Warsaw, IN 46580
http://www.zimmer.com

IOWA
APAC Customer Services
250 E. 90th St.
Davenport, IA 52806
www.apaccustomerservices.com

Maytag Appliances
403 West 4th St. North
Newton, IA 50208
http://www.maytag.com

Principal Financial Group
711 High St.
Des Moines, IA 50392
http://www.principal.com

State of Iowa
Department of Personnel
Grimes State Office Building
Des Moines, Iowa 50319-0150
*https://www.iowaonline.state.ia.us/
idopapptrack/public/AppOpenings.asp*

KANSAS
Koch Industries, Inc.
4111 East 37th St. N.
Wichita, KS 67220
http://www.kochcareers.com

Lucent Technologies
Multiple locations across the state
http://www.lucent.com

Midland Loan Services
10851 Mastin, Suite 300
Overland Park, KS 66210
http://www.midlandls.com

Sprint Corporation
2330 Shawnee Mission Pkwy.
Westwood, KS 66205
http://www.sprint.com

Yellow Services, Inc.
10990 Roe Ave.
Overland Park, KS 66211
http://www.yellowservices.com

TradeNet Publishing, Inc.
1200 Energy Center Dr.
Gardner, KS 66030
http://www.tradenetpublishing.com

KENTUCKY
Federal Aviation Administration
Southern Region Headquarters
Human Resource Management
Division, ASO-14
P.O. Box 20636
Atlanta, GA 30320
jobs.faa.gov

PNC Financial Services Group
500 West Jefferson
Louisville KY 40202
http://www.pnc.com

LOUISIANA
Federal Aviation Administration
Southwest Region Headquarters
Human Resource Management
Division, ASW-10
2500 Meacham Blvd.
Fort Worth, Texas 76137-4298
jobs.faa.gov

MAINE
Federal Aviation Administration
New England Region Headquarters
Human Resource Management
Division, ANE-14
12 New England Executive Park
Burlington, MA 01803
jobs.faa.gov

University of Maine
Office of Human Resources
Orono, ME 04469-5717
http://www.umaine.edu

MARYLAND
Centers for Medicare & Medicaid
Services
7500 Security Blvd.
Baltimore, MD 21244-1850
http://cms.hhs.gov/

Devereux Maryland Resources for
Special Children
1341 Ashton Rd., Suite A
Hanover, MD 21076
http://www.devereux.org

Federal Aviation Administration
Eastern Region Headquarters
Human Resource Management
Division, AEA-10
One Aviation Administration
Jamaica, NY 11434-4809
jobs.faa.gov

Goodwill Industries
9200 Rockville Pike
Bethesda, MD 20814
http://www.goodwill.org

Harford Community College
401 Thomas Run Rd.
Bel Air, MD 21015-1698
http://www.harford.cc.md.us

L N K Corporation, Inc.
6811 Kenilworth Ave
Suite 306
Riverdale, MD 20737-1333
http://www.lnk.com

Lucent Technologies
225 Schilling Circle
Hunt Valley, MD 21031
http://www.lucent.com

Maryland State Retirement Agency
120 E. Baltimore St.
Baltimore, MD 21202
http://www.sra.state.md.us/hr.htm

The Mass Transit Administration
William Donald Schaefer Tower
6 Saint Paul St., 5th Floor
Baltimore, MD 21202-1614
http://www.mtamaryland.com

McCrone, Inc.
207 North Liberty St., Suite 100
Centreville, MD 21617
http://www.mccrone-inc.com

The National Aquarium In
Baltimore
Pier 3 / 501 East Pratt St.
Baltimore, MD 21202-3194
http://www.aqua.org

National Instrument Co., Inc.
4119 Fordleigh Rd.
Baltimore, MD 21215
http://www.filamatic.com

National Security Agency
Recruitment and Staffing, MB
P.O. Box 1661
Ft. Meade, MD 20755
http://www.nsa.gov

U.S. Consumer Product Safety
Commission
4330 East West Hwy.
Bethesda, MD 20814
www.cpsc.gov

U.S. Foodservice
9755 Patuxent Woods Dr.
Columbia, MD 21046
http://www.usfoodservice.com

MASSACHUSETTS
Analog Devices, Inc.
Corporate Headquarters
Three Technology Way
Norwood, MA 02062
http://www.analog.com

Avnet, Inc.
10 Centennial Dr.
Peabody, MA 01960
http://www.avnet.com

Boston College
Human Resources, More Hall 315
Chestnut Hill, MA 02467
www.bc.edu

CAST
39 Cross St.
Peabody, MA 01960
http://www.cast.org

Centers for Medicare & Medicaid
Services
John F. Kennedy Bldg., Rm. 2375
Boston, MA 02203-0003
http://cms.hhs.gov/

Data General Corporation
4400 Computer Dr.
Westboro, MA 01580
http://www.dg.com

Devereux
Multiple locations across the state
http://www.devereux.org

Education Development Center, Inc.
55 Chapel St.
Newton, MA 02158-1060
http://www.edc.org

Federal Aviation Administration
New England Region Headquarters
Human Resource Management
Division, ANE-14
12 New England Executive Park
Burlington, MA 01803
jobs.faa.gov

Lucent Technologies
Multiple locations across the state
http://www.lucent.com

Massachusetts Institute of Technology
77 Mass. Ave.
Cambridge, MA 02139
http://web.mit.edu

Mellon/The Boston Company
One Boston Place, 024-0063
Boston, MA 02108
http://www.mellon.com

New England Research Institutes
9 Galen St.
Watertown, MA 02472
http://www.neri.org

Perot Systems Healthcare Services
20 Overland St.
Boston, MA 02215
http://www.perotsystems.com

PNC Financial Services Group
16101 Southwest 72nd St.
Westborough MA 01581
http://www.pnc.com

State Street
P.O. Box 351
Boston, MA 02101
http://jobs.statestreet.com

MICHIGAN
Compuware Corporation
31440 Northwestern Hwy.
Farmington Hills, MI 48334-2564
www.compuware.com

EDS
Staffing, 5th Floor
700 Tower Dr.
Troy, MI 48098
http://www.eds.com

Federal Aviation Administration Great Lakes Region Headquarters
Human Resource Management
Division, AGL-18
2300 East Devon Ave.
Des Plaines, IL 60018
jobs.faa.gov

Ford Motor Company
Recruiting - ATS
P.O. Box 6248
Dearborn, MI 48126
http://www.ford.com

Kelly Services
999 West Big Beaver Rd.
Troy, MI 48084
http://www.kellyservices.com

Michigan Technological University
1400 Townsend Dr.
Houghton, MI 49931
http://www.admin.mtu.edu

Perot Systems-Recruiting
28333 Telegraph Rd., Suite 275
Southfield, MI 48034
http://www.perotsystems.com

Valassis Communications, Inc.
19975 Victor Pkwy.
Livonia, MI 48152
http://www.valassis.com

Wolverine World Wide, Inc.
Employment Office (HC 1-27)
9341 Courtland Dr.
Rockford, MI 49351
www.wolverineworldwide.com

MINNESOTA
7 West Communications
14525 Highway 7, Suite 145
Minnetonka, MN 55345
http://www.7west.com

CaptionMax
530 North Third St., Suite 210
Minneapolis, MN 55401
http://www.captionmax.com

Federal Aviation Administration Great Lakes Region Headquarters
Human Resource Management
Division, AGL-18
2300 East Devon Ave.
Des Plaines, IL 60018
jobs.faa.gov

Hennepin County Human Resources
A-400 Government Center
300 South 6th St.
Minneapolis, MN 55487
http://www.co.hennepin.mn.us

Hickory Tech Corporation
221 East Hickory St.
P.O. Box 3248
Mankato, MN 56002-3248
http://www.hickorytech.com

Honeywell Inc.
Employment Response Center
P.O. Box 524; MN12-3260
Minneapolis, MN 55440
http://www.honeywell.com

Hopkins School District 270
1001 Highway 7
Hopkins, MN 55305
http://www.hopkins.k12.mn.us

Northwest Airlines
5101 Northwest Dr.
St. Paul, MN 55111-3034
http://www.nwa.com

Perot Systems-Recruiting
625 Fourth Ave. South
Mail Stop 1290
Minneapolis, MN 55415
http://www.perotsystems.com

PNC Financial Services Group
1700 West 82nd St.
Minneapolis, MN 55431
http://www.pnc.com

Pro Staff
Regional Office - MN
600 S Hwy. 169, Suite 1575
St. Louis Park, MN 55426
http://www.prostaff.com

SearchAbility
3675 Ihduhapi Rd.
P.O. Box 308
Loretto, MN 55357
http://www.search-ability.com

MISSISSIPPI
Federal Aviation Administration Southern Region Headquarters
Human Resource Management
Division, ASO-14
P.O. Box 20636
Atlanta, GA 30320
jobs.faa.gov

MISSOURI
AT&T
Multiple locations across the state
http://www.att.com

Centers for Medicare & Medicaid Services
Richard Bolling Federal Building
601 East 12th St., Rm. 235
Kansas City, MO 64106-2808
http://cms.hhs.gov/

Cerner Corporation
2800 Rockcreek Pkwy.
Kansas City, MO 64117
http://www.cerner.com

The Children's Mercy Hospitals and Clinics
2401 Gillham Rd.
Kansas City, MO 64108
http://www.childrens-mercy.org

Federal Aviation Administration
Central Region Headquarters
Human Resource Management
Division, ACE-12B
901 Locust
Kansas City, MO 64106-2641
jobs.faa.gov

Fleishman-Hillard, International
Communications
200 North Broadway
St. Louis, MO 63102
http://www.fleishman.com

John Knox Village
400 NW Murray Rd.
Lee's Summit, MO 64081
http://www.johnknoxvillage.org

Lucent Technologies
1111 Woods Mill Rd.
Town & Country, MO 63017
http://www.lucent.com

Social Security Administration
Human Resources Center
P.O. Box 15458
Kansas City, MO 64106
http://www.ssa.gov

Starz Encore Group LLC
1650 Des Peres Rd., Suite 302
St. Louis, MO 63131
http://www.encoremedia.com

University of Missouri - Columbia
Human Resource Services
201 South 7th St.
130 Heinkel Building
Columbia, MO 65211-1320
http://web.missouri.edu

MONTANA
Federal Aviation Administration
Northwest Mountain Region
Headquarters
Human Resource Management
Division, ANM-14
1601 Lind Ave. SW
Renton, WA 98055
jobs.faa.gov

NEVADA
Federal Aviation Administration
Western Pacific Region
Headquarters
Human Resource Management
Division, AWP-10
P.O. Box 92007
Los Angeles, CA 90009
jobs.faa.gov

U.S. Department of Energy
Nevada Operations Office
P.O. Box 98518
Las Vegas, NV 89193-8518
http://www.nv.doe.gov

NEW HAMPSHIRE
Federal Aviation Administration
New England Region Headquarters
Human Resource Management
Division, ANE-14
12 New England Executive Park
Burlington, MA 01803
jobs.faa.gov

NEW JERSEY
AT&T
Multiple locations across the state
http://www.att.com

Devereux
Multiple locations across the state
http://www.devereux.org

Federal Aviation Administration
William J Hughes Technical Center
Human Resource Management
Division, ACT-10
Atlantic City International Airport
Atlantic City, NJ 08405
jobs.faa.gov

Foster Wheeler Corporation
Perryville Corporate Park
Clinton, NJ 08809-4000
http://www.fwc.com

ILEX Systems
170 Patterson Ave.
Shrewsbury, NJ 07702
http://www.ilex.com

Johnson & Johnson
501 George St.
P.O. Box 16597
New Brunswick, NJ 08906
http://www.jnj.com

KPMG LLP
Three Chestnut Ridge Rd.
Montvale, NJ 07645
http://www.kpmgcareers.com

Lucent Technologies
600-700 Mountain Ave.
P.O. Box 636
Murray Hill, NJ 07974-0636
http://www.lucent.com

Nabisco, Inc.
100 Deforest Ave.
East Hanover, NJ 07936
http://www.nabiscoworld.com

NECA
80 South Jefferson Rd.
Whippany, NJ 07981
http://www.neca.org

Our Lady of Lourdes Medical
Center
1600 Haddon Ave.
Camden, NJ 08103
http://www.lourdesnet.org

PNC Financial Services Group
Two Tower Center
East Brunswick, NJ 08816
http://www.pnc.com

Prudential Insurance Company
National Staffing Organization
100 Mulberry St.
Gateway Center 4, Floor 2
Newark, NJ 07102
http://www.prudential.com

Quality Systems & Software, Inc.
200 Valley Rd., Suite 306
Mt. Arlington, NJ 07856
http://www.qssinc.com

Starz Encore Group LLC
70 Hudson St.
Hoboken, NJ 07030
http://www.encoremedia.com

TruGreen ChemLawn
Multiple locations across the state
http://www.trugreenchemlawn.com

NEW MEXICO
Federal Aviation Administration
Southwest Region Headquarters
Human Resource Management
Division, ASW-10
2500 Meacham Blvd.
Fort Worth, TX 76137-4298
jobs.faa.gov

University of New Mexico
Albuquerque, NM 87131
http://www.unm.edu

NEW YORK
Bristol-Myers Squibb Company
345 Park Ave.
New York, NY 10154
http://www.bms.com

Brookhaven National Laboratory
Human Resources Division
Bldg. 185
P.O. Box 5000
Upton, NY 11973-5000
http://www.bnl.gov

Centers for Medicare & Medicaid Services
26 Federal Plaza, Rm. 3811
New York, NY 10378-0063
http://cms.hhs.gov/

Devereux New York
Route 9 North
P.O. Box 40
Red Hook, NY 12571
http://www.devereux.org

Diversified Investment Advisors
Human Resources
4 Manhattanville Rd.
Purchase, NY 10577
http://www.divinvest.com

E-R Model Importers, Ltd.
1000 South Main St.
Newark, NY 14513
http://www.ermodels.com

Ernst & Young
5 Times Square
New York, NY 10036-6530
http://www.ey.com

Federal Aviation Administration Eastern Region Headquarters
Human Resource Management
Division, AEA-10
One Aviation Administration
Jamaica, NY 11434-4809
jobs.faa.gov

Gay Men's Health Crisis
119 West 24th St.
New York, NY 10011
http://www.gmhc.org

IBM Corporation
New Orchard Rd.
Armonk, NY 10605
http://www.empl.ibm.com

Lockheed Martin
Attention: Staffing
Ocean, Radar & Sensor Systems
P.O. Box 48 40, EP7-G40
Syracuse, NY 13221-4840
http://www.lmco.com

Lucent Technologies
666 5th Ave.
New York, NY 10103
http://www.lucent.com

PricewaterhouseCoopers LLP
1301 Avenue of the Americas
New York, NY 10019
http://www.pwcglobal.com

Salomon Smith Barney
388 Greenwich St., 7th Floor
New York, NY 10013
http://www.smithbarney.com

Starz Encore Group LLC
2875 Union Rd., Suite 21-22
Cheektowaga, NY 14227
http://wwww.encoremedia.com

Verizon Communications
1095 Avenue of the Americas
New York, NY 10036
http://www.verizon.com

NORTH CAROLINA
ALLTEL Corporation
10100 Sardis Crossing Dr.
Charlotte, NC 28212
http://www.alltel.com

AT&T
Multiple locations across the state
http://www.att.com

Cross Sales & Engineering Company
P.O. Box 18508
Greensboro, NC 27419-8508
http://www.crossco.com

DukeSolutions, Inc.
230 S. Tryon St., Suite 400
Charlotte, NC 28202
http://www.DukeSolutions.com

Federal Aviation Administration Southern Region Headquarters
Human Resource Management
Division, ASO-14
P.O. Box 20636
Atlanta, GA 30320
jobs.faa.gov

Lord Corporation
111 Lord Dr.
P.O. Box 8012
Cary, NC 27512-8012
http://www.lordcorp.com

Lucent Technologies
Mt Hope/I85 P.O. Box 20046
Greensboro, NC 27420
http://www.lucent.com

North Carolina State University
Office for Equal Opportunity
Box 7530
North Carolina State University
Raleigh, NC 27965-7530
http://www.ncsu.edu

Option One
1221 Woodridge Center Dr.
Suite 150
Charlotte, NC 28217
http://www.option-one.com

Research and Evaluation Associates, Inc.
6320 Quadrangle Dr., Suite 180
Chapel Hill, NC 27514
http://www.rea-inc.com

SAS Institute, Inc.
SAS Campus Dr.
Cary, NC 27513
http://www.sas.com

Wachovia Corporation
Staffing Services
401 Linden St. NC30014
Winston-Salem, NC 27101
http://www.wachovia.com

NORTH DAKOTA
Federal Aviation Administration Great Lakes Region Headquarters
Human Resource Management
Division, AGL-18
2300 East Devon Ave.
Des Plaines, IL 60018
jobs.faa.gov

OHIO
Access Equality Incorporated
613 Schuyler Dr.
Kettering, OH 45429
*http://home.earthlink.net/
~coyotestairs/*

Central Ohio Transit Authority
1600 McKinley Ave.
Columbus, OH 43222
http://www.cota.com

Crown Equipment Corporation
44 South Washington St.
New Bremen, OH 45869
www.crown.com

Federal Aviation Administration Great Lakes Region Headquarters
Human Resource Management
Division, AGL-18
2300 East Devon Ave.
Des Plaines, IL 60018
jobs.faa.gov

Lucent Technologies
6200 East Broad St.
Columbus, OH 43213-1569
http://www.lucent.com

OCLC Online Computer Library Center, Inc.
6565 Frantz Rd.
Dublin, OH 43017-3395
http://www.oclc.org

Ohio State University Employment Services
250 Northwood/High Building 2231
North High St.
Columbus, OH 43201
http://hr.osu.edu

Ohio State University Medical Center Career Opportunities
1375 Perry St.
Columbus, OH 43201
http://www.osumedcenter.edu

PNC Financial Services Group
201 East Fifth St.
Cincinnati OH 45202
http://www.pnc.com

Procter and Gamble
P.O. Box 599, T N 4
Cincinnati, OH 45201-0599
http://www.pg.com

OKLAHOMA
Federal Aviation Administration
Mike Monroney Aeronautical Center
Human Resource Management
Division, AMH-200
6500 South MacArthur Blvd.
Oklahoma City, OK 73169
jobs.faa.gov

Federal Aviation Administration Southwest Region Headquarters
Human Resource Management
Division, ASW-10
2500 Meacham Blvd.
Fort Worth, TX 76137-4298
jobs.faa.gov

Lucent Technologies
7725 W. Reno Ave.
Oklahoma City, OK 73127
http://www.lucent.com

OREGON
City of Eugene
Human Resource & Risk Services
777 Pearl St., Room 101
Eugene, OR 97401
http://www.ci.eugene.or.us/jobs/default.htm

Federal Aviation Administration Northwest Mountain Region Headquarters
Human Resource Management
Division, ANM-14
1601 Lind Ave. SW
Renton, WA 98055
jobs.faa.gov

Portland Habilitation Center
5312 NE 148th Ave.
Portland, OR 97230
http://www.phcnw.com

St Vincent DePaul Staffing Services
1205 NE Broadway
Portland, OR 97213
http://www.svdpstaffing.com

TriMet (Tri-County Metropolitan Transportation District of Oregon)
4012 SE 17th Ave.
Portland, OR 97202
http://www.trimet.org

PENNSYLVANIA
Armstrong World Industries, Inc.
P.O. Box 3001
Lancaster, PA 17604
http://www.armstrong.com

Bender Consulting Services, Inc.
Penn Central West III, Suite 223
Pittsburgh, PA 15276
www.benderconsult.com

Centers for Medicare & Medicaid Services
Suite 216, Public Ledger Bldg.
150 S. Independence Mall
West Philadelphia, PA 19106
http://cms.hhs.gov/

The Children's Hospital of Philadelphia
Career Services
34th & Civic Center Blvd.
Philadelphia, PA 19104
http://careers.chop.edu

Devereux
Multiple locations across the state
http://www.devereux.org

Federal Aviation Administration Eastern Region Headquarters
Human Resource Management
Division, AEA-10
One Aviation Administration
Jamaica, NY 11434-4809
jobs.faa.gov

JDS Uniphase
200 Precision Rd.
Horsham, PA 19044
http://www.jdsuniphase.com

Lucent Technologies
Union Blvd.
Allentown, PA 18103
http://www.lucent.com

Pennoni Associates Inc.
One Drexel Plaza
3001 Market St., 2nd Floor
Philadelphia, PA 19104
http://www.pennoni.com

Pennsylvania State University
Employment and Compensation
Division Office of Human Resources
120 South Burrowes St.
University Park, PA 16801-3857
http://www.ohr.psu.edu

PNC Financial Services Group
Multiple locations across the state
http://www.pnc.com

Primavera Systems, Inc.
3 Bala Plaza West, Suite 700
Bala Cynwyd, PA 19004
http://www.primavera.com

SAP America
3999 West Chester Pike
Newtown Square, PA 19073
http://www.sap.com

Starz Encore Group LLC
Multiple locations across the state
http://www.encoremedia.com

TruGreen ChemLawn
Multiple locations across the state
http://trugreenchemlawn.com

USDA, ARS
North Atlantic Area
Administrative Office
600 East Mermaid Lane
Wyndmoor, PA 19038-8598
http://www.ars.usda.gov

Westinghouse Electric Company
Staffing & University Relations
P.O. Box 355
Pittsburgh, PA 15230-0355
www.westinghouse.com

Willow Valley Retirement Communities
100 Willow Valley Lakes Dr.
Willow Street, PA 17584
www.willowvalleyretirement.com

RHODE ISLAND

Federal Aviation Administration
New England Region Headquarters
Human Resource Management
Division, ANE-14
12 New England Executive Park
Burlington, MA 01803
jobs.faa.gov

SOUTH CAROLINA

Federal Aviation Administration
Southern Region Headquarters
Human Resource Management
Division, ASO-14
P.O. Box 20636
Atlanta, GA 30320
jobs.faa.gov

Westinghouse Savannah River
Company
Aiken, SC 29808
http://www.srs.gov

SOUTH DAKOTA

Federal Aviation Administration
Great Lakes Region Headquarters
Human Resource Management
Division, AGL-18
2300 East Devon Ave.
Des Plaines, IL 60018
jobs.faa.gov

TENNESSEE

Federal Aviation Administration
Southern Region Headquarters
Human Resource Management
Division, ASO-14
P.O. Box 20636
Atlanta, GA 30320
jobs.faa.gov

FFC Services, Inc.
4010 Pilot Dr.
Memphis, TN 38118
http://www.ffcfuelcells.com

Home & Garden Television/Cinetel
Studios/Scripps Productions
9701 Madison Ave.
Knoxville, TN 37923
http://www.scripps.com

Oak Ridge National Laboratory
P.O. Box 2008
Oak Ridge, TN 37831-6216
http://www.ornl.gov

TEXAS

Advocacy, Incorporated
7800 Shoal Creek Blvd.
Suite 171 E
Austin, TX 78757
http://www.advocacyinc.org

Affiliated Computer Services, Inc.
2828 N. Haskell
Dallas, TX 75204
http://www.acs-inc.com

AT&T
Multiple locations across the state
http://www.att.com

Avnet, Inc.
Multiple locations across the state
http://www.avnet.com

Benchmark Hospitality
2170 Buckthorne Place, Suite 400
The Woodlands, TX 77380-1719
http://www.benchmarkhospitality.com

Centers for Medicare & Medicaid
Services
1301 Young St., Room 714
Dallas, TX 75202-4348
http://cms.hhs.gov/

Dallas County Community College
District
Employment Services
701 Elm St.
Dallas, TX 75202
http://www.dcccd.edu

Devereux
Multiple locations across the state
http://www.devereux.org

EDS
5400 Legacy Dr.
Staffing H4-GB-35
Plano, TX 75024
http://www.eds.com

Federal Aviation Administration
Southwest Region Headquarters
Human Resource Management
Division, ASW-10
2500 Meacham Blvd.
Fort Worth, TX 76137-4298
jobs.faa.gov

The Gallup Organization
1016 La Posada, Suite 290
Austin, TX 78752
http://www.gallup.com

Lucent Technologies
3000 Skyline Dr.
Mesquite, TX 75149
http://www.lucent.com

NationsBank
901 Main St., Suite 4700
Dallas, TX 75202
http://www.bankofamerica.com

Nokia
6000 Connection Dr.
Irving, TX 75039
http://www.nokia.com

Perot Systems-Recruiting
2300 W. Plano Pkwy.
Plano, TX 75075
http://www.perotsystems.com

SBC Communications Inc.
175 E. Houston
P.O. Box 2933
San Antonio, TX 78299-2933
http://www.sbc.com

Starz Encore Group LLC
17304 Preston Rd, Suite 460
Dallas, TX 75252
http://www.encoremedia.com

Texas Higher Education
Coordinating Board
P.O. Box 12788
Austin, TX 78711
http://www.thecb.state.tx.us

Texas Instruments
P.O. Box 650311
M/S 3979
Dallas, TX 75265
http://www.ti.com

Walter P. Moore and Associates, Inc.
3131 Eastside, 2nd Floor
Houston, TX 77098-1919
http://www.walterpmoore.com

UTAH

Federal Aviation Administration
Northwest Mountain Region
Headquarters
Human Resource Management
Division, ANM-14
1601 Lind Ave. SW
Renton, WA 98055
jobs.faa.gov

VERMONT

Federal Aviation Administration
New England Region Headquarters
Human Resource Management
Division, ANE-14
12 New England Executive Park
Burlington, MA 01803
jobs.faa.gov

University of Vermont
232 Waterman Building
85 S. Prospect St.
Burlington, VT 05405
http://www.uvm.edu

VIRGINIA
Alexandria, City of
Personnel Services Department
301 King St.
Alexandria, VA 22314
http://www.ci.alexandria.va.us/city/
city_employment.html

American Association of Motor
Vehicle Administrators
4301 Wilson Blvd., Suite 400
Arlington, VA 22203
http://www.aamva.org

American Diabetes Association
National Office, Human Resources,
1701 North Beauregard St.
Alexandria, VA 22311
www.diabetes.org

American Management Systems,
Inc.
4050 Legato Rd.
Fairfax, VA 22033
http://www.amsinc.com

AT&T
Multiple locations across the state
http://www.att.com

Axiom Resource Managment
5203 Leesburg Pike, Suite 300
Falls Church, VA 22311
http://www.axiom-rm.com

Booz-Allen & Hamilton
8283 Greensboro Dr.
McLean, VA 22102
http://www.bah.com

CACI International
1100 North Glebe Rd.
Arlington, VA 22201
http://www.caci.com

Capital One Financial Services
Multiple locations across the state
http://www.capitalone.com

Central Intelligence Agency
Recruitment Center
P.O. Box 4090
Reston, VA 20195
http://www.cia.gov

Colonial Williamsburg Foundation
Attn: Recruiting FSO/HR
P.O. Box 1776
Williamsburg, VA 23187-1776
http://www.colonialwilliamsburg.org

DCS Corporation
1330 Braddock Place
Alexandria, VA 22314-1660
http://www.dcscorp.com

Defense Contract Audit Agency
8725 John J. Kingman Rd.
Suite 2133
Ft. Belvoir, VA 22060-6219
http://www.dcaa.mil/

Federal Aviation Administration
Eastern Region Headquarters
Human Resource Management
Division, AEA-10
One Aviation Administration
Jamaica, NY 11434-4809
jobs.faa.gov

Food and Nutrition Service, USDA
Human Resources Division
3101 Park Center Dr., Room 424
Alexandria, VA 22302
www.fns.usda.gov

Jefferson Lab
12000 Jefferson Ave.
Newport News, VA 23606
www.jlab.org

Lucent Technologies
8110 Gatehouse Rd.
Falls Church, VA 22042
http://www.lucent.com

MAXIMUS
2000 Duke St., 2nd Floor
Alexandria, Virginia 22314
http://www.maximus.com

NAI Personnel
8245 Boone Blvd., Suite 690
Vienna, VA 22182
http://www.naipersonnel.com

National Science Foundation
Division of Human Resource
Management
4201 Wilson Blvd., Suite 315
Arlington, VA 22230
http://www.nsf.gov

National Wildlife Federation
8925 Leesburg Pike
Vienna, VA 22184-0001
http://www.nwf.org

The Nature Conservancy
International Headquarters
4245 N. Fairfax Dr., Suite 100
Arlingon, VA 22203-1606
http://www.nature.org

Norfolk Southern Corporation
Three Commercial Place
Norfolk, VA 23510
http://www.nscorp.com

Perot Systems-Recruiting
1801 Robert Fulton Dr.
Reston, VA 20191-4351
http://www.perotsystems.com

U.S. Department of Defense
The Human Resource Services
Center
5001 Eisenhower Ave.
Alexandria, VA 22333-0001
http://www.defenselink.mil/

U.S. Fish and Wildlife Service
4401 North Fairfax Dr.
Arlington, VA 22203
http://www.fws.gov

WASHINGTON
Bates Technical College
1101 South Yakima Ave.
Tacoma, WA 98405-4895
http://www.bates.ctc.edu

Bellevue Community College
Human Resources
3000 Landerholm Circle, S.E.
Bellevue, WA 98007-6484
http://www.bcc.ctc.edu

Centers for Medicare & Medicaid
Services
2201 Sixth Ave., Room 911
Seattle, WA 98121
http://cms.hhs.gov/

Central Washington University
400 E. 8th Ave.
Ellensburg, WA 98926-7497
www.cwu.edu

Everett Community College
2000 Tower St.
Everett, WA 98201
http://www.evcc.ctc.edu

Federal Aviation Administration
Northwest Mountain Region
Headquarters
Human Resource Management
Division, ANM-14
1601 Lind Ave. SW
Renton, WA 98055
jobs.faa.gov

Fremont Public Association
1501 North 45th St.
Seattle, WA 98103
http://www.fremontpublic.org

Lake Washington Technical College
11605 132nd Ave.
Kirkland, WA 98034
http://www.lwtc.ctc.edu

SAFECO
SAFECO Plaza, T-17
Seattle, WA 98185
http://www.safeco.com

State of Washington
Department of Information Services
1110 Jefferston St.
P.O. Box 42445
Olympia, WA 98504-2445

Department of Personnel
P.O. Box 47500
Olympia, WA 98504-7500
http://access.wa.gov

Department of Revenue
P.O. Box 47463
Olympia, WA 98504-7463
http://dor.wa.gov

University of Washington
Seattle, WA 98195
http://www.washington.edu

Western Washington University
516 High St.
Bellingham, WA 98225
http://www.ac.wwu.edu

Zones, Inc.
1102 15th St. SW, Suite 102
Auburn, WA 98001
http://www.zones.com

WEST VIRGINIA
Federal Aviation Administration
Eastern Region Headquarters
Human Resource Management
Division, AEA-10
One Aviation Administration
Jamaica, NY 11434-4809
jobs.faa.gov

**InfoCision Management
Corporation**
168 West Main St.
Clarksburg, WV 26301
http://www.infocision.com

WISCONSIN
Dueco, Inc.
N4 W22610 Bluemound Rd.
Waukesha, WI 53186
http://www.dueco.com

Fairbanks Morse Engine
701 White Ave.
Beloit, WI 53511
http://www.fairbanksmorse.com

Federal Aviation Administration
Great Lakes Region Headquarters
Human Resource Management
Division, AGL-18
2300 East Devon Ave.
Des Plaines, IL 60018
jobs.faa.gov

**Foth & Van Dyke and Associates,
Inc.**
2737 South Ridge Rd.
Green Bay, WI 54304
www.foth.com

GE Medical Systems
3000 N. Grandview Blvd
Waukesha, WI 53188
www.savelives.gecareers.com

Industries for the Blind
3220 W. Vliet St.
Milwaukee, WI 53208
www.ibmilw.com

Michels Corporation
817 W. Main St.
Brownsville WI 53006
http://www.michels-usa.com

Omni Tech Corporation
N27 W23676 Paul Rd.
Pewaukee, WI 53072
http://www.omnitechcorp.com

Wisconsin Electric Power Company
333 W. Everett St., A125
Milwaukee, WI 53290
http://www.we-energies.com

WYOMING
Federal Aviation Administration
**Northwest Mountain Region
Headquarters**
Human Resource Management
Division, ANM-14
1601 Lind Ave. SW
Renton, WA 98055
jobs.faa.gov

Index

Symbols

7 West Communications, 260

A

AARP, 256
abilities, assessing, 3–21
Academy for Educational
    Development, 256
Accenture, 257
accepting a job offer, 216–221
Access Equality Incorporated,
    262
accommodations, 237–251
    adaptive equipment, 239–240
    deaf/hearing loss, 242–249
        alarms, 245
        audiotape transcription,
            248
        communicating, 243–245,
            247
        environmental sounds,
            245–246
        noises, 246
        vehicles in workplace, 247
        videos, 248
    epilepsy, 249–250
    facility modifications, 239
    inexpensive, 242
    job duties, 238–239
    new products, 241
    product modifications,
        240–241
    special equipment, 240
    work schedule, 238–239
achievement assessment, 14–16
achievements on resumes, 68–69
ACSG, Inc., 258
action verbs on resumes, 62–63
Adult Basic Learning
    Examination (ABLE), 14
Advanced Management
    Technology, Inc. (AMTI),
    256

Advocacy, Incorporated, 264
Aetna U.S. Healthcare, 255
Affiliated Computer Services,
    Inc., 264
agoraphobia, 238
AIDS/HIV, 8, 232, 238
Alabama employers, 253
Alaska employers, 253
alcoholics, 102
ALLTEL Corporation, 254, 262
AltaVista, 165
Alternative Resources
    Corporation, 258
America's Job Bank, 136
American Association for the
    Advancement of the
    Sciences (AAAS), 41
American Association of Motor
    Vehicle Administrators,
    265
American Association of People
    with Disabilities, 156
American Council of the Blind,
    256
American Diabetes Association,
    265
American Eagle Federal Credit
    Union, 255
American Institute of Certified
    Public Accountants, 138
American Institutes for Research,
    256
The American Legion, 258
American Management Systems,
    Inc., 265
American Purchasing Society,
    138
American Welding Society, 138
Americans with Disabilities Act
    (ADA), 205–216
    actions to take, 209–210
    charges of discrimination,
        210–212
    results of, 211–212

time limits, 211
timing, 212
discrimination covered by,
    208–209
employment provisions, 206
Equal Employment
    Opportunity
    Commission (EEOC),
    210–213
questions about, 214–216
relief/remedies of
    discrimination, 212–213
Title I, 206
Title II, 206,
who is covered, 206–208
Analog Devices, Inc., 254, 259
APAC Customer Services, 258
applications, 157–159
apprenticeships, 40
aptitude assessment, 14–16
ARAMARK Uniform Services,
    254
Arizona employers, 253 -254
Arkansas Department of Parks
    and Tourism, 254
Arkansas employers, 254
Armed Services Vocational
    Aptitude Battery (ASVAB),
    15
Armstrong World Industries,
    Inc., 263
Asperger's syndrome, 9
assertiveness, 43–48
assessment
    achievement, 14–16
    aptitude, 14–16
    assertiveness, 44–45
    career, 14–20
    interests, 16–17
    Internet instruments, 19–20
    self, 3–14
assistive devices, 8
Association of Administrative
    Professionals, 138

asthma, 9
AstraZeneca, 256
AT&T, 253–255, 257–258, 260–262, 264–265
attention deficit disorder (ADD), 9, 68
Automotive Service Industry Association, 138
Avnet, Inc., 253–254, 257, 259, 264
Axiom Resource Management, 265

B

Bar Association of San Francisco, 254
Bates Technical College, 265
Bell Technologies, Inc., 257
Bellevue Community College, 265
Benchmark Hospitality, 264
Bender Consulting Services, Inc., 263
Berkeley Policy Associates, 254
bonuses, sign-on, 219
Booz-Allen & Hamilton, 265
Boston College, 259
Bristol-Myers Squibb Company, 261
Brookhaven National Laboratory, 261
The Brookings Institution, 256
Burson-Marsteller, 256
Business for Social Responsibility, 254
Business Leadership Network, 133, 156
buzzwords in resumes, 64

C

CACI International, 265
California Department of Rehabilitation Central Office, 254
California employers, 254
California State Department of Transportation (Caltrans), 254
California State University, 254
Campbell Interest and Skill Survey, 19

Candescent Technologies Corporation, 254
Canon Computer Systems, Inc., 254
Capital One Financial Services, 265
CaptionMax, 260
career centers, 132–133
Career Directions Inventory, 16
Career Interest Inventory (CII), 15
The Career Interests Game, 19
The Career Key, 19
Career Occupational Preference System Interest Inventory (COPS), 16–17
Career Service Authority, 255
CareerBuilder, 137
careers
    achievement, 14–16
    aptitude, 14–16
    assessment, 14–20
    autobiography exercise, 3–4
    computer-based guidance systems, 18
    counselors, 14
    exploring, 23–38
    informational interviewing, 34–36
    instruments for people with disabilities, 18–19
    interest inventories, 16–17
    Internet instruments, 19–20
    misinformation, 23–24
    Occupational Information Network, 26–31
    Occupational Outlook Handbook (OOH), 31–33
    professional associations, 34
    reference publications, 26–33
    researching, 24–33
    starting own business, 36–37
    trade groups, 34
Careers and the DisABLED magazine, 135
CareerSearch, 164
CAST, 259
Centers for Medicare & Medicaid Services, 254–260, 262–265
Central Intelligence Agency, 265
Central Ohio Transit Authority, 262

Central Washington University, 265
cerebral palsy, 9, 239, 241
Cerner Corporation, 260
characteristics, assessing, 12–13
chemical sensitivity, 9
Chicago Board of Trade, 258
The Children's Hospital of Philadelphia, 263
Children's Mercy Hospitals and Clinics, 260
Choices CT, 18–19
CHOICES Hospice Triage, 258
chronic fatigue syndrome, 9
chronic illness, 9
chronological resumes, 55–75
    action verbs, 62–63
    activities, 67–68
    athletics, 65–67
    awards, 68–69
    buzzwords, 64
    education, 58–60
    experience, 60–63
    military experience, 64
    objective, 56–58
    personal information, 71–72
    professional associations, 69
    references, 69–71
    samples, 72–75
    skills, 65
    vital statistics, 55–56
Cisco Systems, Inc., 254
college career centers, 132–133
Colonial Williamsburg Foundation, 265
Colorado employers, 255
Colorado State Government, 255
communication, 230
    accommodations for hearing loss, 242–249
    e-mail, 120
    on-the-job, 230
    public speaking, 48–50
    speakers' clubs, 50
    telephone, 113–119
The Communitarian Network, 256
Community Development Commission, 254
Compuware Corporation, 260
conflict, fear of, 45
Connecticut employers, 255

Construction Technology Labs, 258
contacts, tracking, 139–140
cooperative education (co-op), 41–42
Corporation for National and Community Service, 256
corVISION MEDIA Inc., 258
cover letters
  block left style, 95
  contact information, 89–90
  content (what), 93–94
  finish, 95
  format, 95
  full block style, 95
  indented style, 95
  online help, 106
  purpose (why), 90–92
  response wanted, 94–95
  samples, 95–105
    ad with contact information, 96–98
    blind ad, 98–99
    combination with resume, 101
    disability with resume, 101
    lead from friend, 104–105
    personal contact, 100
  writing, 89–106
Cox Communications, Inc., 254
Cross Sales & Engineering Company, 262
Crown Equipment Corporation, 262
CSX Technology, 257
curiosity, 186
Cystic Fibrosis, 68

D

Dallas County Community College District, 264
Data Focus Corporation Company, 254
Data General Corporation, 259
DCS Corporation, 265
deaf/hard of hearing, 10
  accommodating, 242–249
Deere & Company, 258
Defense Contract Audit Agency, 265
Delaware employers, 256

Deloitte & Touche Tax Technologies, 258
Department of Labor (DOL), 132, 156, 253–266
depth perception, 10
Devereux, 254–257, 259, 261–264
dexterity limitations, 241
diabetes, 10, 239
Differential Aptitude Test (DAT), 15
dinner interviews, 192–195
disabilities
  agoraphobia, 238
  AIDS/HIV, 8, 232, 238
  alcoholism, 102
  Asperger's syndrome, 9
  assessing, 8–12
  assistive devices, use of, 8
  asthma, 9
  attention deficit disorder, 9, 68
  cerebral palsy, 9, 239, 241
  chemical sensitivity, 9
  chronic fatigue syndrome, 9
  chronic illness, 9
  coworkers' adjustments to, 232–233
  Cystic Fibrosis, 68
  depth perception, 10
  dexterity limitations, 241
  diabetes, 10, 239
  disfigurement, 10
  hearing, 10, 239–240, 242–249
  learning, 10
  missing digit, 10
  missing limbs, 10
  on-the-job, 232–233
  psychological/emotional, 11
  seizure disorders, 102, 233, 249–251
  speech, 11
  Tourette's syndrome, 11, 68
  transportation issues, 10
  traumatic brain injury, 11
  visible to others, 11
  vision, 11, 241
Disability Rights Education and Defense Fund, Inc. (DREDF), 254
DisabilityInfo.gov, 136
disclosing disability, 94–95, 167–169, 171
Discover program, 18

discrimination, 205–216
  Americans with Disabilities Act, 205–216
  charges of, 210–212
  Equal Employment Opportunity Commission (EEOC), 210–213
  relief/remedies, 212–213
  spouses with disabilities, 216
disfigurement, 10
District of Columbia employers, 256
Diversified Investment Advisors, 262
Dress for Success, 189
Dueco, Inc., 266
DukeSolutions, Inc., 262
Dunn & Bradstreet's Million Dollar Directory, 165

E

E.I. du Pont de Nemours and Company, 256
e-mail
  networking, communicating by e-mail, 120
  resumes, 88
E-R Model Importers, Ltd., 262
EDS, 260, 264
education
  apprenticeships, 40
  cooperative (co-op), 41–42
  experiential, 39–40
  financial aid, 20–21
  internships, 40–41
  practicum, 42
  service learning, 42
  student teaching, 42
  volunteer experiences, 42–43
Education Development Center, Inc., 259
emotional/psychological disabilities, 11
employment agencies, 130–132
Employment and Training Administration, 26
Entry Point, 41
epilepsy
  accommodating on the job, 249–251
  seizure disorders, 102, 233

Ernst & Young, 262
Everett Community College, 265
Excite, 165

F

The Facility Group Inc., 257
Fairbanks Morse Engine, 266
fears, 45–46
Federal Aviation Administration
    (FAA), 253–266
Federal Bureau of Investigation
    (FBI), 256
Federal Communications
    Commission (FCC), 256
feedback, 204
FFC Services, Inc., 264
financial aid, 20–21
Fleishman-Hillard, International
    Communications, 261
FlipDog, 137
Florida employers, 257
fonts for resumes, 86
Food and Nutrition Service,
    USDA, 265
Ford Motor Company, 260
formatting of resumes and cover
    letters, 86, 95
Fortune Magazine's 500, 165
Foster Wheeler Corporation, 261
Foth & Van Dyke and Associates,
    Inc., 266
Fremont Public Association, 265
functional resumes, 76–82
    education, 77
    experience, 77–79
    objective, 76–77
    samples, 80–82

G

The Gallup Organization, 264
Gateway Café, 135
Gay Men's Health Crisis, 262
GE, 255
GE Medical Systems, 266
George Washington University, 256
Georgia employers, 257
goals, 3–21, 150
Goodwill Industries, 256, 259
Google, 165
guilt, 186–187

H

Harcourt Brace School
    Publishers, 257
Harford Community College,
    259
Harrington O'Shea Career
    Decision-Making System-
    Revised (CDM-R), 17
The Hartford, 256
Hawaii employers, 257
Health Systems Research, Inc.,
    256
hearing disabilities, 10, 239–240,
    242–249
HEATH Resource Center, 21
Hennepin County Human
    Resources, 260
Hickory Tech Corporation, 260
HirePotential, Inc., 255
hobbies listed on resumes, 71–72
Home & Garden Television/
    Cinetel Studios/Scripps
    Productions, 264
honors and awards listed on
    resumes, 68–69
Honeywell Inc., 260
Hoover's Handbook, 165
Hoover's Online, 165
Hopkins School District 270,
    260
Hyperion Solutions Corporation,
    254

I

IBM Corporation, 262
Idaho employers, 257
Idealist, 43
ILEX Systems, 254, 261
Illinois employers, 257–258
Indiana employers, 258
Industrial Development Agency,
    37
Industries for the Blind, 266
InfoCision Management
    Corporation, 266
InfoSeek, 165
Ingalls Memorial Hospital, 258
Innovative Interfaces, 255
insecurity, 45–46
insurance, 235–236
interest inventories, 16–17

Interest Inventory (USES II),
    15–16
Internet job leads, 133–134
internships, 40–41
InternWeb.com, 41
interviews
    accessibility issues, 167–169
    appointment log, 141–143
    arriving for, 189–191
    assertiveness, 43
    disabilities, disclosing, 171
    dressing for, 188–189
    follow up, 201
    guidelines for, 172–173
    illegal questions, 185
    informational, 34–36
    interviewer's emotions,
        186–187
    online resources, 195
    preparing for, 131–137, 188
        contacts, 166
        research, 162–167
    rehearsing, 169–171
    sample questions, 174–185
    second, 191–195
    styles, 185–186
Iowa employers, 258

J

JDS Uniphase, 263
Jefferson Lab, 265
JIST Publishing, 87, 106, 195
Job Accommodation Network
    (JAN), 4, 11, 237, 242
Job Corps, 40
JobAccess, 135
jobs
    applying for, 155–160
        application forms,
            157–159
        cover letters, sending,
            156–157
        networking, 155–156,
            159–160
        online, 157
        resumes, sending, 156–157
    disability and, 232–234
    initiative, 231
    insurance, 235–236
    keeping, 225–236
        attitude, 226–227

office politics, 227–230
seeking opportunities,
230–232
leadership, 176, 230–232
leads, 127–138
Business Leadership
Network, 133
career centers, 132–133
Department of Labor, 132
employment agencies,
130–132
Internet, 133–136
newspaper, 127–130
trade publications, 137–138
vocational rehabilitation
offices, 133
searching for, 139–153
contacts, tracking, 139–140
government jobs, 153
not-for-profits, 152–153
smaller companies, 152
time management, 140–153
JobStar, 106
John Knox Village, 261
Johnson & Johnson, 261

K
Kansas employers, 258–259
Kelly Services, 260
Kensington Technology Group,
255
Kentucky employers, 259
KLA-Tencor, 255
Koch Industries, Inc., 258
KPMG LLP, 261

L
Lake County Government, 258
Lake Washington Technical
College, 266
leadership skills, 176, 230–232
learning disabilities, 10
LNK Corporation, Inc., 259
Lockheed Martin, 262
Lord Corporation, 262
Loronix Information Systems,
Inc., 255
Louisiana employers, 259
Lucent Technologies, 255–259,
261–265

lunch/dinner interviews, 192–195
Lycos, 166

M
*Macmillan's Directory of Leading
Private Companies*, 165
Maine employers, 259
Maintenance Warehouse (A
Home Depot Company),
255
Maryland employers, 259
Maryland State Retirement
Agency, 259
The Mass Transit
Administration, 259
Massachusetts employers,
259–260
Massachusetts Institute of
Technology, 260
MAXIMUS, 265
Maytag Appliances, 258
Mellon/The Boston Company,
260
mentors, 122–125
Mesa, AZ Police Dept., 254
McCarron-Dial System (MDS),
18
McCrone, Inc., 259
McDonald's Corporation, 258
Michels Corporation, 266
Michigan employers, 260
Michigan Technological
University, 260
Midland Loan Services, 258
military experience, 64
Minnesota employers, 260
missing digits/limbs, 10
Mississippi employers, 260
Missouri employers, 260–261
Mitchell International, 255
Mitsubishi Electric & Electronics
USA, Inc., 255
modifications for employees
with disabilities
facilities, 239
products, 240–241
Monster.com, 106, 137
MonsterTrak, 137
Montana employers, 261
Morton College, 258
Motorola, 258

N
Nabisco, Inc., 261
NAI Personnel, 256, 265
National Aeronautics and Space
Administration, 256
National Aquarium of Baltimore,
259
National Association of
Broadcast Employees and
Technicians (NABET-
CWA), 256
National Business and Disability
Council, 135
National Instrument Co., Inc.,
259
National Journal Group, Inc.,
256
National Science Foundation,
265
National Security Agency, 259
National Wildlife Federation, 265
NationsBank, 264
The Nature Conservancy, 265
NECA, 261
negotiating the offer, 216–219
networking, 109–125, 159–160
assertiveness, 43
candidates, 111
communicating by e-mail, 120
communicating by telephone,
113–119
contacts, 139–140, 166,
204–205, 234
establishing, 111–122
first ring, 112–113
mentors, 122–125
numbers game, 110
organizing, 121–122
second ring, 113
"six degrees of separation,"
110
Nevada employers, 261
New England Research Institutes,
260
New Hampshire employers, 261
New Jersey employers, 261
New Mexico employers, 261
New York employers, 261–262
New York State Department of
Labor, 88, 106
newspaper job leads, 127–130
Nokia, 264

nonassertiveness, 45–46
Norfolk Southern Corporation, 265
North Carolina employers, 262
North Carolina State University, 262
North Dakota employers, 262
Northern Arizona University, 254
Northwest Airlines, 260
not-for-profit companies, 152–153

O

Oak Ridge National Laboratory, 264
objectives on resumes, 56–58, 76–77
Occupational Information Network (O*NET), 26–31, 37, 162
Occupational Outlook Handbook (OOH), 31–34, 37, 138, 162
OCLC Online Computer Library Center, Inc., 263
offers of employment, 216–221
Office of Apprenticeship Training, Employer and Labor Services, 40
Office of Disability Employment Policy, 135–136
Office of the Comptroller of the Currency, 256
office politics, 227–230
Ohio employers, 262–263
Ohio State University
    Employment Services, 263
    Medical Center Career Opportunities, 263
Oklahoma employers, 263
Omni Tech Corporation, 266
Opportunity Medical Complete, 258
optical character recognition (OCR), 84
Option One, 262
Oregon employers, 263
Our Lady of Lourdes Medical Center, 261
Overseas Private Investment Corporation, 256

P

Pennoni Associates Inc., 263
Pennsylvania employers, 263
Pennsylvania State University, 263
Perot Systems Healthcare Services, 255, 260
Perot Systems–Recruiting, 255, 257, 260, 264–265
personal information on resumes, 71–72
personality characteristics, 12–13
Personality Inventory, 20
Pitney Bowes Inc., 256
pity from interviewers, 187
PNC Financial Services Group, 256–257, 259–261, 263
Portland Habilitation Center, 263
positive attitude, 205, 226–227
powerful action words on resume, 62–63
practicum, 42
prejudice, 187
PricewaterhouseCoopers LLP, 262
Primavera Systems, Inc., 263
Principal Financial Group, 258
Pro Staff, 260
Procter and Gamble, 263
professional associations, 34
Prudential Insurance Company, 261
psychological/emotional disabilities, 11
public speaking, 48–50
Purdue University, 87, 258

Q

Quality Systems & Software, Inc., 261
questions during interview, 174–185
    commonly asked, 174
    competency-based, 175
    illegal to ask, 185
    sample answers, 175–186
Qwest, 255

R

Raytheon Systems Company, 255
record keeping during job search, 150

recruiters/interviewers, 166–167, 185–187
references listed on resumes, 69–71
rejection, 202–216
    discrimination, 205–216
    feedback, 204
    networking contacts, 204–205
    thank-you notes, 202–203
research, 162–167
    career field, 162–163
    companies, 163–166
    interviewers, 166–167
    recruiters, 166–167
        competing organizations, 164
        contacts, 166
        news accounts, 164
        online, 165–166
        public relations literature, 163
        third-party publishers, 164–165
Research and Evaluation Associates, Inc., 262
resumes, 53–88
    aesthetics, 85–87
    chronological, 55–75
        action verbs, 62–63
        activities, 67–68
        athletics, 65–67
        awards, 68–69
        buzzwords, 64
        education, 58–60
        experience, 60–63
        military experience, 64
        objective, 56–58
        personal information, 71–72
        professional associations, 69
        references, 69–71
        samples, 72–75
        skills, 65
        vital statistics, 55–56
    combination with cover letters, 101
    correspondence log, 145–147
    e-mail, 88
    font, 86
    functional, 76–82
        education, 77
        experience, 77–79

objective, 76–77
samples, 80–82
information not to include, 83
Internet and, 87–88
length, 85–86
online resources, 87–88
paper color, 85
posting to the Web, 86–87
salary requirements, 83
scannable, 84
text formatting, 86
Rhode Island employers, 264
Roaring Fork Transit Agency, 255
Rogers Corporation, 256
RR Donnelley & Sons, 258
Rutgers, 106

S

SAFECO, 266
SAP America, 263
SAS Institute, Inc., 262
SBC Communications Inc., 258, 264
scannable resumes, 84
SCO, Inc., 255
search engines, 165–166
SearchAbility, 260
self-assessment
career autobiography exercise, 3–4
characteristics, 12–13
disabilities, 8–12
feedback, 7, 13–14
skills, 4–7
values, 13–14
weaknesses, 7
Self-Directed Search, 17, 19
seizure disorders, 102, 233, 249–251
SERVEnet, 43
Service Corps of Retired Executives (SCORE), 37
service learning, 42
SIGIPlus, 18
SIRS Mandarin, Inc., 257
Six Continents Hotels, Inc., 257
"six degrees of separation," 110
skills, assessing, 3–21
Small Business Administration, 37

Social Security Administration, 261
Solomon Smith Barney, 262
Sony Electronics Inc., 255
South Carolina employers, 264
South Dakota employers, 264
speech disabilities, 11
Sprint Corporation, 258
SRI International, 255
St. Vincent DePaul Staffing Services, 263
Standard & Poor's Reports, 165
Starz Encore Group LLC, 255–258, 261–264
State of Iowa, 258
State of Washington, 266
State Street, 260
Stichler Group, Inc., 255
Strong Interest Inventory, 17
student teaching, 42

T

T-square evaluation (pros and cons), 37–38
telephone
accommodations for hearing loss, 243–244
contacting people by, 113–119
telephone log, 148–149
Tennessee employers, 264
Tests of Adult Basic Education (TABE), 15
Texas employers, 264
Texas Higher Education Coordinating Board, 264
Texas Instruments, 264
thank-you letters, 197–203
rejection, 202–203
samples, 199–200, 203
writing, 197–198
time management, 140–153
appointments and interviews, 141–143
goal setting, 150
job search, 144, 151–153
government jobs, 153
not-for-profits, 152–153
smaller companies, 152
record keeping, 150
resume/correspondence log, 145–147

telephone log, 148–149
time usage, 144
Toastmasters International, 50
Tourette's syndrome, 11, 68
Towers Productions, Inc., 258
trade groups, 34
trade publications, 137–138
TradeNet Publishing, Inc., 259
TRAK Microwave Corporation, 257
transportation issues, 10
TransUnion, LLC, 258
traumatic brain injuries, 11
TriMet (Tri-County Metropolitan Transportation District of Oregon), 263
TrueCareers, 106
TruGreen ChemLawn, 256, 261, 263
TRW Inc., 255
turning down a job offer, 221

U

Union Rescue Mission, 255
United Cerebral Palsy Employment and Training, 136
United States
Coast Guard, 257
Consumer Product Safety Commission, 259
Department of Agriculture (USDA), Agricultural Research Service (ARS), 263
Department of Defense, 265
Department of Education, 257
Department of Energy, 261
Department of Justice, 257
Department of Labor, 26, 31, 132, 253–266
Department of State, 257
Department of the Interior, 195
Department of the Navy, 257
Employment Service General Aptitude Test Battery (GATB), 15–16
Environmental Protection Agency, 257

United States (*cont.*)
  Fish and Wildlife Service, 265
  Foodservice, 259
United Technologies
    Corporation, 256
University at Buffalo, 87, 106
University of Maine, 259
University of Missouri–
    Columbia, 261
University of New Mexico, 261
University of South Florida, 257
University of Vermont, 265
University of Washington, 266
Urban Institute, 257
Utah employers, 264

V

Valassis Communications, Inc.,
    260
values, assessing, 13–14
Vault Reports, 165
Verizon Communications, 262
Vermont employers, 264–265
Virginia employers, 265

visible disabilities, 11
vision disabilities, 11, 241
vocational counselors, 14, 26
vocational rehabilitation offices,
    133
volunteering, 42–43
VPA, Inc., 255

W

W. W. Grainger, Inc., 258
Wachovia Corporation, 262
Walter P. Moore and Associates,
    Inc., 264
want ads, 127–128
Washington employers, 265–266
weaknesses, assessing, 7
Web sites
  posting resumes to, 86–87
  search engines, 165–166
Wells Fargo Bank NA–Orange
    County Phone Bank, 255
West Central Florida Area
    Agency on Aging, 257
West Virginia employers, 266

Western Washington University,
    266
Westinghouse Electric Company,
    263
Westinghouse Savannah River
    Company, 264
William and Mary College, 195
Willow Valley Retirement
    Communities, 263
Wisconsin Electric Power
    Company, 266
Wisconsin employers, 266
Wolverine World Wide, Inc., 260
Workforce Recruitment
    Program, 41
World of Work Inventory
    (WOWI), 16
Wyoming employers, 266

X–Z

Yahoo!, 166
Yellow Services, Inc., 259
Zimmer, Inc., 258
Zones, Inc., 266